The
Vein
of
Gold

Also by Julia Cameron

The Artist's Way

The Money Drunk
(co-authored with Mark Bryan)

The Vein of Gold

A Journey to Your Creative Heart

Julia Cameron

PAN BOOKS

First published in 1996 by G P Putnam's Sons, New York, USA.

This edition published 1997 by Pan Books
an imprint of Macmillan Publishers Ltd
25 Eccleston Place London SW1W 9NF
and Basingstoke

Associated companies throughout the world

ISBN 0 330 35285 7

9 8 7 6 5 4 3

A CIP catalogue record for this book is available from the British Library

Printed and bound in Great Britain by Mackays of Chatham PLC, Chatham, Kent

This book is dedicated to
Domenica Cameron-Scorsese,
my artist-daughter,
and
to the creative spirits
of her beloved grandparents:
James William Cameron,
Dorothy Shea Cameron,
Luciano Charles Scorsese,
and Catherine Cappa Scorsese,
whose artistry
runs in her veins.

Contents

The Kingdom of Spirituality

Acknowledgments

For their help in incubating and supporting my work, I would like to acknowledge the following people:

First of all, I wish to thank Mark Bryan for his innovative thinking, compassionate teaching, and creative support. He has been for me a believing mirror.

Additionally, I want to thank the Cameron clan, especially Elizabeth Cameron-Evans, for her artistry and inspiration.

The Cameron clan: Mom, Dad, Connie, Jaimie, Libby, Chris, Lorrie, Pegi, for their artistry and inspiration.

And then, my soul clan: Mitchell Canoff, for his "eye" and his "I."

Rosario Carelli, for the drumbeat of his consciousness.

Armando Casillas, for his travels and sense of direction.

Alexander Cassini, for his eyes and ears.

Miel Castagna, for her fiery heart.

Jim Casteel, for his experienced ears.

Sonia Choquette, for her wisdom and generosity.

Kathy Churay, for her help and clarity.

Jay Cocks, for his "I" and his "eye."

Richard Cole, for his chivalry and creativity.

Mauna Eichner, for her incomparable eye.

Rhonda Flemming, for her festive friendship and inspiration.

Natalie Goldberg, for her example and generosity.

Rosemarie Greco, for her wisdom and warmth and music.

Erin Greenberg, for her deft, intuitive, and intelligent support.

Jennifer Greene, for her artful heart.

Gerard Hackett, for his friendship, logic, and loyalty.

Martha Snyder Hamilton, for her friendship and gentle guidance.

Pam Hogan, for her courage and spiritual generosity.

Anthony Hopkins, for his spiritual and creative principles in action.

Michael Hoppé, for his healing music.

Elberta Honstein, for her lantern heart.

Be Hubbard, for her compassionate help.

Ezra Hubbard, for his creative help and spirit.

Jo Ann Iannotti, for her "I" and her "eye."

Aloma Ichinose, for beauty and the eye of the beholder.

Chris James, for voicing peoples' dreams.

Ellen and Derek Jameson, for their kind and festive hearts.

Jan Johnson, for her editorial guidance.

ACKNOWLEDGMENTS

xiv

Arnold Jones, for his wisdom, wit, and compassion.

David Koral, for service above and beyond the call of duty.

Bill LaVallee, for his irreverent spirit.

Michele Lowrance, for her clarity and creativity.

Laura Leddy, for her loving friendship and fine mind.

Larry Lonerghan, for his kindness and insight.

Ellen Longo, for spiritual (and fiscal) clarity.

Howard Mandel, for his vision and commitment.

Billy May, for blazing a trail of (grace) notes.

Julianna McCarthy, for her fire and her ice.

Joseph McClellan, for his sublime ears and a musical heart.

Kekuni Minton, for living sound, body and mind.

Karma Nabulsi, for her spiritual hospitality.

James Navé, for his art and his heart.

John Newland, for his passionate clarity.

David Nichols, for his radical heart.

John Nichols, for his art and his example.

Al Okas, for excellent ears and generous guidance.

Birgitta Royall. Name tells all.

Susan Schulman, my beloved friend (and agent), for her discernment, acuity, compassion, and vision.

Martin Scorsese, for his creative DNA.

Gayle Seminara, for her dynamic leadership and artistry.

Sambhu, for his compassion and music.

Tami Simon, for her service to the healing world of music.

Terrell Smith, for her compassionate heart.

Jeremy Tarcher, my beloved friend (editor and publisher), for his inspired guidance and artist's soul.

Jo Dean Tipton, for her creative example and loving heart.

Ed Towle, for his friendship, compassion, and creativity.

Jenny Trindel, for her support and calm administration.

Patrick Tully, for his protective and artistic heart.

Chris Vinella, for his friendship and artistry.

Dori Vinella, for her friendship and spiritual support.

Robert Welsch, for his inventive, committed, and creative work.

Tim Wheater, Imagemaker, Magellan, for his mission, his music, and his magic.

Jacqueline Woolsey, for her wit and her witness.

Peter Ziminsky, for his strength, clarity, loyalty, and humor.

Zuleika, for her heart.

Finally, I wish to thank those I have omitted and those who have chosen to help me anonymously.

*Wherever you are is
the entry point!*

KABIR

Setting Out

The book you are about to embark on is a pilgrimage, a journey of healing. In Native American traditions, you might call this a vision quest. My Celtic roots prefer the simpler term: quest.

Name this journey as it serves you.

Some of you will conceive this quest as a spiritual journey. You will consciously use your creativity to encounter your Creator. For others, the journey may be viewed psychologically. You are questing for wholeness and a healthy autonomy from the expectations of others. Still others of you may politicize your process. You will experience this work as a radical act, a severing of ties with outmoded hierarchies that have subverted your own considerable powers.

The journey I guide you on will be your journey, not mine. I would be lying if I told you the journey would always be easy, or comfortable. I expect—and so should you—that other words will apply: fascinating, arduous, magical, difficult, rewarding, and above all, personal.

All of us are far richer than we imagine. None of us possesses a life devoid of magic, barren of grace, divorced from power. Our inner resources, often unmined and even unknown or unacknowledged, are the treasures we carry, what I call our spiritual DNA.

When I speak of "spiritual DNA," I am talking about a stamp of originality that is as definite and specific as my blue eyes, blond hair, medium height. Just as our physical potentials are encoded at conception, it is my belief that we also carry the imprint, or blueprint, of our gifts and their unfolding. Often we have far more gifts than we imagine. For example, a love of music may indicate a gift for it as well—a gift we may not have developed due to the circumstances of our birth. Similarly, many voracious readers are closet writers, afraid to step into the arena of their dreams. This arena, the panoply of a more colorful self, is our spiritual DNA, the treasure chest we bring into the world and are charged with developing.

The tricky part is recognizing it.

For a decade and a half, I have taught a process of creative individuation and emergence, The Artist's Way. (Many of you may be familiar with my first creativity book by that name.) When people ask

Making art is a journey.
MEINRAD CRAIGHEAD

I am still learning.
MICHELANGELO

If the first response to inter-dependence and to our shar-ing the common, grace-filled soup of the cosmic womb is to celebrate, the second re-sponse is to heal.
MATTHEW FOX

We live in a time in which most people believe there is not much inside them, only what teachers, parents, and others have put there.
MICHELL CASSOU AND
STEWART CUBLEY

me what it is like to work with people seeking their creativity, I tell them it's like being a prospector. After all these years, I still find it exciting to catch a glimpse of gold. Finding our gold and mining it is what this book is about. Through alignment with this vein of gold, we are able to manifest our lives in a richer way. It is, however, less a matter of productivity than a matter of alchemy. Alchemy is a process of transformation.

At its essence, art *is* an alchemical process. By practicing art, by living artfully, we realize our vein of gold. What I refer to as "the vein of gold," Egyptians referred to as "the golden ray." It is the individual, indisputable, indestructible connection to the divine.

The vein of gold in every life is located in the heart of that life. The heart is the origin of creative impulses. If that heart has been wounded, it must be healed for our vein of gold to flow freely. That is why this book must be a pilgrimage of healing, a journey home to the self. As we travel further and further into our own interiors, we will be taking the dross of our lives—the disappointments, wounds, and burdens—and we will make them into gold through the power of creativity. All of our lives are already golden—in potential—if we are willing to do the necessary work of transformation.

The Artist's Way was a book of reunion and discovery: "Ah-hah! I do have inside me an artist, an inner youngster, who had been lost to me!" That artist self, the Creative Child, or Divine Child as it is called in spiritual tradition, had been stolen away. The recovery of that inner artist, like the recovery of a kidnapped, lost, or missing child, was a cause for great celebration. "I've got you back! I can barely believe it! Think of all the wonderful things we will be able to do together. . . ." Those were heady and lovely feelings. This book is about putting those feelings into action.

If *The Artist's Way* was a book of discovery and reunion, *The Vein of Gold* is a book of healing and rehabilitation. "I've found you, but you've been beaten, battered, starved, malnourished, neglected, discounted, and disowned. I must restore you to health so we can have our adventures. . . ."

To restore our artist-child to health, we must be willing to go to any lengths—just as we would for a child of flesh and blood. This means that like parents of an ailing child who make a journey to

Mecca—or the Mayo Clinic, for that matter—we must be willing to undertake a pilgrimage, with all the challenges that implies.

If this sounds daunting, like an awful lot of *work*, let me assure you that what we are going to undertake is something radically different from what you might conceive. Because our aim is to strengthen and heal a creative *child*, we will be undertaking instead a whole lot of play. On our autobiographical pilgrimage to the self, we will explore our lives through tools that may seem like child's play: movement, writing, sight, sound, and silence. We will create, recreate, and recreate. We will work, yes, but we will really learn to play.

Many of the tools of this book may appear frivolous to your adult self. They are far from frivolous. This is a book of deep, thorough creative healing—and the tools are creative ones. It is the use of creativity which heals the creative wound. Nothing else works. Creative recovery is *not* an intellectual process. Our adult self merely "understands" a wound. Our creative artist, that inner creative child, must actually *heal* it. The job of your adult self, for the course of this book, will be to walk your creative child back into health. You will notice that I have used the word "walk." I have done so deliberately.

A pilgrimage is a physical process, a process that engages our heart and soul, not merely our well-honed intellect. What this means is *that the tools of* Vein of Gold *will be more deeply felt, and therefore more deeply resisted*, than the tools of *The Artist's Way*. The dark horseman of intellectual skepticism (also known as doubt) will be your constant traveling companion.

As you explore the Kingdoms of Story, Sight, Sound, Attitude, Relationship, Spirituality, and Possibility, you will be learning simply to "do" and you will be learning by simply doing. Ironically, by allowing yourself to make what you conceive of as "bad art" or even "crafts," you will heal yourself and give yourself the necessary strength and humility required to make good art. In other words, by working with these childlike beginner's tools, you will be reawakening in yourself your artist's right to a child's wonder and sense of play. It is from that freedom that your mature creativity must be born. In other words, in order to go forward, you must first go back.

The tradition of pilgrimage is as old as religion itself.
DR. LAUREN ARTRESS

Skepticism, as I said, is not intellectual only; it is moral also; a chronic atrophy and disease of the whole soul.
THOMAS CARLYLE

Pilgrims are persons in motion passing through territories not their own—seeking something we might call completion, or perhaps the word clarity *will do as well, a goal to which only the spirit's compass points the way.*
RICHARD H. NIEBUHR

To create is always to learn, to begin over, to begin at zero.
MATTHEW FOX

It is, of course, my hope, that you will choose to work—and play—with these tools. If you do, you will reclaim your keys to the creative gifts locked within you. You will discover that the keys have been yours all along. This means, of course, that it is not my place to name you an artist. Such power would be lovely, but it does not reside with me. You are the one who must name yourself. You are the one who must seek—and claim—your creative destiny. No one can do that for you, but you can do it for yourself.

"This doesn't make sense. It's not productive. This is like kindergarten. What does all of this craft have to do with art?"

These whispered doubts are like the trolls who hide under the bridge in fairy tales so that the traveler is afraid to pass.

"Where is this getting me? This is a waste of my valuable time!" the skeptic will protest when presented with a spiritual tool such as walking. I just don't *get* this!"

This is not a book that can be "gotten" by reading it. This book cannot be read and evaluated any more than India or Bangkok or Jerusalem can be experienced without going there. A travel book is a travel *book*. I am asking you to take the journey instead. The tools of this book are rigorous, albeit playful. They require commitment and engagement. In other words, this is not a book of creative theories. It is a book of creative practice. Again, these tools cannot be read and evaluated, they must be worked.

Can you feel the hackles of your intellect rising at this suggestion? Are you dubious, even a little angry? If so, that's good. Anger is energy. We have located some energy and energy can be used for change.

"Change," of course, is the polite, modern word for transformation, and transformation occurs through action: "Faith without works is dead."

This insistence on learning through doing, on healing through feeling, may make your skeptic furious.

"This is a lot of bunk! I don't see how this could possibly work! It's just so silly. . . ." Your skeptic has been trained to think this way.

"No pain, no gain," is a truism of therapy circles as well as fitness spas. "Go for the burn," we are taught, and so we roast on the spit of self-examination, turned in on ourself with excruciating intensity. Habituated by decades of therapy, we believe in what we conceive of—and experience—as "inner work": most often undertaken through talk therapy. We have an idea that insights and healing must come to us through our intellect. We seek to understand our wounds intellectually and alleviate them through that understanding. We attempt to think our way into right actions rather than act our way into right thinking.

It is time we approach self-healing in a more heart-centered and holistic way. This book asks you to experiment with the idea of growth and healing occurring through the process of "inner play." I ask you to resist your own resistance, doubt your own doubts, and take the risk of moving through and beyond your own intellectualism. For many of you this will be very frightening at first, like stepping out onto the ice or the dance floor when you are not sure you will be able to perform well. ("Well" is the voice of your Perfectionist, the Skeptic's sidekick who insists on perfection rather than progress.)

So? Perform anyway. "Just do it."

When I speak of a "vein of gold," many people think in terms of productivity. "Once I find my vein of gold, I'll strike it rich." It is more accurate to think of the vein of gold as a heart vessel, carrying the precious cargo of the flow of our true nature. Viewed this way, we don't need to "get" rich. We already are rich. This is a book about coming to that recognition; therefore, these tools are about process, not product. Once we undergo the process of healing and valuing ourselves, once we know our own worth, then we will be able to know the worth of what we create and can therefore create more freely.

From my perspective as teacher and witness, transformation is available to anyone willing to pick up spiritual tools and use them for creative unfolding.

Why do I specify *spiritual* tools? Couldn't we call the tools in this book something else? We could, but I believe we would be short-changing ourselves and mincing words as well.

As long as we remain closed to the possibility of spiritual help in our unfolding, we are choosing to operate off the battery pack of our limited resources. When we open to spiritual assistance—however

With everyone born human, a poet—an artist—is born, who dies young and who is survived by an adult.

CHARLES-AUGUSTIN
SAINTE-BEUVE

A frontier is never a place; it is a time and a way of life.

HAL BORLAND

Fun has a sacred dimension.
ADRIANA DIAZ

*Creative breakthroughs are
experiential. They don't
come from intellectual
analysis.*
LUCIA CAPACCHIONE

*We are so captivated by and
entangled in our subjective
consciousness that we have
forgotten the age-old fact
that God speaks chiefly
through dreams and visions.*
CARL JUNG

tentatively, however experimentally—we tap into unlimited supply. No longer restricted by the circumstances of our birth (or our current life, for that matter) we are able to receive sustenance, guidance, and even material resources that support our dreams and our flowering.

All of the tools of both *The Artist's Way* and *The Vein of Gold* are instrumental in assisting spiritual opening. In the world of spirit, there are no orphans or stepchildren. Each of us is a child of the Universe with an enormous endowment available for our use. The recovery of that endowment is the reward of working with these playful tools.

This contact with the first—or authentic, or original—self can feel as magical as encountering a deer in a mountain clearing. "Could that magical creature really be *me?*" we may wonder as the first shimmers of self shine through our doubts.

And so we start. We become pilgrims. Because our pilgrimage is an internal one, to the riches locked within our own hearts, we become prospectors and miners as well.

In order to arrive at paydirt, the valuable ore they are seeking, miners must sift through and discard a great deal of worthless material known as "the overburden." In personal terms, our individual overburden can obscure the gleam of a creative gift.

Buried under the negative (or simply ignorant or misleading) interpretations of others, the glistening veins of our talents, dreams, and aspirations must be actively sought in order to be found. Like miners, we will dig for these secret lodes of riches. We will pick out the nuggets of self we find hidden below our surface lives. We will haul these treasures to light, clean them off, and claim them. Each bit of authenticity we are able to own constitutes a part of our vein of gold. Once uncovered, the original self is vital and vibrant—not at all the colorless, lackluster depressive so many of us have felt ourselves become!

This book is about becoming—*recognizing*—your original self. Recovering your original self is a withdrawal process, one in which we pull our energy back into our core, depositing it within our self, in our center, where we can access it for our dreams and goals. In other words, we withdraw our energy from any mis-investments in the priorities, expectations, and interpretations of others. It is with this recognition as the goal that I devised the set of tools you will be using to excavate your vein of gold. And for many of us, finding ourselves may take quite a bit of digging!

We don't always know what makes us happy. We know, instead, what we think *should*. We are baffled and confused when our attempts at happiness fail. We get the dream job and it is a nightmare. We find we miss the dead-end job we left behind. We finally purchase a swank new condo with high-rise views, only to find we miss the old back porch on the railroad flat we shed like a seedy coat.

What's going on here? Shouldn't we be smarter? How could we be so . . . dumb?

We are dumb, no question, but only in the sense of being mute. We are mute when it comes to naming accurately our own preferences, delights, gifts, talents. The voice of our original self is often muffled, overwhelmed, even strangled, by the voices of other people's expectations. The tongue of the original self is the language of the heart. It is the purpose of this book to amplify that voice.

That's what we'll be doing in the exercises that follow: Working with autobiographical writing, collage, mask-making, doll-making, spiritual disciplines such as walking meditation, song, and silence, we will ask ourselves the questions, "Who am I? What do I love? In what directions do I choose to extend myself?" Some of our answers and explorations will be surprising. This book may at times feel like a maze or a labyrinth.

"How is this going to pay off? Why isn't she teaching me something?" the skeptic will shrill.

This book is not about *my* teaching you something. It is about your teaching yourself. This book is not about my answering questions. It is about your asking and answering questions yourself. You are both the traveler and the destination. Your destiny is the arrival at your internal truth, the place within you that's so still, so central, and so *you* that you are the midpoint—the eye and the "I."

In this fulfillment, we have the active partnership of what I call the Great Creator. Others call this power God or Higher Power or Christ or Great Mother, or simply the Tao or the Force. While each of us may name or envision or experience this power differently, working with the tools of *The Artist's Way* and *The Vein of Gold* does es-

To believe your own thought, to believe that what is true for you in your private heart is true for all men—that is genius.

RALPH WALDO EMERSON

If you are seeking creative ideas, go out walking. Angels whisper to a man when he goes for a walk.
RAYMOND INMON

Art is a definite way of knowledge or approach to truth. . . .
PETER ROGERS

tablish the spark of connection and the eventual sense of an ongoing collaboration in which our plans and dreams are both manifested and improved through the power of this creative source.

The tools and understandings of this book are the fruit of thirty years as an active artist. I could tell you that I have been a *working* artist, but that would not be true. What I have been is a *playing* artist, and it is in that sense of play that I have found the keys to continual, abundant creativity.

In *The Artist's Way*, a reconnection to the inner artist was established. (The pivotal Artist's Way tools are reviewed in this book to be absolutely certain they are in place for those who have worked the Artist's Way and to put them in place for those who have not. You will find them in the next chapter, "In Your Backpack.") The process of inner healing both proceeds and inaugurates productivity. An artist, in order to function fully, must be both vulnerable *and* resilient. This requires spiritual autonomy, and that is the gift of the healed heart.

The vein of gold is the sense of self connecting to self that comes when we are utterly true to ourselves. It is, in short, a sort of power beam that we can access in our heart of hearts. This beam is the dazzling light of spiritual clarity: we see our gifts as God-given and realize how to actualize them. When we are centered in our hearts, when we act in accordance with our truest nature, we access and express our vein of gold. We do it automatically, creatively, and consistently. It is the aim of this book to so strengthen and heal the inner artist that such living becomes an everyday reality.

Most of us are not raised to actively encounter our destiny. We may not know we have one. As children, we are seldom told we have a place in life that is uniquely ours alone. Instead, we are encouraged to believe that our life should somehow fulfill the expectations of others, that we will (or should) find our satisfactions as they have found theirs. Rather than being taught to ask *ourselves* who we are, we are schooled to ask others. We are, in effect, trained to listen to others' versions of ourselves. We are brought up in our life *as told to us by someone else!* When we survey our lives, seeking to fulfill our creativity, we often see we had a dream that went glimmering because we believed, and those around us believed, that the dream was beyond our reach. Many of us would have been, or at least might have been, done, tried *something*, if . . .

If we had known who we really were.

But how were we to know? We were being told stories that didn't tell us all of the possible happy endings—or even all of the possible meanings of the stories themselves. The Ugly Duckling did not know it was a swan because it had never seen another swan.

Turned in on itself, creativity becomes both a consolation and a source of isolation. Many an imaginary playmate was invented from the yearning for shared creative adventures. The bottled-up wish for a more magical life is often the unspoken grief carried by the creative adult who has forgotten, abandoned, or marginalized the creative child he used to be. That child had stories to tell and knew it. Those stories, buried below the surface of our life, are still waiting to be mined and told—first to us and then to others.

All of us have lives striped in our own colors. All of us have stories embedded within our official life story that are the stories of our own truest heart. The trick—the one we will be practicing in these pages—is to separate out our version of our story, our version of ourself. The pilgrimage we are making is to our own core, our own reality, our own sense of self and self-expression.

Art provides a healing force which aids both the maker and the viewer. . . .

RICHARD NEWMAN

Although the tools we will use are often three-dimensional, involving not only sight but also sound and touch, this book is, at its base, a book about stories. It is about the stories others tell about you, and the stories you tell yourself. As we work, we will be asking, "What stories do I tell about myself? What stories do others tell about me?"

You may find your stories quite different from the stories told about you. Or the stories may be the same, but the meanings assigned to them very different. As you work with your life stories, you may find yourself seeing your character quite differently and realizing that you yourself can alter the plot you have been living out.

And yet, for all its involvement with story, this is not a book about writing. It is, more accurately, a book about *righting*: we will right the wrongful images we have of ourself. We will use tools of many descriptions to change our faulty descriptions of ourself.

Some of you may enjoy thinking of these tools in mythic terms: the tasks of Hercules, just smaller. The word I use for many of them is "challenging," often because they seem so whimsical that your Skeptic will rear its head and howl.

Remember that your Skeptic is the dragon at the gate. The riches you are seeking lie within. You must evade, even slay, your Skeptic to enter your heart. And yet your Skeptic is not your enemy. Your Skeptic is the adversary that will make you strong. Each time you grapple with your doubt, each time you doff your intellectualism to experience a tool rather than analyze it, each time you choose to actualize rather than theorize your creativity, you will move ahead.

I am asking you to experiment, to employ these tools by entering them experientially. Their benefit lies in discovering their result not in distancing yourself intellectually by trying to figure them out. Many of the tools you resist the most strongly will be those which serve you best. In a spirit of excitement and adventure, I invite you to experiment and see if this is true.

Art is made through a series of moments—choices—leading each to the next. Life is made the same way. When we desire to live artfully, we must live not only consciously but concretely. We must shape our life. This book is a series of healing tools intended as a prescription for artful living.

In Your Backpack:
The Basic Tools

MORNING PAGES

For the duration of this pilgrimage (and I would hope, long beyond
it), I ask you to employ three pages of daily, longhand morning writing called Morning Pages. Yes, they must be longhand. Yes, they
must be done in the morning. (If you have done *The Artist's Way*, you
have done your Morning Pages. Hopefully, you do them still.) You
may think of them as anything from "brain drain" to meditation.

Morning Pages will center you, steady you, empower you, enlighten you. They will comfort you, console you, stimulate you, intrigue you, challenge, irritate, and *activate* you. For Westerners, they
are a potent form of meditation, and like all meditation, they will
make you intimate with yourself, with your personality and all its
fears, foibles, and quirks. Practiced over time, Morning Pages become
a reliable bridge to the Universe itself. Through them you will encounter the workings of your spirituality, the great Creator within,
with all its grace, wisdom, and power.

Here's how you do them:

Every morning, write three longhand pages (single-sided, eight
and a half by eleven inches) of whatever comes into your head. Not

*It is necessary to write, if
the days are not to slip
emptily by.*

VITA SACKVILLE-WEST

*This is the practice school of
writing. Like running, the
more you do it, the better
you get at it.*

NATALIE GOLDBERG

13

*My painting is always
ahead of my understanding.
It is a sort of teaching
process for myself, a way of
spiritual knowledge.*

PETER ROGERS

*Only a mediocre writer is
always at his best.*

W. SOMERSET MAUGHAM

art. Not thought. Just . . . stuff. As my friend Timothy says, "We *all* have our stuff."

Stuff like, "My back hurts. I forgot to call Joanne back. I need to do laundry. Did I forget to buy Tide? I hate what Terry said about me at the meeting yesterday. He's so self-serving. Maybe I need to keep a file of just what *I've* done on this project. . . . Do I need to buy dog food?"

Sometimes joyous, sometimes sad, the Morning Pages may be whiny, petty, full of gripes. Conversely, some of the stuff may be far larger. "I sense Dad's in more pain than he is letting on," or "I could propose we go a whole new direction with this project and it just might be perfect. . . ."

Sometimes they pinpoint realizations about what's working for you. "You know, for once I think I am pretty happy. Those Daily Walks may be really helping." Alternatively, they may hold flights of fancy.

"I'd love to go to Australia."

"Wouldn't it be fun to write a musical?"

"I could bike to work most days."

"It would be fun to *combine* my photographs and poems."

Not all insights need to be dazzling. Not all days need to hold insights at all. In other words, the point of doing the pages is doing the pages: process, *not* product. Think of them as playing scales. Yes, they take time, but by prioritizing how we spend our time, they give us time as well.

Have I emphasized Morning Pages must be done by hand? I know that is inconvenient, unpleasant, time-consuming, archaic. I ask you to do them that way because it works.

What does that mean?

Why By Hand?

We prick our finger and sign in blood. It is an oath to tell the truth. In a darkened room we touch our fingertips, and when we draw them apart, they trail particles of light. There is an energy to the hand, an energy of blood, of truth, and knowledge that is deeper than skin. Blood is the body's ink. We write our lives in it. The blood remembers what the mind forgets, and when the blood remembers, it tells the hand.

Writing by hand is not merely writing. It is "righting." If we follow our hand, which both leads and follows our thoughts, that hand will point to the trail. (Since we are on a pilgrimage, this is important!)

Writing by hand is like walking somewhere, instead of whizzing there in the car. We notice landmarks. We retain a sense of direction. Writing by hand will show us True North and the false directions and switchbacks that have occurred, the shortcuts that saved us nothing and took us nowhere.

Remember, the hand holds a map in its palm; its fingers, holding a pen, become the tools of a cartographer. We write, and as we do, we see the right lineaments of our life. Each word is a new arrival, a place to stand on, like a musical note.

"But, Julia! I type a lot faster than I write!"

I understand. But speed is not always desirable. We are after a process that will allow for depth *and* distance, not just speed. Writing by machine may accumulate pages, but I am not sure if those pages accumulate enough depth. In the end, the pages are better when they are made by hand.

We are on a pilgrimage, and writing by hand allows us to examine more closely the journey we are taking. We write our views, and the term is quite literal. We *see* how we feel. We see our life by the way we finger it.

Palmists will tell you your life is written on your hand. Handwriting experts will tell you that the loops and loopholes of character are in your handwriting. I would say you help determine your life through your hand, writing. Line by line, by hand, we are able to make a handmade life.

"But, Julia! I'm a talker! Can't I talk my pages into a tape recorder?"

Words can be wrapped on tape and spooled into a ball. This will capture the thread of what you are saying, but the danger is that such isolated threads can make lies of whole cloth. The tongue is slippery, slick, evasive. The hand—nimble perhaps, but humble—seldom lies.

I don't wait for moods. You accomplish nothing if you do that. Your mind must know it has got to get down to work.

PEARL BUCK

*Just as appetite comes by
eating, so work brings
inspiration.*
IGOR STRAVINSKY

*Work and play are the same.
When you're following
your energy and doing what
you want all the time, the
distinction between work and
play dissolves.*
SHAKTI GAWAIN

A touch is a touch no matter how we disguise it. And so, writing by hand, we touch the truth. It knuckles under.

"But the truth changes!" you tell me.

Yes, it does. It changes under our hand. We call it "writing," and as you will see, it does right things. We begin with a version of reality that is neat, slick, and clean—a sheet of paper. When we move our hand across our experience, something more complicated happens. We see where we have told ourselves one thing while feeling quite another. By writing lines on a page, we begin to read between them. We sink below the surface of events to the interior mystery of our feelings, intuitions, motives, and lessons.

Although an occasional rereading of the Morning Pages can be very valuable, they are not meant to be pored over and reexamined obsessively. Pressing themes will emerge—and reemerge later if we have not dealt with them.

As a rule of thumb, allow some weeks to accumulate before you do reread your pages—and *never* allow anyone else to read them. When you read, read as if you were your own closest friend looking for sources of pain and happiness. Be alert for recurring themes, concerns, and causes for celebration.

I lived for years in Greenwich Village. Only when I found myself writing my delight in window boxes, city cats, and city dogs did I realize that my daily flora and fauna reports might indicate that a more rural life was called for. It was the Morning Pages that helped me break my denial. Officially, I was a terminally hip downtown artist, urban and urbane. At heart, I longed for country roads, sunflowers, and chicory.

As I write this, I live in a small mountain town where we drive to the post office to get our mail. Nearly every day, I get a letter like the one below from someone whose Morning Pages led him to an altered life:

"I've been working with them now for nearly nine months. I've moved back into my photography, out of a bad relationship, into a great guest house, and I'm actually doing improv. . . ."

We are *all* doing improv. Our lines are a musical composition of our and the Universe's devising. Morning Pages teach us to hear our cues, follow our promptings, enter and exit with grace, play our songs with heart.

Remember: do not obsess on your pages as literary material. They are intended not as art but as artifact: the pottery shards of your month of July. Remember that writing your Pages, not reading them, is the heart of this tool's value.

∼∼ Task: Morning Pages. ∼∼

Each day, every day, get up early and write your Morning Pages. Again, remember that they are not meant to be art. (In fact, they need not even be legible to anyone but yourself.) Do not use a tiny little notebook. It will crimp your thoughts. A hard-bound, eight-and-a-half-by-eleven notebook serves me nicely—although some people prefer spiral-bound.

Everywhere I go, I find a poet has been there before me.
SIGMUND FREUD

Artist Dates

Stefan Grapelli once remarked, "Great improvisors are like priests. They are always listening to their god." The second tool is a listening tool, a weekly period of assigned solitude that I call the Artist Date.

I now know how to plan my life and direct my path because God is doing this for me by doing it through me.
ERNEST HOLMES

Shamanic healing is a journey. It involves stepping out of our habitual roles, our conventional scripts, and improvising a dancing path.
GABRIELLE ROTH

In Morning Pages, we are like a radio set tuned to send: we notify ourselves and the Universe of our likes, dislikes, and dreams. This is busy work. It siphons off steam and it creates a vacuum into which new thoughts and impulses can move, if we let them. That is where our listening tool comes in.

Life flows like a river. We can skim the surface or plunge more deeply into our experience. It is solitude that encourages and permits the experience of depth. No wonder so many of us avoid it. The currents of our emotions frighten us. We sense powerful forces moving in the depths of our being. These forces often frighten us, and so we avoid contact. We become distracted by the surface of our lives. Our thoughts scuttle and dart like water bugs skating on the glassy sheen of current events. Leading lives of quick, shallow contacts, we yearn for something deeper, but even the yearning may disturb us.

For this reason, the second tool involves creative deepening. As those who have studied creativity know, breakthroughs occur when focused, rational thought and activity are followed by a period of release. This is why we get up from our desks frustrated and exhausted, decide to shower and—bing!—there's the answer. This is why good solutions emerge not in our office, but as we merge five lanes left in traffic, or as we pause in our manic writing and rewriting of our thesis to hand-polish our boots for the first time this winter.

The Artist Date, an hour or longer weekly block of time spent on yourself and with yourself, doing something festive, is intended to engender release. Release, in turn, engenders inspiration.

In Manhattan, a particularly magical Artist's Date for me was a visit to the Compleat Traveler, a small, treasure-laden store on the corner of Thirty-fifth Street and Madison Avenue. Filled with everything from maps of Ireland, Polynesia, and the Isle of Wight to vintage books on Marco Polo and the Himalayas, it is a world where time and distance conspire and conjoin.

Aquarium stores, museums, cathedrals, flea markets, or five-and-dimes . . . vintage films, lectures on the odd, the improbable, or merely interesting . . . musical performances by traveling Tibetan monks, a trip to a quiet, riverside spot—any of these can function as an Artist Date.

And yet, many of us are too busy and too intellectually self-defended to allow such small gateways for inspiration to gain entrance. Longing for change, we nonetheless avoid the avenues through which it might come to us. We fill our quiet time with business or busy-ness. We do not know how to relax, or even that we should.

In our product-driven society, work, especially networking, makes us feel important and *product*ive. Of course it may also make us feel cranky, put upon, overtired, frustrated, thwarted, bored, and miserable—but who has time to think of that? Who *wants* time to think of that?

We do. We just may not know that we do.

In the term "Artist Date," note that "date" is of equal weight with the word "artist." In other words, preplanning and anticipating the experience are central to properly working with this tool. We are training ourselves in the art of self-initiated nurturance. Our dates need not be highbrow, elaborate, or expensive, but we must be careful not to stand ourselves up. We are *romancing* our creative urges. Nothing kills a romance more quickly than a few broken promises.

Ah, but I was so much older then, I'm younger than that now. BOB DYLAN

Let the beauty we love be what we do. RUMI

When the eye wakes up to
see again, it suddenly stops
taking anything for granted.
FREDERICK FRANCK

We are shaped and fashioned
by what we love.
JOHANN WOLFGANG VON
GOETHE

Artist Dates, in conjunction with Morning Pages, perform major adjustments in spiritual chiropractic. That is, they tend to align us with a flow of what might be called luck, coincidence, or good orderly direction. (What Dr. Carl Jung termed "synchronicity.") We tend to be in the right place at the right time, encountering not only support, but also opportunity. Ideally, an Artist Date is a time for receiving inflow—new images from some festive activity; new perspectives from the time alone, free from the input of familiar sources; new currents of thought and activity triggered through the operation of synchronicity.

Despite their obvious advantages, don't expect Artist Dates to be an easy matter. Most of us are skilled spiritual anorectics, and we are adroit at avoiding self-nurturing. Set an enjoyable Artist Date and then watch your killing side swing into action with sudden self-imposed deadlines and wet-blanket agendas, all designed to sabotage your creative solitude. Visiting friends, needy spouses, friends on the rocks—all may suddenly become sidecars to your solo adventure. Before your wondering eyes, a hundred valid excuses (but no good reasons) will suggest themselves to help you postpone, evade, dilute your expedition.

Make no mistake, Artist Dates are like blind dates: we hope for the best, fear the worst, and undertake them, if at all, with a sense of duress more often than elation.

Please do them anyway.

I admit that time alone, deliberately undertaken, can be threatening. I admit it can be hard to arrange and could even seem as though I am a stickler for details. After all, what could be wrong with a trip to the ballet *à deux?*

Simply this: you are not after the thoughts and companionship of others. You are after the thoughts and companionship of your soul.

With daily Morning Pages and a weekly Artist Date in place, the exercises, tasks, and expeditions this book requires—some psychic and some physical—are far more easily undertaken. You might consider them spiritual sit-ups. They render you strong, flexible, and fit. These attributes will serve you well as you undertake the pilgrimage necessary to find and mine your vein of gold.

∼ Task: Do a Weekly Artist Date. ∼

Each week, every week, take your creative consciousness out on a pre-
planned, festive expedition. Again, remember that this need not be
"high art." It is more important that this be soul food for you, however you define it. Remember that art is an image-using system and
that you are to use this time to consciously stock your imagination.
Think of it like a pond, filled with deep and swirling images. You
want to keep it stocked so that when you go to draw upon it it will not
be overfished.

Clusters: Your Traveling Companions

This pilgrimage will work perfectly well for you if you undertake to do it alone. It is my experience, however, that you might find it more enjoyable to have traveling companions. I call such a group of kindred souls a "creative cluster."

Now what do I mean by a creative cluster? I mean a group of people who are interested in supporting each other's creativity by banding together and undertaking this journey as a group. There does not need to be any leader or facilitator, although there can be. (See the appendix at the end of the book for guidelines.) A cluster can be as small as two people or as large as you wish.

The main thing to remember about cluster work is that it is intended to be supportive, not competitive, and that it is based on sharing actual work with the tools (the solution) instead of merely griping about the obstacles (the problem)! It is a way of sharing experience and staying on the trail.

In terms of choosing clustermates, all that is required is that you find someone to play with you. That someone (or someones) should be positive and reliable. They should also be committed to expanding their own creative potential, not just to fixing *you* up. Remember that a cluster is a circle of equals joined together for a common cause: to help each other recover from creative discouragement. I like to call clustermates "believing mirrors." They mirror back a belief in your creative unfolding.

It is an important function of a creative cluster to remind us that creativity is an act of the soul, an expansion and extension of divine creative force, and not just some "ego trip" we are indulging in.

In Chicago, a cluster that I led years ago still gathers regularly every Tuesday night. What they do on those Tuesday nights is continue to teach and expand and support each other. In this way, Maureen is cheered on to rewrite her script about World War II women in aviation. Ginny gets enthusiasm for her television talkathon shows. Pam receives feedback about her theatrical career. Ilyce gets a cheering section for her books.

Now, as it happens, this cluster is made up primarily of writers, but a cluster can and often should be more multicolored than that. You don't have to be a declared artist to start a cluster or join one. You simply need to have a desire to try being more creative.

When I asked some recent students what they found most valuable about clusters, their responses varied, although all, *without exception*, agreed they were valuable.

Kathy told me, "Clusters were valuable because sharing experience took the skeletons out of the closet and they didn't rattle quite as loudly. It brought compassion and empathy."

Joan felt, "Clusters are awesome and enlightening. They reminded me of many things I had forgotten."

Melissa said quietly, "They created an opening space. The intimacy was in most cases incredible."

Andrew observed, "Clusters affirm the humanness in all of us yet acknowledge our individuality."

There is a decade-old twelve-step program, Arts Anonymous, which has been forming its own creative clusters and generating powerful support and literature. They are headquartered in New York, and many people in Arts Anonymous find that the tools of their program work well with the tools of *The Artist's Way* and this book.

We did not all come over on the same ship, but we are all in the same boat.

BERNARD BARUCH

Invent your world. Surround yourself with people, color, sounds, and work that nourish you. SARK

*I accept the Divine Presence
as now bountifully expressing peace and harmony
in my life.*
ERNEST HOLMES

*Without connection there is
something dangerous and
wrong about the world.*
DAVID NICHOLS

~ Task: Cluster List. ~

Make a list of people with whom you could form a creative cluster. Although geographic proximity is nice, it is not always a prerequisite. Clusters have worked by phone and even by letter. (In England, they seem to have begun chiefly that way.)

Once you have your potential cluster list in hand, you may want to move on to contacting people and actually setting up a cluster. If so, you would plan to meet once a week. (Again, be sure to see the appendix at the back of the book for cluster guidelines.) If not, simply save your cluster list and remember that you can phone the people on it if you find at any point in the process of this book you need a little cheering on. In fact, it would be my suggestion that you phone one or two of your cluster list to specifically ask them if they would serve as that sort of support for you. A pilgrimage, after all, is a strenuous undertaking, one in which companionship and support may be pivotal.

My longtime teaching partner Mark Bryan twice ran the grueling Chicago marathon. Both times he felt his capacity to successfully finish was owed in part to the loyal support of his friends who showed up near race's end and cheered his every exhausted step.

As for myself, as I work through a book, play, or screenplay, I often alert my friends: "Prayers are welcome. I'm in the homestretch. Help! Send good thoughts!" Their positive energies function as booster rockets for my own. Please use your cluster list in the same way.

Your Mode of Transportation:
Walking

One of the most powerful tools for a *spiritual renewal* is a simple and overlooked one. It is so simple and so commonplace that people mistake it for metaphor. We say, "I am walking my way back into my creativity," but we do not realize that this is a literal statement. Walking is the most powerful creative tool that I know. Although it has fallen into disuse in our hurried times, it may be the most powerful spiritual practice known to man. Because, for the purposes of this book, creativity and spirituality are indistinguishable, we will walk for inspiration and integration.

A creative life is a process, and that process is digestion. We speak of "food for thought" but seldom realize that as artists we need *thought* for food. Walking, with its constant inflow of new images, gives us new thoughts that nourish us. It replenishes our overtapped creative well and gives us a sense of . . . well, wellness.

Yes, art is an interior process, but it is also an exterior one. We are seeking images and we see them both through our physical eyes and our mind's eye. All too often, in the name of our art, we lock ourselves away from new experiences and shut ourselves off from both sight and insight. Holed up working, we wonder what happened to our imagination's sense of play.

Travelers, there is no path, paths are made by walking.
ANTONIO MACHADO

Solvitur ambulando. . . . It is solved by walking. . . .
ST. AUGUSTINE

25

. . . Learn to see, and then you'll know that there is no end to the new worlds of our vision.

CARLOS CASTANEDA

Father Earth is the Green Man of the Craft, the God who is pictured crowned with leaves and twined with vines, the spirit of vegetation, growing things, the forest.

STARHAWK

Walking opens us up. It feeds us. Image by image, it spoons up for us a broth or soup of soul food, which sustains us as we do the work necessary to shape and reshape our lives. In other words, we can walk our way out of "problem" and into "solution."

If I am snagged on a story line, I walk it out. If I am stymied about what to work on next, I walk until it comes to me. When I am tangled in the plot lines of my work or my life, I take a walk and allow the walk to sort things out.

Creativity is a spiritual process, one in which we speak of "inspiration." When we talk about inspiration we are talking about drawing breath. Walking makes our breathing rhythmic and repetitive. As our breath steadies and soars, so does our thought. Great spiritual traditions know this. English pilgrims traveled by foot to Canterbury. Muslims braved the trackless Sahara to visit Mecca. Across cultures and continents, walking is an ancient and literal form for pursuing a spiritual path.

Druids and Wiccans quest by walking. Tibetans make circular pilgrimages around Kalais, the sacred mountain that is Shiva's birthplace. (The Tibetan word for human is *a-Gro ba*, "a go-er," "one who goes on migrations.") Native Americans walk for vision quests. Jesus the Nazarene did the same thing, venturing into the desert for forty days and forty nights to glimpse and prepare for what his future held. All of us make a pilgrimage whenever we set ourselves outward bound for inner voyaging. Walking is the simplest way to do this.

John Muir, explorer, conservationist, and nature mystic, once wrote ruefully, "I only went out for a walk, and finally concluded to stay out till sundown, for going out, I found, was really going in."

Theologians speak of "the ground of being" as a synonym for God. I believe that the ground is the being of God, and it speaks to our *souls* through our *soles*. Do not think I am kidding here. Please do not imagine that the puns are merely facile.

Several years ago, I went through a spiritual passage during which I "saw" that the earth was a living being which stored all of our collective experiences, every footfall and whisper, every passion, hope, heartbreak, dream that any of us had ever embodied. To learn of these things, we had only to listen carefully enough to the earth. Through it, our ancestors spoke to us. I remember telling my friends to leave me alone and let me just sit out under my apple tree to listen and learn. I remember telling them that if they wanted to spend time with me just then, we could *walk* the land and talk. (My friends became concerned for my sanity, but I felt I was watching and listening to something very important.)

In the time since this passage, I have let my fingers do some walking as well. I have many books now which are underlined and scribbled in. I've found "my" insights recorded by others as their own spiritual passages or parts of their spiritual tradition. "I saw that!" my margins exclaim, or "Yes!"

I now know that I am far from alone in believing that walking with our soles is really walking with our souls. Our internal horizons stretch with our external ones. We walk into expanded possibility: If you can bear it, the soles of our feet lead us to the feats of our souls.

Cultural ecologist Joan Halifax writes, "People have traveled over this Earth with a heart of inquiry for millennia. They have sung through the land as a living being, offered themselves, their steps, their voices and prayers as acts of purification that opened them to an experience of connectedness."

In his masterful book *Songlines,* the mystic travel writer Bruce Chatwin reminds us, "In Islam, and especially among the Sufi orders, *siyahat* or 'errance'—the action or rhythm of walking—was used as a technique for dissolving the attachments of the world and allowing men to lose themselves in God."

The English poets were (and probably remain) great walkers. They were also mystics, and the intersection of the two paths is no accident.

It is no coincidence that many poets are both mystics and walkers. It is no coincidence that poetry is divided into feet, and we speak of feet as comprising poetic meter. Meter is the gait of a poem. The gait of a poem is often the "gate" we use to enter spiritual realms. Great poets like Blake and Rumi and Roethke walk us through the gate or veil that separates us from knowing our spiritual power. When we are tapped into this power—and walking is a direct way to do this—our creativity expands far beyond what we may think of as our known "ceiling." This has been true for artists throughout the ages.

The song and the land are one.   BRUCE CHATWIN

All of the larger-than-life questions about our presence here on earth and what gifts we have to offer are spiritual questions. To seek answers to these questions is to seek a sacred path.

DR. LAUREN ARTRESS

When we pay attention to nature's music, we find that everything on the earth contributes to its harmony.

HAZRAT INAYAT KHAN

The world is charged with the grandeur of God.

GERARD MANLEY HOPKINS

When I rest my feet, my mind also ceases to function.

J. G. HAMANN

Our nature lies in movement; complete calm is death.

BLAISE PASCAL,
Pensées

In his book *Conversations on Dante*, Osip Mandelstam explains, "The *Inferno* and especially the *Purgatorio* glorify the human gait, the measure and rhythm of walking, the foot and its shape. The step, linked to the breathing and saturated with thought: this Dante understands as the beginning of prosody."

But you do not have to be a poet to undertake walking! Walking, by its rhythmic nature, makes all of us poets. We see the flash of a bluebird. The jackhammer socks out a rhythm we take on as our own jive. Life sings along our circuitry as we invite it in by venturing out into it. Chatwin reminds us that the Greek word *melos* means "limb," hence "melody."

When Walt Whitman sang "the body electric," it was the planetary body, the planetary song, which had begun to sing through his body. Although we have lost touch with our capacity to do so, we, too, can experience this same mystical connection. Even one month of walking will convince you that this is so.

As much as anything else, walking is an exercise in heightened listening. As we walk, we awaken our neural pathways and make them more sensitive. This is what sound healer Don Campbell refers to as "an acute sensing in an awakened, powerful internal space." All kinds of revelations follow.

Yet we do not need to leave our environments to experience the benefits of walking. When I am in an extremely intense urban environment—say, midtown Manhattan—I will take my Daily Walk and my Walkman, using a tape like Tim Wheater's *Timeless*. Wheater spends yearly time in Australia and the music shows it, moving past urban noise pollution and into the timeless realm where eternal questions can be raised and, if not resolved, at least examined. With the expansive and effervescent tape unspooling in my ears, I will thread my way past construction sites and urban blight, taking it in but also seeing something beyond it.

In other words, walking is a form of meditation.

When we are too heady, too full of the chatter and clatter of our stress-filled lives, our spiritual energy returns to us through our feet. We walk on the ground and we ground ourselves by walking. Zen Master Dogen called this "the walking of the self."

In Britain, Druids walk "the old tracks," pathways that crisscross the land. Called ley lines, these pathways (what the Chinese geomancers would call "dragon lines") are energy routes or currents. Viewed psychically, they resemble luminous ribbons or serpents of light. Seekers walking the energy lines experience a realignment in their own energies. If we will allow it, the physical world is a great spiritual teacher.

"But, Julia! I don't have time for walking," you may be thinking. "My life doesn't move at that pace!" Such resistance is normal.

Philip Carr-Gomm, who is currently chief of the Order of Bards, Ovates, and Druids, explains the technique: "Central to the idea of druidry is the idea that we should 'listen to the land'—that it can speak to us and guide us if we are able to open ourselves to it." Walking allows us to explore such multisensory guidance from the physical world. As a culture, we have confused velocity with accomplishment. We "run" ourselves ragged. Convinced that if we just do more and go faster we will succeed, we often lose the pulse of our own lives. We can find it again by walking.

Very often, walking our own neighborhoods or countryside, we can encounter and recognize places and routes which "feel good to us." Sometimes, a little exploration will reveal that we are walking the local ley lines. Properly named or not, such places, walked in a spirit of openness, yield tremendous spiritual clarity.

When I lived in Los Angeles I always took my problems to a particular road to sort them out. There, on a ridge inland from Malibu and a little to the north of it, I always experienced greater calm and a heightened sense of perspective.

"Of course you did," I was told years later. "That's where the ley lines are and all the Native American sacred sites were!"

In Britain, ley lines are characterized and identified by the spiritual sites located along their lengths and particularly at their intersections. There you will find a Christian shrine, built upon a pagan shrine, built upon a Paleolithic shrine. Through the eons, people have sensed the "rightness" of certain locales for spiritual purposes. Even in a city, overlaid by several hundred years of commerce, such sites are discernible. Walking such sites—walking with our spiritual

Our elders used to tell us that all holy sites are endowed with ancient wisdom. These centers have innate powers. JOSEPH RAEL

The sun shines not on us, but in us. The rivers flow not past, but through us, thrilling, tingling, vibrating every fiber and cell of the substance of our bodies, making them glide and sing. JOHN MUIR

It is good to collect things, but it is better to go on walks. ANATOLE FRANCE

The song still remains which names the land over which it sings. MARTIN HEIDEGGER

sights in place as well—is what Carr-Gomm refers to as "listening to the ancestral voices that speak through landscape."

(City-dwellers may wish to walk "point to point," stopping in to a church or synagogue at intervals en route.)

In *Songlines*, Chatwin details the Aboriginal beliefs:

> The Ancestors sang the world into existence . . . each totemic ancestor while travelling through the country was thought to have scattered a trail of words and musical notes along the lines of his footprints. . . .

The "trail of music" is both what we hear and what we make as we walk. Like the ancestors before us, we name our experience as we walk. We name both our internal and our external landscape. We have an experience of resonance, of "sounding out" our lives in relation to the physical world.

Hawaiians speak of each of their islands as having a separate tone. My own experience is that each of them has a different vibration, like the after-sound when you have tapped a drumhead. *All* land has a tone to which we can respond, a note by which we can orient ourselves, like finding our place on a musical scale. In other words, the land has its own song and you will hear it as you walk. Not only that, by learning to hear the land's song, you will recognize your own life song and learn what creates harmony and dissonance for you.

∾ Task: Walk Daily. ∾

Twenty minutes is enough. You may just want to get off the transit system one stop early or walk one stop before you get onto it at night. Your Daily Walk can be a part of your lunch hour, the way you start or unwind from your day. When you do it and how you do it matters less than *that* you do it! (Treadmills and Stairmasters provide exercise, but they do not provide an image flow. Consider them a last resort.)

When they are in nature, people sense intuitively that the other kingdoms are living in harmony with universal law. In such an environment, it's easier for the heart to open, to become softer and live in tune with the earth.

WABUN,
Sun Bear's medicine helper

It is the child that sees the primordial secret in Nature and it is the child of ourselves we return to. The child within us is simple and daring enough to live the Secret.

LAO-TZU

ᔕ Task: Walk an Hour-Long Walk Weekly. ᔕ

Use this longer walk to explore territory that is either new or very interesting to you. You may wish to drive to the country and walk there. If you live in the country, you may wish to go to the city and walk there. The idea is to stretch both your legs and your territory. You are using this walk to fill your image bank because art is an image-using system and you will be drawing heavily on your image bank in the weeks to come.

ᔕ Task: Walk Prayerfully. ᔕ

At least once a week, on one of your Daily Walks, use the time to exercise your gratitude. Consciously list and vocalize your gratitude for everything about your life that you enjoy. At first, this will require real spiritual exertion and may feel quite difficult. (Also saccharine!) What you are actually doing is gaining altitude so that you see your life from a higher perspective, where you are able to recognize many more choices.

This practice creates a dramatic shift in consciousness and often in mood. As the mystic Meister Eckhart noted, "If the only prayer you say in your whole life is 'thank you' that would suffice."

Earth with her thousand voices praises God.
SAMUEL TAYLOR COLERIDGE

For you can look at things while talking or with a radio going full blast, but you can see only when the chatter stops.

FREDERICK FRANCK

The secret of the receptive Must be sought in stillness; Within stillness there remains The potential for action.

ZHOU XUANJIING

The Gateway: Entering the Imagic-Nation

Many of us resist walking because it "doesn't really get us any-where," except perhaps physically. We recognize that it might be good exercise, but we tend to dismiss it as a "pastime," even a hobby. We say to ourselves skeptically, "I go out for this Daily Walk and I come back and nothing's changed except that I've wasted half an hour." We think this way because we view walking as primarily a physical process. It is much more than that.

As we walk, we cross the bridge into the realm of desire and imagination. I call this realm the "Imagic-Nation." The term is very specific, suggesting as it does that it is through *images* that we popu-late our own kingdoms, create our own lives. "Ask and you shall re-ceive; believe and it shall be opened to you."

By consciously "walking" into our Imagic-Nation on a daily basis, we are able to generate desired forms in the material world. We can bring our ideal into the real by crystallizing the ideal with enough imaginative weight that it takes on a concrete form. It does not matter whether we are attempting to bring in a novel, a movie, a new studio to work in, an improved relationship with a spouse or friend, or a better state of health. What we can conceptualize and inhabit on the imaginative realm, we can manifest and materialize on the physical one. There are creative powers larger than our own which will consciously assist us in shaping our destinies and desires—if we will seek their involvement. This is what we do as we walk in our Imagic-Nation.

Some artists call this "seeking the muse." It doesn't really matter what you call the process. What matters is that we learn to *do* the process. It is a sort of climbing, or crossing over, that in spiritual traditions is often conceptualized as "climbing a ladder" or "crossing a bridge." The physical act of walking makes this crossing over very easy, almost automatic. I experience it as a small shift that I can feel in the back of my head, just above the base of the spine. *You don't need to physically feel it for it to occur.*

Another way to think it is to imagine it as a sort of "linking up"—like a small aircraft refueling by connecting to a larger aircraft in midair. What we want to do is consciously attach our individual consciousness to what might be called "greater consciousness." Then, in that expanded state, we allow our imaginations to play with what we would like to actually effect. This inner "play" creates an outer change.

Leonardo da Vinci knew this. Walt Disney knew this. Contemporary artists like George Lucas and Steven Spielberg know this. Physicists now know this. "Primitive people" and their shamans have always known this. We sophisticated ones are late to the party, rediscovering some very old techniques.

For more than 40,000 known years, Aborigines have walked in Dreamtime. In this "timeless" dimension, they dream toward the future and the future dreams back. In this realm, they alter the future by altering the way they dream back at it. We can do the same thing. Walking allows the body to move into Dreamtime. (Or, as I prefer to call it, the "Imagic-Nation.")

As we walk toward our future it also moves toward us, much the way clouds move toward an aircraft. We catch glimpses of it like photographic images flashing briefly through the soup of our consciousness. As we continue to *walk,* the briefly flashed image becomes clearer; now it is more like an image emerging from a mirage. We

Sometimes, I think
The things we see
Are shadows of the things to
*   be;*
That what we plan we
build . . .

PHOEBE CARY

Yes, creation is moving to-
ward us; life is moving to-
ward us all the time. We
back away, but it keeps push-
ing toward us.

JOAN HALIFAX

You have the power in the present moment to change limiting beliefs and consciously plant the seeds for the future of your choosing. As you change your mind, you change your experience.

SERGE KAHILI KING

The shamanic state of consciousness, however, is dominated by the alpha wave cycle.

MICHAEL DRAKE

Art is prayer.

JOSEPH ZINKER

wonder, "Is this dream a trick of my mind's eye—or could it be real?"

It is real. Just not yet material. Desire (energy), coupled with imagination, creates form. In other words, we enter into a "place" or "space" where we are able to effect change. Metaphysically, this is called the "causal plane."

As we keep on walking, the dream takes on solidity. We are bringing it into form one step at a time. Just as the Aborigines have always known, as the Hawaiian kahunas have known, the dream of our future is both sacred and malleable. By entering our Imagic-Nation and walking within the realm of imagination on a daily basis, we can encounter the shape of our probable future and shape a different one by changing how we think. We can think, "What if I . . . ?" and "Wouldn't it be nice if . . . ?" and "I think it would be possible to . . ."

Many books on shamanism explore and explain Dreamtime at some length. For our purposes we can simply think of it as a sort of channel of consciousness, a band or wavelength where both time and events are flexible. In that realm, positive dreams take on reality. At first you may want to think of it as playing make-believe, or call it "watching an inner movie." No matter how you conceptualize it, it is an altered state of consciousness that is available to us through crossing a sort of bridge either sonically or rhythmically. Walking is an easy way to move into it.

As we align our own thinking to more positive possibilities, they shift toward probability. Expanding with our stride, our minds begin to experience broader horizons, wider possibilities. This expansion and yearning create not only the possibility of change but change itself. Our clarity in limning a desired outcome catalyzes that outcome. Theologian Pierre Teilhard de Chardin saw this clearly: "Matter is transparent and malleable in relation to spirit."

It is almost as though the laws for creative manifestation are laid out for us, but in code. For example, all of us use the phrase "seeing is believing," but we use it as if what we see is already in tangible, solid form. My feeling is that the phrase is intended as a creative direction or law: "*See*, and then you will *believe*." In other words, see first with your mind's eye. The act of such seeing *causes* the tangible form to materialize.

For many of us, this is a difficult concept at first, trained as we are to believe in a God outside of us who might find our dreams and desires suspect or uppity. And yet when we posit ourselves as co-creators—extensions, if you will—of an inner creative force that manifests through us, we are only agreeing with Goethe, who asked, "What sort of God would it be who only pushed from without?"

In other words, consider the possibility that our dreams and desires are the voice of our soul, the God-voice awake within us, dreaming of expression and expansion through our daring and our faith. We walk into that faith, that daring, a step at a time. As we do so, we pass through the portal into Imagic-Nation.

It could fairly be said that when we enter Imagic-Nation, we enter the realm of mind over matter. Or, to put it differently, the realm where mind appears to create matter. You may want to think of it as a form of magnetism. A clear dream takes shape and draws form to itself like metallic shavings.

Teacher Shakti Gawain puts it almost identically: "When we create something, we always create it first as a thought form. . . . The idea is like a blueprint; it creates an image of the form, which then magnetizes and guides the physical energy to flow into that form and eventually manifest it on the physical plane."

Because walking is a step-by-step process, a regular and rhythmic process, it allows both halves (a figure of speech) of the brain to talk with each other. When we walk, the information from our intuitive, artist's brain and the information from our rational brain get a chance to converse. It works a little like this.

Rational brain: "What about this?" (The funny way Fred is acting, the trouble at the office, your mother's health . . .)

Artist brain: "Mmmm."

Rational brain: "I'm talking to you. I said, 'What about this!' "

Artist brain: "Nice blue jay. Great pinecone . . . I'd try this . . ."

I am not alone in noticing that time spent in the Imagic-Nation is a great problem solver—and the problems to be solved need not always be artistic ones. As Soren Kierkegaard warned,

If you just set people in motion, they'll heal themselves.
GABRIELLE ROTH

Keep your sense of proportion by regularly, preferably daily, visiting the natural world.
CAITLIN MATTHEWS

Walking wisdom is natural and lets you learn complex things easily.
W. A. MATHIEU

Above all, do not lose your desire to walk: every day I walk my-self into a state of well-being and walk away from every illness; I have walked myself into my best thoughts, and I know of no thought so burdensome that one cannot walk away from it . . . but by sitting still, and the more one sits still, the closer one comes to feeling ill. . . . Thus if one just keeps on walking, everything will be all right.

*Prepare your mind to
receive the best that life has
to offer.*
ERNEST HOLMES

*Dancers need music, but
walkers are their own music.*
W. A. MATHIEU

*Imagination connects us
with the web of power and
the spirit in all things.*
JOSE STEVENS, PH.D., AND
LENA S. STEVENS

From my perspective, healing is essentially a creative process: we create a new state of health. As an artist, I am not alone in finding Daily Walks a key to productivity and balance. Although they may not articulate it in these terms, many artists have discovered the link between walking and walking their art into the world.

Actress Jessica Lange walks with her dogs through the wood-lands. Writer Natalie Goldberg hikes through the sagebrush. Who knows how much these walks have helped to shape their clear-eyed, distinctive careers?

Brenda Ueland, the brilliant teacher who wrote *On Becoming a Writer,* said, "Think of yourself as an incandescent power, illumined and perhaps forever talked to by God and his messengers." She added, "I will tell you what I have learned myself. For me, a long five- or six-mile walk helps. And one must go alone and every day."

When author John Nichols was writing *American Blood*—to my eye, the best and most powerful Vietnam novel ever written—he took long daily walks. "I was the healthiest I've ever been," Nichols told me. "I needed to be to write that book. It was the walks."

At home in New Mexico, my routine around walking involves taking my dogs on crack-of-dawn rambles through piñon foothills. The Sacred Mountain often is still wrapped in clouds. Magpies and wild bluebirds dart through the piñon. Overhead, giant crows and ravens laugh at our progress. We walk for about an hour, climbing to a circle of fir trees on a ridge overlooking the valley. We stop for a wondering moment, feel the power of the land, then head back home.

On the days when I walk, my day unfolds with powerful syn-chronicity. I have talked not just with God, but with both sides of my-self. Perhaps most important, the land has talked to me. I love the clarity and the flow such walking brings to me. Just as Morning Pages create a step-by-step trail into the interior of our own thoughts, so does walking move us into intimacy with ourselves one step at a time. In other words, when we walk into the outer world, we are moved into the inner one as well.

In periods of intense pain, I walk it out. In times of elation, when I can't embody my emotion properly, I walk it out. I walk to meditate and "hear," and I also walk to pray and "speak." It is on my long solitary walks that the Universe gets an earful from me and vice versa.

Walks are the generators for me of what I call my "alpha ideas." (So named not only because they are "A level" ideas but also because the aerobic aspect of walking generates alpha waves, which are characterized by their creative nature.) These alpha ideas are the ideas that seem to come from a higher source than myself, suggesting better solutions to my creative or daily problems than my ordinary thinking does. If walking allows me to enter the Imagic-Nation by crossing a bridge, climbing up a ladder, or scrambling up a tree, alpha ideas are the fruit that I return with from my visits there.

Task: Manifesting—Enter Your Imagic-Nation.

Walk and work with improving the plot of your inner movie for one month. Do this and watch the shape of your life shift. Use the step-by-step rhythm of your walk to create a new path.

Think about what you'd like more of, what you'd like less of, what would make you happier, which things make you glad. Then try focusing, especially, on this phrase, "It would be really lovely if . . ."

Be careful to keep your attention focused on imagining—and delighting in—positive shifts. As Sonia Choquette reminds us, "If we give something our *attention*, we rest our creativity on it. . . . If we put our attention on the wrong things, they steal our energy and leave us impotent while pulling unsavory experiences into our lives." (In metaphysical terms, this is the explanation for why those things we most fear "come to pass.")

You may find to your astonishment that your thoughts habitually stray toward ominous imaginings. If they do, simply shepherd them

Your body is the ground metaphor of your life, the expression of your existence. It is your Bible, your encyclopedia, your life story.
GABRIELLE ROTH

Magic has often been thought of as the art of making dreams come true; the art of realizing visions. Yet before we can bring birth to the vision . . . we have to see it. STARHAWK

There are no terrestrial or cultural boundaries in the otherworlds; the knowledge that you find there is universal in application.
CAITLIN MATTHEWS

There are wildernesses to be tamed within, and hostile beings we may encounter, but even those respond better to a touch of the silk glove than to the slap of the gauntlet.
STEPHEN LARSEN

Invention is the natural outcome of creative thinking.
SARK

"in" far enough to *feel* and process feelings, then shepherd them back to the sunnier side of the street. Over time, you will discover that positive thinking is a form of spiritual muscle which you can develop through gentle daily practice. Positive results will follow.

There is no need for you to believe any of this. My suggestion is simply that you try walking and mulling over your life. Experiment by making a list of twenty things you would like to have manifest in your life. These things can be material, spiritual, intellectual, or artistic: a new reading chair, a better attitude toward your job, more clarity around your thesis, a more creative ending for that short story. . . .

Read the list daily and use it as thinking material on your Daily Walks. Post the list where you see it, *walk the list daily*, and watch your life for results.

CREATIVITY COMMITMENT

In launching into your journey, it often helps to commit yourself in an official manner. You may wish to use this contract or devise one of your own making. Sign it, date it, amend it if necessary:

I, _____, realize that I am entering a rigorous inner process which will both test and liberate me. I commit myself to the three pivotal tools of creative self-care: Morning Pages, Daily Walks, and Artist Dates.

I, _____, acknowledging a responsibility for spiritual balance as the tools of this book, raise and resolve issues and emotions, commit myself to adequate sleep, nutrition, exercise, solitude, and personal compassion.

_____
Name

_____
Date

Guidelines

1. Be self-loving. Eat and sleep. Watch for overuse of caffeine, sugar, alcohol, and drugs. Any of these can block or impede your process.

2. Do your Morning Pages and take a twenty-minute Daily Walk. Take a weekly Artist Date.

3. Experience this process. Do not analyze it. Allow yourself to do the exercises rather than debate them. Practice Beginner's Mind. These tools are intended for the long haul.

4. Hold your own counsel. You are working to contact yourself. Listen to your own responses. For the duration of the journey, don't talk about or "process" the tools with others, except for support. Avoid debate.

5. Remember you will need both your "inner child" and your "inner adult" to do this work. Get them into dialogue. Allow them to walk each other through resistance.

When we conceive a new idea we are thinking directly from the creativity of God. God is both the inventor of a game and those who play it, the author and the actor, the song and the singer.

ERNEST HOLMES

The
Kingdom
of Story

According to the Hopi, Spider Woman sang the world into existence a word at a time. According to the New Testament Book of John, "In the beginning was the word." Ethiopians believe God created both the world and himself by saying his own name. The Egyptian god Thoth created the world through language. Indians believe the same thing: "Nada Brahma: the world is sound." Australian Aboriginals believe that the world came into existence when it was named in song by the ancients—one word, one note, one thing at a time. As Chatwin writes in *Songlines:*

> . . . each Ancestor opened his mouth and called out, "I am!" "I am—snake . . . cockatoo . . . honey-ant. . . . The Ancients sang their way all over the world. They sang the rivers and the ranges, salt pans and sand dunes. . . . They wrapped the whole world in a web of song; and at last, when the earth was sung, they felt tired. . . .

As this brief scan demonstrates, we would be hard-pressed to find a spiritual tradition that does not believe in the creative power of the word. Is it any wonder, if the word is so powerful it can create all we see about us, that it can also have an enormous impact on the creation of our own self-image? Hardly.

When we realize that our word-shaped self-image generates and selects our life experience, we begin to realize the importance of story. "The way we describe our lives and understand them is ultimately and inextricably connected to the way we live them," writes Mandy Aftel. In undertaking our creative pilgrimage, in seeking our vein of gold, we therefore begin with the Kingdom of Story.

The Narrative Time Line

The road to authentic art is through the self. More specifically, it lies through the heart, not the head. Your loves, your hates, your scars, glories, fears, losses, triumphs—your heart is the heart of the matter. Heart is where the art is.

We often talk about creative self-expression without realizing that the creative flows from the self into expression. If our self is still hidden from our view, invisible and inaudible to us due to its being cloaked in the interpretations of others, we may quite naturally fear we have nothing to say. In order to be really creative—or so we believe—we should have traveled around the world, lived in Paris, been arrested in Morocco, perhaps shot drugs or enemy soldiers. . . . In order to be a *real artist* . . . In short, we're afraid that we're boring, not colorful enough, too "ordinary."

Nonsense. Your own life is full of great stuff. You will find out which stuff as we go. You will write your life and "right" it. The point of writing a narrative of your life is to make the narrative truly of *your* life. Writing down the facts and your reaction to them will help you to begin clarifying *your* version of you.

My life story—as told to me—is that I was born on a snowy, crystalline winter day, my mother's favorite kind. That is not how I would begin. What I remember begins when I was a toddler. I am wriggling under a fence to pick wildflowers among some dangerous neighborhood cows.

The difference in the two beginnings is important. In the first, my mother is the storyteller. I am her Julie, another jewel in her crown of seven children. My mother's version of life emphasizes her love of beauty, order, serenity, perfection: a *crystalline* winter day. In my version, life is messier, warmer, full of adventure and delight. In my version, risk is tied to reward. Risk the wild dairy cows, reap the wildflowers.

In other words, my mother's memory and my own center on differing chords, each expressing the melodies of our own personalities. My mother was a melancholic harp. Myself, I followed the piper. Mischief and merriment, the tendrils of earthly delight, enticed me. It is no coincidence that the Pied Piper and Peter *Pan* figured large in my childhood imagination. My mother's favorite fairy tale was "The Snow Queen." Her dreams and imagination differed from my own.

My mother told another story about me. It centered on her reading *Alice in Wonderland* to me. I loved the book and evidently thought I'd love the experience even more. Naturally, when I spotted some wild mushrooms, I couldn't wait to get my teeth into them. I remember being rushed to the hospital. I remember the nice red-haired nurse and the experience of having my stomach pumped. My mother remembered my "scaring her to death."

In my mother's account, this proved I was a wild and unpredictable and even dangerous child. When I remember this episode, I don't remember the terror. What I remember is spotting those mushrooms and feeling intense curiosity. Would eating a mushroom really make me smaller . . . ?

While my mother yearned for serenity and order—in a house with seven children!—I craved adventure and expansion. I wasn't trying to thwart my mother. She wasn't trying to wet-blanket me. Our needs, personalities, and spiritual agendas differed. For the sake of love and household harmony, we worked to accommodate each other.

This is true for many of us. Too often, we take on the coloration of parental dreams without realizing they have shaded our own. In

In every adult there lurks a child—an eternal child, something that is always becoming, is never completed, and calls for unceasing care, attention, and education. That is the part of the human personality which wants to develop and become whole. C. G. JUNG

The world is full of people that have stopped listening to themselves or have listened only to their neighbors to learn what they ought to do, how they ought to behave, and what the values are that they should be living for.

JOSEPH CAMPBELL

*Whenever two people meet
there are really six present.
There is each man as he sees
himself, each as the other
person sees him, and each
man as he really is.*
WILLIAM JAMES

*The quest for a story is the
quest for a life.*
JILL JOHNSTON

this way, a pharmacist who is an unfulfilled doctor may see a surgeon in his son. Conversely, the mother who suppressed her acting gifts may turn an unconsciously blind eye to the dazzling actress trying to emerge in her daughter.

I want to be clear that often it is not that we are consciously, willfully molded into false selves. We are merely shaped into selves that others find more acceptable or comprehensible.

Let me share yet another story gleefully told and retold by my family—an example, again, of my "craziness." (I am telling as many stories as I am to show how persuasively the official versions of ourselves may be built and why it is so hard, at first, to disbelieve them.)

I was five years old when I walked out the back door onto our flagstone patio and found a great green tomato worm, oozing greenish blood, severed into two separate, wriggling parts. My mother's gardening hoe had dealt the blow. I took one look, raced into the house, emerged in a wink with a box of Band-Aids, and taped that worm together again.

"When it crawled off in two directions, you cried and cried," the story goes. Again, this story told my family I was "crazy." That's one interpretation. Until I began working with the tools you will use in this book, I tended to accept this interpretation. Working with my story myself, I found another. Now this story tells me I am a healer by nature.

It is my belief that the stories we *choose* to tell and cherish about ourselves are the true stories, the road map to the real, lantern-hearted self. Until we do the work of excavating, claiming, and owning our own life stories, we run the very real risk of seeing ourselves, describing ourselves, and *proscribing* ourselves as others see fit. We go along with their plot lines for what is our life story. This is both dangerous and damaging. How often have you known someone to accept limitations that to your eye are illusory? How cheered are you when someone—be it Rocky or your own cousin—has the clarity and courage to become larger than their circumstances would suggest.

We must learn to deconstruct the negative story lines that hamper our growth. One woman I know had spent a life feeling she was Cinderella. Working with her Narrative Time Line, she suddenly realized that her own myth was far closer to that of the Ugly Duckling.

She was not the shunned sister. She was the unrecognized swan. This "click" of recognition led her to stop waiting for Prince Charming and begin, instead, to seek the company of swans. (It was there that Prince Charming found her.)

"But, Julia!" I am often asked, "what if I'm not really creative? What if I get unblocked and I'm dull?"

That is one question, but I am no longer sure it is the right one. I think the real question is, "What if I have gifts and abilities and in this lifetime I never find the courage to use them?" That is the real question, the real tragedy.

"But what if the real me is some mousey, Milquetoast . . . ?"

"What if the real you is fascinating and you just don't trust it?"

And so we start. We start where we must start: at the beginning. We write autobiographies not as an art form, but in order to mine them further for detail that will serve us in *any* art form we choose. We want access to our lives as material.

Our vulnerability can feel excruciating. Even reliving our vulnerability at a remove of thirty years can feel excruciating. This is why it is worth noting that in reviewing our story we have the chance to rewrite it as well. Let me give a specific example.

When Carolyn was eighteen and a newcomer at college, she was nominated for homecoming queen. At the time, she took it as a cruel joke. A wallflower member of a large family filled with pretty sisters, the resident brain ("Carolyn Egghead") at her high school, she went off to college unprepared for the fact that she was just as pretty as her vivacious sisters, and that as an anonymous freshman at her new college, no one knew her as an egghead to make fun of her on that count, either. They were taking her at "face" value.

Writing her Narrative Time Line, Carolyn came to the homecoming nomination and found herself awash with conflicting emotions:—grief, pride, anger.

"I wanted to call my mother and say, 'Why didn't you ever tell me I was pretty? I'd have liked being pretty!' "

Instead, Carolyn found herself always awkwardly at odds with men and their motives. "My self-image was Carolyn Egghead. Imagine my shock when a man made a pass at me. I thought it was done out of pity."

We do not learn by experience, but by our capacity for experience. BUDDHA

*As we begin to become aware
of the narrative patterns
around which we structure
our lives, we learn how
to take charge, revise,
refine, and even completely
rewrite them.*

MANDY AFTEL

*When we look into the mir-
ror we see the mask. What is
hidden behind the mask?*

DIANE MARIECHILD

The pity was that Carolyn did not get to enjoy her prettiness. When men expressed sexual interest, it came at her from left field, startling her and throwing her off base. Working with her time line, Carolyn came to the belated but nonetheless delightful realization that she had always been pretty as well as smart. Since she had always envied pretty girls, thinking of herself as a sort of egghead duckling, she felt a considerable shift in self-perception.

Writing our stories, cause and effect very often reveal themselves in unexpected ways. For years, Rose had been ashamed of a period in her early twenties when she had suddenly and inexplicably turned promiscuous, sleeping with a half dozen of her male friends.

"It wasn't a case of my sleeping with people I didn't know. It was a case of my sleeping with people I knew all too well. I was lucky that any of my friendships survived—much less me!"

Writing her Narrative Time Line, Rose made a series of unex-pected connections: "Oh, my parents' marriage ended and my friend overdosed and that's why I went around the bend . . . I'm not so crazy!"

For the first time, her promiscuous period was comprehensible to her. For the first time, she felt compassion for her younger self in-stead of shame. It was comfort and security, not sex, that she had been seeking (hence friends and not strangers), but they all had been so young, confused, and hormonally driven. . . .

Realizations like this may tempt you to pause, poised on the point of your newest insight. Don't pause. Insights like these, while per-sonally wonderful, are a side issue. They are very nice, but they are not the point. The point of all this is a creative recovery. That means we must re-cover a lot of territory. So keep your hand moving.

Think of your Narrative Time Line like driving coast to coast. If you pause at every scenic spot, you won't get west of Pennsylvania. (And you can always go back there later if you want, which is exactly what we will be doing with a later tool called "Cups.")

It is crucial in writing your Narrative Time Line to keep on mov-ing. Write quickly and without editing. This is not an essay or a grammar lesson. Nothing could be further from the truth. This is therapeutic, but it is not therapy. Think of it, instead, as archaeology. *You* are what we are digging for. Keep it simple. This is not meant to be art. You may find it a powerful, cathartic experience to write out the facts of your life. You may, on the other hand, find yourself distanced emotionally, even bored. Do not be fooled. *Keep writing.*

Do not strain after emotion. On the other hand, if emotion overtakes you, know that however strong it is, it will pass through you like a wave. Let yourself bob on the currents of this writing without feeling you have to troll through the depths. As the old television detective Joe Friday put it, "Just the facts, ma'am. Just the facts."

Sometimes the facts include an important shift in perspective: "Then we moved to the beloved Libertyville house . . . Wait a minute! I didn't love it! Not at first. I was lonesome there. It took me three years to make any friends. . . ."

Do not be discouraged if at first getting it down on the page feels cold and makes you feel vulnerable. I understand. However, my experience has been that the real result of writing an autobiography is strength: the first glimmerings of compassion and self-acceptance.

Writing his Narrative Time Line, Michael saw for the first time that his love of writing had been all but snuffed out by the hostile criticism of his high school English teacher. To his surprise, he saw that his writing had stayed in his life in many hidden forms—letters to friends, political activism in which he wrote speeches, helping others with grant proposals. Instead of beating himself up for not writing all those years, he realized that he had in fact always written, and protected his writing from criticism by doing it anonymously. For the first time he felt compassion for his fragile self, and respect, too, for the survivor side that had kept him writing through it all.

When I was teaching at Northwestern University, I came across the work of writer and teacher Carol Bly, who required that all of her short-story students write an autobiography. What a great idea, I thought, assigning the same to my screenwriting students. Her reasons for this undertaking were the unearthing of a real voice, a goal I held in common with her. What emerges from this process is a capacity for work of great originality and specificity.

I soon found, however, that there was another fruit of this process that was arguably of equal value: not only does writing a Narrative Time Line yield material, it generates personal strength. Artists need not only their material but also the strength to handle it. I have been

You need only claim the events of your life to make yourself yours.
FLORIDA SCOTT-MAXWELL

assigning Narrative Time Lines and my variations on them ("Cups," more on which later) ever since.

Let me say at this point that I know that this tool can feel daunting. Even knowing the potential rewards, it can be hard to do the actual writing. If you get stuck or want to prime the pump before plunging in, try this:

Divide a piece of notebook paper into three parts horizontally. Label the top third, "Years 1–5." The middle is "Years 5–10." The bottom third is "Years 10–15." On additional pieces of paper, move through your life in five-year increments up to your current age, jotting notes to answer these questions:

Where did you live?

Who were your major players?

Any significant pets?

Favorite food?

Favorite game?

Favorite music?

Favorite friend?

Favorite toys?

Favorite hobbies?

Favorite interests?

Favorite clothes?

What were your major events?

What are your dominant memories?

Do not be alarmed if some answers are hard to come by. This is a seeding exercise. By raising these questions, we stimulate a flow of memories. They may not emerge immediately. Be patient. Don't worry about that. You are simply priming the pump. *Eventually* you will find a richer flow of images and identity.

Even without formally writing on your life, the mere act of jotting notes will begin to connect the dots of a fragmented self. When

I think of me between five and ten, I see myself hauling red wagonloads of wild violets home from the woods to our doorway. I remember young me, hands blistered from the wagon handle, lugging
load after load, transplanting them to make fairy rings around the
base of our oak trees. You see, my sad mother loved violets, and I believed that if I could just transplant enough heavy wagonloads, I
could lighten my mother's heart.

All of us have stories like this. The act of remembering them
helps right our vision of ourselves. And so I urge you, in your notes,
to be specific. Remember.

At age eight, you moved away from your beloved best friend. In
the official family version, the move was a great success for all of you.
You got out of the city and into the splendors of suburbia, "to that
wonderful house where we all were so happy. . . ."

Were you?

Maybe you missed your friend. Maybe the rolling suburban lawn
meant nothing to you after the action and adventure of city alleys.
This is *your* story. Remember that. Don't judge what you are noting
down. If a memory comes back to you—the peculiar cowboy lamp
with the buckskin fringed shade, your ranch-style bunk beds—trust
that memory and jot it down: Lamp. Bunk beds. The smell of lilacs
outside your ten-year-old self's bedroom may be the gateway to a lifelong love of flowers. To nurture yourself effectively as an adult, you
may *need* flowers, potpourri—a house of scents as well as sensibility.

On a recent teaching trip to Minnesota, I was running my morning rounds through the city streets when I spotted a lone, lovely violet peeping out through a crack at the bottom of some cement steps.
Instantly I thought of my mother, dead now for fifteen years. I remembered her largest garden: the peonies, rambling roses, and the
tall spears of delphinium, piercing blue. Beyond that, I remembered
me, the sweetness of my child's hope that a wagon full of violets
could make her happy.

As you write, allow yourself compassion. Be sure to remember
that the emphasis given to events is yours and yours alone. The loss of
a pet parakeet out the window may have loomed larger to your young
self than gaining a baby brother. Don't judge yourself for this! Being

*Our own life is the instru-
ment with which we experiment with Truth.*

THICH NHAT HANH

*Especially as artists, we have
to celebrate our memories.*

MEINRAD CRAIGHEAD

You already have the pre-cious mixture that will make you well. Use it.
RUMI

teased about your singing voice in eighth-grade chorus may have silenced a singer's heart. Allow yourself to claim the memory at the same level it claims you!

Years one to five may take twelve pages or only two. Pace yourself gently but steadily. As a rule of thumb, Narrative Time Lines profitably run between five and twenty-five thousand words. Ten to fifteen thousand seems to suit a lot of people nicely. The danger in using too few words is that you may still be serving up the canned version of yourself, as capsulized by family and friends. The danger in too many words, too much detail, is discouragement about finishing. We're looking for a balance between brevity and overkill, between:

(a) "I got divorced the year I was twenty-nine" and

(b) "Sally, on that Tuesday, the third Tuesday of March, right after my twenty-ninth birthday, squeezed the toothpaste in the middle . . . foreshadowing our divorce later that year."

If a memory is strong for you, trust that. You are all that matters. If an incident has weight for you, then it is significant. Trust yourself in this. Each of us has special stories to tell, and the audience we require is our own loving attention.

Suzanne, writing notes for her early twenties, wrote down the fact of her sister's accidental death. Moving on to jot down other notes, she saw that many of her favorite things had left her life along with her favorite sister. For the first time, she saw clearly how darkness had settled over life, and she saw too that it was guilt as well as grief that had shadowed her days. She and her sister had shared many joys. Grieving her sister, she packed away many of her enthusiasms just as she had packed away her sister's clothes.

Remember that insights often come to us as flashes. In doing her notes, Suzanne saw her life illuminated. Later, writing out her Narrative Time Line, as we will be doing in future weeks, a thaw came to Suzanne's heart. The Charles Aznavour records she and her sister had found so riveting—couldn't she listen to them again? Couldn't she, twenty years later, now allow herself to take the trip to Paris that she and her sister had planned long ago? She could and she did; she went for both of them.

In losing her sister, Suzanne had lost much of herself. In claiming her past, Suzanne found herself present for her future.

A word here: not all of us have lives that contain events as traumatic as a sibling's sudden death. Some of us enter our Narrative Time Lines convinced we are the owners of boring stories. We believe others have lived in Technicolor while we have merely dabbled in pastels. Reentering the lives we have considered drab, we are often surprised to find that as we really focus on them, honoring them with our attention, our very lives seem to become richer, more saturated with color and meaning.

I am thinking now of my friend Laura, a kindergarten teacher, who undertook her Narrative Time Line with the conviction her own life was simple as a children's coloring book, hackneyed as a nursery rhyme.

"I've been a teacher for twenty years," she told me. "My life is children. I'm like Mary Poppins."

Under her startled hand, Mary Poppins discovered a life rich in forgotten and misplaced passions: an abandoned gift for playing the cello, a love for dance, a zealous interest in Cretan culture, a love of Middle Eastern food . . . A life, in short, with at least as much spice as it had sugar.

Remember: While writing is the act of saying, "I, I, I," it is equally true that writing is the act of saying "he, she, they," and then telling it like we saw it.

"He hit me."

"She stole my boyfriend."

"They moved in next door."

Practice letting yourself leave in all the interesting little hooks that spring to mind: "My aunt Bea. She always smelled like talcum powder and lemons."

Be gentle with yourself about the vagaries of memory. The flashes that emerge may startle you. Think of them as heat lightning: you are warming to the task of meeting yourself. In tracing your

The deepest secret in our heart of hearts is that we are writing because we love the world.

NATALIE GOLDBERG

There is danger in singing
someone else's song.
DON G. CAMPBELL

Human beings ought to com-
municate and share all the
gifts they have received
from God.
MEISTER ECKHART

Narrative Time Line, you are looking for landmarks, yes, but you will also find more subtle tracery of your heart's trail. What did you love? Ask yourself that about anything from clothing to college studies. The answer is another tiny nugget of your authentic self.

Take the question of pets.

When I was a child, my grandparents and my parents raised boxer dogs. As an adult, my heart still leaps up at the sight of a boxer puppy. Poodles, beagles, German shepherds may cheer me, but a good baby boxer thrills and transports me. It is a trick of memory: I am in the backyard, playing with our two boxers, Sean and Clooney. We are gamboling across the lawn. Clooney attacks dandelions, sending puffs of snow into the air—no, Sean is skidding through snowdrifts and then I am in my snowsuit, sledding, with Sean harnessed by scarves to my Red Flyer sled.

You may notice as you write that slowly and almost imperceptibly your emphasis is shifting as your own recollections take over. Notice that as you recall places and events, you may reconnect to a younger self and even feel the energy of that self: glad, sad, isolated, zany. . . .

At this point, let us note (as we will again and again!) that the word "original" contains the seed word "origin." In writing out our Narrative Time Line, we outline our land of origin. We strengthen our color and our unique personal frequency. By owning our life, we make it our own. By writing our Narrative Time Lines, we give permission to the self to do/have/make/be something special.

Here are a few of the "Ah-hahs!" that students have had working with this tool:

"My ah-hah after the fact was how cruel and judgmental I have been with myself about my life."

"My ah-hah was more compassion toward self and family."

"I saw how much denial I have had about my family. They are not available to me."

"I saw a theme in my life between being in control and being silly."

"I never allowed myself to be the important one in a relationship."

"I don't feel ruled by my past—and it was really fun to do!"

"I thought perhaps my 'real' father might not have really been my father and you know what? It does not matter!! I am who I am all by myself!!"

"I let go of old grief and anger."

"I was actually able to look at my life a little more objectively and remember more of the good things and not dwell so much on the negative. I also began to see a thread of connection to so much unconscious behavior."

"Ah-hah! A warmth from revisiting myself!"

"I was surprised that after seemingly constant self-exploration the last two years, there was even more dirt to dig up!"

"Realization that highlights and traumas had karmic overtones!"

"How vast and varied and many-lived my life has been. Also a great mine for writing material."

You will work on this task for the next two to three weeks. From our Narrative Time Lines, we gain a sense of personal continuity and:

> permission to say the unsayable.
>
> permission to think the unthinkable.
>
> permission to make the previously unmakeable art.

In other words, although the Narrative Time Line is not in and of itself "art," it is the wellspring from which our art flows.

Director Martin Scorsese remembers that above his childhood bed in New York's Little Italy was painted God's all-seeing eye. This eye missed nothing of young Martin's thoughts and activities. It loomed large in his youthful imagination, so pursuing him that for a while he entered a seminary to make peace with God's demanding omniscience.

Is it any coincidence that as a mature filmmaker Scorsese makes films centering on themes of guilt and redemption? He doesn't think so.

Novelist John Nichols, who lost his mother to an untimely death when he was still a toddler, forged a heartbreaking novel of an aban-

We must capture our personal and idiosyncratic language so that we may speak about our personal and idiosyncratic life.

PETER LONDON

As you begin to pay attention to your own stories and what they say about you, you will enter into the exciting process of becoming, as you should be, the author of your own life, the creator of your own possibilities.

MANDY AFTEL

doned child, *The Wizard of Loneliness,* in his artistic reworking of that loss.

My own sister Libby, a brilliant portrait painter, turned her skills to "painting through the memories" in order to put behind her a difficult adolescence. In the process, she generated a series of autobiographical oils, featuring her and her childhood mare, which remain among her best and most original work. It was also the first glimmering of the fact that she would be able to specialize in the exceedingly difficult task of combined child and animal portraiture.

For all of us, by claiming our own memories, we gain access to the creative energy that they contain. Memories become a source, not only of inspiration, but of fuel. In other words, they give us not only ideas but also the power to carry them out. Real art is made from the inside out, not the outside in. For this reason, self-disclosure must begin with the disclosure of self to self. This self-initiated self-disclosure requires privacy and attention. Those are the gifts of the Narrative Time Line.

However confused the scene of our life appears, however torn we may be who now do face that scene, it can be faced, and we can go on to be whole.

MURIEL RUKEYSER

∽ Task: Filling In Notes. ∽

This week, every day, work on filling in your Narrative Time Line notes. If you find that the act of jotting down notes moves you straight into writing, skip ahead and dive right into writing.

∽ Task: Post a Sign on Your Mirror. ∽

"Yes, I *can* do my Narrative Time Line!"

∽ Task: Contact Someone and Commit. ∽

Call or write someone on your cluster list. Explain what it is you are undertaking and commit, officially, to doing it. You may wish to set up a weekly check-in with them.

～ Task: Do Your Narrative Time Line. ～

Working with your time line notes or simply plunging in, begin to get your life on paper. Write very fast, from the top of your head, perhaps setting a clock and only allowing an hour per session, although you can do more if it is comfortable. (Many people experience the time line rushing through them.)

I am often asked if the time line can be done in place of Morning Pages. The answer is no, no, and no! The Morning Pages are a very important anchor in your present life. Do not abandon this grounding line. Think of them as a rope you have tied around your waist to keep you safe and connected no matter how deeply you travel into the mine of your past experiences.

Ultimately, literature is nothing but carpentry. With both you are working with reality, a material just as hard as wood.
GABRIEL GARCÍA MÁRQUEZ

～ Task: Filling In Blanks. ～

Please fill in the blanks on the age periods that apply to you. Do this in addition to your own work on Narrative Time Line notes.

Years 1–5

As a young child, my favorite playmate was _____.

What I remember about my playmate is _____

_____.

As a young child, my favorite toy was _____.

I remember my favorite game was _____.

We lived _____

_____.

Our house was _____

_____.

I remember liking to go_____

_____.

In my family, we had lots of _____.

My brothers and sisters _____

_____.

My pets _____

_____.

*It doesn't matter who my fa-
ther was; it matters who I
remember he was.*
ANNE SEXTON

Years 5–10

As a child, my favorite subject was _____.

I thought my teachers were _____.

My best friend _____.

I liked _____.

My favorite teacher was _____.

I remember _____

_____.

The teacher I hated was _____.

I was praised in school for my _____.

My parents seemed to feel I was _____

_____.

My own feeling is that I was _____

_____.

Years 10–15

As a pre-adolescent, I began _____

_____.

I loved to_____._____.

My favorite adventure was _____

_____.

My friends were _____.

Alcohol and drugs were _____.

Sex was _____.

My parents _____.

In my family I was considered _____.

My friends called me _____.

What I did to amuse myself was _____.

Years 15–20

As a teenager, I considered myself _____.

What made me feel less isolated was _____.

The friend I had fun with was _____.

I experimented with _____.

My job as a teenager was _____.

My own sense of myself was _____.

My relationship to alcohol, drugs, sex, and food was _____

_____

_____

_____.

My teen hangout was _____.

What I did to amuse myself was _____

_____.

*One writes to make a home
for one's self, on paper, in
time, in others' minds.*

ALFRED KAZIN

What my friends and I did for amusement was _____
_____.

Years 20–25

At college age, my self image was _____
_____.

*There are only two or three
human stories and they go
on repeating themselves as
fiercely as if they had never
happened before.*

WILLA CATHER

My closest friends were _____.

What I wanted to do was _____.

What I studied was _____.

I found a new interest in _____.

College felt to me like _____.

My relationship to alcohol, drugs, sex, and food was _____
_____

_____

_____.

During this time my relationship to my mother _____
_____.

During this time, my relationship to my father _____
_____.

The music and movies and books and other cultural enjoyments were
_____.

Years 25–30

In my twenties, I generally felt _____
_____.

My close friendships _____

_____.

I undertook _____.

I became aware or started to believe _____

_____.

I began to have trouble with _____.

I got a better perspective on _____.

My self-esteem _____.

My spiritual life _____.

I defined myself primarily by _____.

I felt my options _____.

I think of the self that I write about as being made of words. He's been recon-structed constantly, over and over again, out of words.

CHARLES WRIGHT

Years 30–40

In my thirties, I began to feel _____.

My life seemed somehow _____.

I think this was because _____

_____.

My friendships seemed to _____.

I found myself _____.

I developed a deeper interest in _____.

Hobbies _____.

My life was dominated by my _____.

I considered myself _____.

I began to wish _____.

*Life can only be understood
backward, but it must be
lived forward.*
NIELS BOHR

Years 40–50

As I entered my forties, I found _____

_____.

I was surprised at how _____

_____.

I yearned to just _____.

I told myself _____.

I discovered I could _____.

My friendships now _____.

I used my time _____.

Increasingly I turned to _____.

I found a deeper sense of _____.

The world felt _____.

Years 50–60

Moving into my fifties, my spiritual life _____

_____.

My daily patterns _____.

I made peace with _____.

I felt anger at _____.

I chose to _____.

I began with _____.

I turned to _____.

I found I _____.

My view of life _____.

I began to actively seek _____.

Years 60–70

At sixty, I found I could _____.

What surprised me was _____

_____.

I liked feeling _____.

I felt liberated from _____.

My regrets became _____.

My clarity about _____.

My sense of fair play demanded _____

_____.

I looked to _____.

I found I could no longer _____.

I chose to _____.

*The aim of every artist is to
arrest motion, which is life,
by artificial means.*
WILLIAM FAULKNER

*Properly understood as a
question of focus, unconditional love is the creative
process.* PETER ROGERS

Years 70–80 and onward

After I turned seventy, my interest in _____

_____.

My focus on _____.

My feeling of _____.

My passion for _____.

My joy in _____.

My release of _____.

My concern about _____.

My return to _____.

My acceptance of _____.

My curiosity about _____.

"Cups": The Key to Self-Disclosure

In your travels along your Narrative Time Line, you have doubtless hit sections that were painful or simply highly charged emotionally to remember. These sections are the ideal raw material for the tool I call "Cups."

Be compassionate as your Creator is compassionate.

JESUS

What, precisely *is* a Cup and what might it contain? A Cup is a "scoop" of time, emotion, and memory ladled from your Narrative Time Line to be examined more closely. As a rule, a Cup might run from a thousand to several thousand words. (Estimate that a double-spaced typed page runs between 250 and 300 words.)

While some Cups will center on painful memories or secrets, others may simply focus on parts of ourselves that have been misplaced or forgotten. When Cokey was writing her Narrative Time Line, she remembered her childhood love of daredevil bike riding, and so she wrote a Cup on "Speed." In it, she traced the greased-lightning child in her who piloted her bike pell-mell and loved to drive her adult car like a female Mario Andretti—much to the chagrin of her family, who thought it wasn't seemly for "Mom" to drive with such assertive expertise. "Speed" was an important part of her, Cokey realized. She loved her own crisp competence, slicing through traffic or the workload on her desk. Writing her Cup allowed her ownership of her own daring and prowess.

65

Another effective way to approach Cups is to take a look at the list which I call "Deadlies." Write a "Jealousy Cup" or a "Greed Cup." Scan your Narrative Time Line to see if "Pride" has ever been your undoing or if there is a Cup of "Anger" simmering somewhere.

Short and to the point, Cups are remarkably cathartic and healing. If a memory has special poignancy—the last holiday with my mother, the night before my first child was born, the moment I knew we would get married—that memory is an ideal idea for a Cup.

Cups can be used to process grief and ventilate betrayal. They can be used to open up and aerate a family secret. Here is a small excerpt from one of the most valuable of my own:

V U L N E R A B I L I T Y

I come from a family where both fragility and tenacity are well-hewn family traditions. I hospitalized both of my parents and, in their absence, took an active role in raising my siblings. My parents' hospitalizations, in the dark days before lithium and antidepressants, were succeeded, post-lithium, by halcyon decades trouble-free. Incredible as it sometimes seemed, their stability was maintained by a simple dab of salt.

There were side effects, but we lived with those gratefully. My mother suffered weight gains. My father's hands shook badly. After my mother's death, we watched him for any telltale signs of "windup" but we loved him fiercely, if a little protectively, perhaps the same way he, our waning patriarch, loved us.

None of us inherited Mom or Dad's fragility. Not one of us. Seven out of seven, we stood sane and sound. This was an article of faith among all of us. Our batting average: astounding. Perhaps we watched each other a little closely—hypervigilant, scanning each other's lives with the acute peripheral vision we had collectively developed to "field" any shifts in our parents' psyche.

"How did he sound to you?" We would double-check each other, reporting in our phone calls to our elders.

Or, "Mom sounded good."

(Writing this, I see that the unvoiced alternative was always present, looming amid the shadows we collectively surveyed and discounted.)

A decade, sometimes a decade plus, *with no hospitaliza-tions* . . . we didn't exactly get breezy—yes, we did. We reported in like we were lofting a Frisbee on a long holiday afternoon.

"How's Dad?" Toss. Back to you.

"Sounded good." Toss. Back to you . . .

Writing this Cup, I was able to gain some objectivity in looking at my own family history and some compassion and insight into my own determination that things be "safe"—read: "stable"—for my daughter. I should also add that for me, this Cup contained the kernel of a play. While Cups are not intended as "art," they often become the seedbed for art. By grounding the excessive emotional charge that events may contain for us, they free us to use that material as the building blocks of art. In addition, the same grounding process allows us the grace of more artful living.

Let me explain.

Until we possess our own version of ourselves, we are prone to all manner of mishaps. Chief among these is what I dub blurting. (Psychologists call it "spilling.") No matter what you call it, the behavior in question is the sudden, seemingly inadvertent or inappropriate sharing of highly personal information—an act triggered by someone else's stimulus and our overeager response. Very often, someone else's confession sparks the unwitting self-disclosure we might have chosen not to make.

"I had an abortion. It was terrible."

"Really? Me, too. Yeah. It was."

Or, "My boss is real piggy."

"No kidding. So's mine."

Sometimes such self-disclosures are harmless. Frequently, however, they leave us gnashing our emotional teeth: "I wish I hadn't said that!"

So why did we?

When we haven't processed our life and feelings, they surprise us by leaping from hiding. Perhaps the best analogy is a phenomenon known to fighters of forest fires. Very often the surface fire will appear to be squelched, only to have the fire leap into sudden visibility far beyond the firebreak. How did that happen?

We are healed of our suffering only by experiencing it to the full.

MARCEL PROUST

Detail is electric.

BONNI GOLDBERG

Learn to trust your own judgment, learn inner independence, learn to trust that time will sort good from bad—including your own bad.

DORIS LESSING

When we write from experience we harvest our lives.

BONNI GOLDBERG

As those firefighters know from grim experience, fires can burn unchecked through the root system underground. This is what our emotions do when we keep them buried from ourselves. The anger that hasn't been faced from an old affair suddenly flares out and sabotages a lovely new love. We may not have faced how bad that abortion made us feel, or just how badgered we really felt by the ill-concealed advances of our piggy boss.

When we work regularly with the tools of autobiographical self-expression, the private act of self-disclosure affords us the public luxury of privacy. Privacy differs from secrecy. It has little to do with hiding something and far more to do with protecting something—ourselves. What our privacy protects is not our dignity; that is inviolably ours as a soul. What our privacy protects is our Creative Child.

Whenever we self-disclose prematurely or inappropriately, we feel ourselves slip out of power and into victim status. Suddenly "they" (our listeners) "have something on us." That something, the revelation we weren't really ready to share, becomes something we are ashamed of having shared. Shame impacts creativity. It makes it difficult to create. Shame shuts us down, shuts us out, shuts us off.

What a shame!

Writers like John Bradshaw and Anne Wilson Schaef tell us that ours is essentially a shame-based society. Shame, and its handmaiden, guilt, are used to manipulate and silence those who would declare that the emperor has no clothes—or needs new ones.

As artists, we are perpetually seeking to penetrate the veil of cultural prescriptions and arrive at personal truth. In order to do this, we need to be brave enough with—and open enough to—our own internal territory that our art can express it. In other words, we must be able to face down shame and *choose* self-disclosure. This takes courage. All of the tools you are using in the Kingdom of Story involve finding the courage to speak our own truth.

Both our Morning Pages and our Narrative Time Lines afford us the sacred enclosure of privacy and self-containment. Inviting ourselves into self-encounter through these tools, we learn our areas of vulnerability and of strength, our needs for self-compassion or further self-scrutiny. Ironically, it is as we become known to ourselves that we can risk authentic and timely self-disclosure to others.

It is one of the paradoxes of self-exploration that as self-knowledge and self-acceptance increase, self-disclosure becomes both more possible and more discretionary. What *is* certain is that you will no longer need, ask, or rely on others to tell you who you are. Their version of you may or may not interest you any longer. You will have your own version of you. When you know who you are and what you are about, you may or may not choose to tell others. "Cups" are a very profound way of telling yourself who you are.

A Cup might be:

Our family had a secret . . .

My closest childhood friend . . .

My greatest regret . . .

My secret vice . . .

My best childhood Christmas . . .

My most beloved relative . . .

My favorite pet . . .

My worst betrayal . . .

My deepest fear . . .

My secret dream . . .

My closest call . . .

My deepest gratitude . . .

Some writers confuse authenticity, which they ought always to aim at, with originality, which they should never bother about.

W. H. AUDEN

~~ Task: List Five Secrets. ~~

Secrets are very often episodes for which we feel a sense of shame and confusion. "I don't know how I got into that situation," we say to ourselves. "And I really wish I hadn't," or "I don't know why I did that—and I sure am sorry I did."

Sometimes, the reverse is true. "I don't know if I want anybody else to know about this, but I sure did enjoy doing that. . . ."

Loaded with negative energy, loaded with positive energy—secrets are loaded with energy, period, and energy is what gives vitality to our lives and our art. List five of your secrets here and be sure to mention them in your Narrative Time Line. Now choose one of your secrets and enter it fully to write a Cup. Remember that, like the Morning Pages, your Cups are for your eyes only, so write freely.

1. _____

2. _____

3. _____

4. _____

5. _____

Singing is a special code that identifies us as human—our collective password.

W. A. MATHIEU

～ Task: Make a Narrative Time Line ～ Photo Album for Yourself.

Working with your Narrative Time Line and whatever photos you have, "illustrate" your memories. Get a color Xerox of a favorite photo. Ask your copy shop if they can make "picture of you as a child" stationery.

Words Do It

Those who do not have power over the story
that dominates their lives, power to retell it, to
rethink it, deconstruct it, joke about it, and
change it as times change, truly are powerless,
because they cannot think new thoughts.

SALMAN RUSHDIE

One of my favorite fairy tales is "The Ugly Duckling." As the story goes, a certain perfectly lovely young swan was raised amid a group of ducklings. The young swan had a long, beautiful neck—swans do. The young ducklings—all the ducks, for that matter—had shorter, stouter necks and considered the young swan a freak, an "ugly duckling." Having no information to the contrary, never having seen another swan, the young swan also found itself to be an inferior duckling. Of course it was! It was never meant to be a duckling at all. God had intended it as a glorious swan.

Your own words are the bricks and mortar of the dreams you want to realize. Your words are the greatest power you have. The words you choose and use establish the life you experience.

SONIA CHOQUETTE

Many intensely creative children experience the Ugly Duckling Syndrome. Because their nascent talents tower above the talents of those around them, they are regarded as freakish. Very often their talents are mirrored back in a distorted fashion, the mirror being the eye of the beholder.

Andrea, a very musical child, was told by her novice singing

71

*Over and over, we have to go
back to the beginning. We
should not be ashamed of
this. It is good. It's like
drinking water.*

NATALIE GOLDBERG

teacher that she was a "bad alto" and encouraged to pipe down while the other students were told to pipe up. In her mid-forties, Andrea attended a creativity workshop in which one of the other students happened to be an opera teacher. When the class tried out a little singing, Andrea confessed her fears as a "bad alto," but she sang anyway. At the break, the opera teacher approached her.

"My dear, you are not a *bad alto*," said the opera teacher gently. "What you are is a coloratura soprano! You are not supposed to be singing down low. Your voice wants to be way up here. Try this."

The opera teacher demonstrated a vocal exercise. Andrea tried it and felt her voice take wing. A soprano! Her heart lifted with her voice.

Told that we are not gifted in certain areas, we are all too ready to believe it. Believing it, we repeat the damning words to ourselves and guarantee our own negative results. "I can't dance," "I can't sing," "I have no color sense," we parrot—without exploring whether the lack is real or merely a part of our familial conditioning.

"I'd love to write a novel but I'm not a writer. . . . I like art but I could never paint. . . . I'm just not musical—even though I love music. . . ."

When I teach the concept of creative ceilings, I often talk about Chicago, a city filled with old buildings that feature wonderful, high, ornate pressed-tin ceilings—ceilings often obscured by a lower, "modern" Styrofoam ceiling. It used to be a game of mine to tap the panels of these Styrofoam ceilings (they weren't really solid) and see what glories they had hiding up above. In many ways, we are a lot like those buildings with the artificially low ceilings. The hidden gifts we believe to be far above our creative capacities are often merely obscured from our view. A tiny whisper of the gift may remain, tapping at our consciousness like a mouse scratching at the ceiling. When we hear the whispered wish of that gift, we say, "Oh, I could never do that! That's so far above my head. . . ."

But is it really? Sometimes, all we need to do is tap—which is the point of the essay you are now reading. As dismaying as it may be to remember the negative words I am asking you to recall, in the act of such remembering lies freedom.

Many creative people suffer from artificially low creative ceilings caused by what they've been told about themselves. Conditioned to believe they will fail in an art form they love, they are either afraid to make even a fledgling attempt or if they do, they judge that attempt so harshly that they abandon their efforts before they have a chance of success. To be blunt, they have been blinded to their own powers by the negative use of language. Let me tell you a story to illustrate this point.

One of the best singers I know was routinely told by his musician father that he "had no ear" and couldn't sing. For three full decades, until he "tried" singing in a creative cluster, this man believed that music was a gift beyond his reach. It took him until his mid-forties to undo the power of his father's words and discover that he did, in fact, have a beautiful, resonant singing voice and a very fine ear, thank you.

"I actually think I do have a voice, Julia," he told me recently. "The other night I was asked to do a radio show about my poetry and I did an improv piece with a poem and my guitar and at the end of it I actually did a little singing. And you know what? The singing sounded fine."

When last I saw him, he was writing songs and performing them, still in the process of unwrapping his newly discovered gift for music—a gift he had owned, in fact, since childhood, although the power of his father's words had convinced him otherwise.

My friend was one of the lucky ones. He was able to retrieve his lost gift and claim it. Many people are less fortunate. Their loss may be buried so deeply, they no longer know that it occurred. As sound healer Don Campbell writes, "Wounded musicians who were told they could not sing in tune or play an instrument may have lost their glorious birthright of knowing the powers that are already in play."

Music is not the only gift that can be lost or buried due to the power of negative words—and sometimes an artistic birthright is not lost but is badly wounded.

A young woman I know, a very gifted actress, is embroiled in battle right now. Even though she has been acting since early childhood—some TV, a few movies, school plays, local theater, some

Our skin is what stands between us and the world.
DIANE ACKERMAN

Great writing can be conjured from great injustice.
LANCE MORROW

Behind every word flows energy.
SONIA CHOQUETTE

Learning is movement from moment to moment.
KRISHNAMURTI

Apparently, sound is a kind of food for the brain and the whole body.
JOY GARDNER-GORDON

professional theater work—her father routinely denigrates all of her efforts as not being "real" acting.

"I have finally realized he is simply, completely, opposed to my acting," she recently told me.

For his part, the father cites parental concern over the "heart-breaks" of his daughter's chosen profession. But how much more heartbreaking is it to have a parent who squelches your dreams, refuses to acknowledge your gifts—even when they are seen and appreciated by others? How long will this young woman be able to hold on to her conviction that she is a "real" actress in the face of her father's oft-spoken words that she is not?

In my years as a teacher, I have been amazed time and again by the power of negative words to dampen and all but extinguish luminous creative gifts. For this reason, "artist abuse" hits me the same way child abuse hits a lot of other people.

From my perspective, artist abuse *is* child abuse because the part of us which creates is, in fact, a vulnerable inner youngster. This luminous inner being—a soul sprite, if you will—is directly connected to the divine and possesses the power to accomplish enormous things. In order to accomplish them, however, this artist-child must be able to survive, overcome, or turn aside whatever negative verbal programming sets an artificially low ceiling on its creative gifts.

As creative beings, we carry a little seed of belief that says, "I'd like to be, I think I am . . . a writer, a painter, a photographer, an actor. . . ."

This seed of desire isn't always welcome news for our families. Hanging on to that kernel of self-belief in the face of well-meaning familial skepticism can be tough. Sometimes parents act as though our desire to make art is an act of sabotage to their dreams for us. This is parental colonialism. They have their own lives to live and we have ours, but as parents they hope to guide us—often in misguided ways.

Steeped in our anti-art mythology, they may know, or think they know, how "terrible" an artist's life can be, how drunk, crazy, promiscuous, and *broke* artists "always" are. So survival as an artist starts very early when our first W.B.'s (Wet Blankets) say, "That's nice, dear, but how do you plan to make a living?"

Children don't come into the world and hatch an artistic career as a diabolical plan to scotch their parents' dreams. No seven-year-old says, "I think I'll really screw the old bastards. I'll be a writer." And yet many creative children (and all children are creative) are construed by family and teachers to be management problems. I was Unruly Julie. (*"Don't be so intense. Calm down. Slow down. Stop being so wild...."*) Composer Michael Hoppé was routinely denigrated as "the Dreamer."

"Oh, Michael, you are such a dreamer," the scornful parental tone rained down on him—and reined him in. Told by his parents that artists were selfish and irresponsible people, he was urged to become a businessman instead of a composer. Being a financial success would yield him, his family, and his world far more happiness and satisfaction than following his musical dreams, he was told. Besides, the family mythology continued, artists were selfish, irresponsible, thoughtless, vain ...

An obedient, dutiful son, Hoppé heeded his parental guidance and became not a composer, but an executive at a large record company, serving his musical dreams at one remove. (A practice I call being a "shadow artist.") Graced with a composer's ears, he brought to his label fine performers and composers, among them Vangelis. All the while, he quietly noodled away in his off-hours, composing his own music, composing his own soul, if not his life, around the music he created himself.

Events might have continued to unfold in this fashion but for a fateful accident. Asked to audition his company's "talent" for a film producer, Hoppé made a tape of his artists' work and sat through a long and difficult meeting as artist after artist was rejected.

"No, no, no, no, no! Don't you have anybody that's right for me?"

Just as the tape was spooling to the end, a snippet of his own music came on. Oh, my Lord. What an embarrassing accident! Hoppé lurched to snap off the machine.

"That's it. That's him! That's our composer!" the producer all but shouted. Hoppé was stunned. Composers were the people he represented! Fortunately, the producer was insistent. In that moment, a composer was not so much born as freed. (Hoppé has subsequently made the Oscar short list for his film compositions.)

The structure of myth exists in the mind and needs only to be tapped.

DEENA METZGER

We must use the power of our words constructively.
STELLA TERRILL MANN

It doesn't have to be a big fire, a small blaze, candle-light perhaps. . . .
RAY BRADBURY

"The dreamer began to follow the dream," Hoppé says, a world of emotion lying in his soft understatement.

Often, when I am teaching, I play Hoppé's heartfelt melodies from *The Yearning* and then stop to remind my students that he was not supposed to compose them. The life of a composer was supposed to remain above his creative ceiling. Our creative ceiling is what we determine by our language.

"I'm just not creative," I have often been told by people whose creativity sticks out all over them—to *my* eye, but not to theirs.

Judi writes wonderful poems, "but not enough of them," she says. Meanwhile, she is one of the best cooks I have ever run across, a fine weaver, and the creator of homes that speak to the spirit and make the heart sing. As a friend she is endlessly, playfully thoughtful. She is forever locating the odd book, the great batch of dried flowers for the hallway, etc.

Do I need to tell you Judi bemoans her lack of creativity? Like many people, Judi believes that artists are an elite tribe of which a "regular person like me" is simply not a member. Like many people, Judi must learn to recognize that creativity is native and natural to all of us. As long as she disqualifies herself in word, she will also do it in deed.

Composer Susan Alexander tells the story of listening to a beautiful piece of music and suddenly asking herself what would make her the most happy in all the world.

"Being a composer!" the answer shot back.

At the time, Alexander was a working mother in her forties and far from the rarefied air she had previously believed composers occupied. On this day, however, she abruptly found herself thinking, "Why not me?" instead of "Not me." With that change of phrase, she had a change of heart and her creative ceiling shot up. Within a week, she had a mentor. Within two years, she had a master's degree in musical composition. When I met her, she was the recipient of a composing fellowship from a university in Michigan. She told me this story as we strolled through the great northern woods.

Creativity is a spiritual essence that can operate in any and all areas of life. The law can be creative and so can the kitchen. When we allow ourselves to bring our full attention to any circumstance, we bring to it the possibility of the creative spark.

It is one of the ironies of my work that very often the phrases used to shame children actually single out for ridicule the very finest parts of their creative DNA. If Michael Hoppé had not been a dreamer, could he have written his yearning romances? No. We are lucky that Hoppé's "Dreamer" survived.

Gifted in ways that our parents or teachers find threatening or disruptive, many of us have been called dreamers, and other things as well. Often, the negative words used to describe us were actually attempts to harness our behavior into the service of parental goals.

"Don't be such a daydreamer . . . clean your room . . ."

"Don't be so loud . . . stop singing and let me watch TV . . ."

"Don't be so sure of yourself . . . let me tell you who you are . . ."

Not all of this controlling was undertaken with malice aforethought. In all probability, very little of it was. Nonetheless, it is worth trekking back to our youth to discover some of the phrases used to make us more cooperative with other people's agendas. (It is also worth noting that silence can speak volumes, and that the withholding of praise or comment for our gifts or creative efforts is also a potent tool of control.)

Kathleen, a gifted textiles designer now in creative recovery, remembers that in her childhood her play with fabric was received not with delight or encouragement but with icy silence.

Justin, a writer who is now coming into his substantial gifts, remembers that in his childhood his writing was harshly criticized and often completely rewritten by his father. Once, when he was assigned to write a poem, his father wrote one "for him" and insisted that his poem be turned in as his son's work—since his son wasn't "much of a writer."

Is it any wonder that both Kathleen and Justin had difficulty knowing and owning the extent of their talents? Silence had been used to disenfranchise one of them. Language itself was used to steal language from the other. Both of them grew up disbelieving their talents because to their parents those talents had not been real.

The power of the word is real whether or not you are conscious of it.

SONIA CHOQUETTE

*Soul loss is regarded as the
gravest diagnosis in
[shamanism], being seen as a
cause of illness and death.
Yet it is not referred to
at all in modern Western
medical books.*
JEANNE ACHTERBERG

*The soul among all creatures
is generative like God is.*
MEISTER ECKHART

As youngsters, when we are judged by outside authority, we often take that judgment into ourselves. The choir teacher who makes fun of a quavering adolescent voice may cause a singer to lose that voice. The college professor who tells his students, "Your job is to convince me you're brilliant" (not to express yourself), may rob his students of their right to self-expression. Even as an adult, the threatened spouse who says, "You really think anybody's going to buy one of those things?" (paintings, sculptures, handmade aprons, photographs) may steal from his or her partner the will to continue making art.

In shamanic tradition, the loss of these parts of ourself is called "soul loss." Any severe artistic shaming is sufficient to cause such a self-displacement, and the results can be catastrophic in terms of both identity and productivity. Our gift for design, our gift for poetry—some part of us is judged and then disowned. This disowned gift goes underground.

Yes, it would be lovely if we were resilient enough to shrug these shamings off, but we often can't.

Since the creative part of us is *always* childlike no matter what our chronological age, we have no sophisticated defenses that are proof against volleys of disparagement. The very vulnerability and openness that makes us creative makes us able to be wounded, hurt, and misled. This is why these epithets must be made conscious. They must be dragged into the light of reason and dismantled like rifles lest we turn them on ourselves.

(Please bear with the work of this essay, however painful you may find it. Resistance to cleaning a wound is understandable, but cleaning a wound is a necessary part of healing it.)

At best, the controlling descriptions issued to us as children are opinions. At worst, they are character assassination. "Get your head out of the clouds. . . . You'll never amount to anything. . . ."

Because these negatives were often instilled in us before we were old enough to see through them or to question the authority from which they came, we may *still* accept these shaming dictums as fact.

As adults we may have learned the knack of considering the source, but that knack is not common among children. For our Creative Child, any of these Creative Monsters is sufficient to trigger shame—and shame *automatically* triggers soul loss. Scolded, discounted, ridiculed, ashamed, the singer or writer or painter goes underground. And this is often only a part of the damage done.

As the Celtic shaman Caitlin Matthews writes, "One of the problematic aspects of soul loss is that when human beings lose a vital part of themselves, they resort to substitutes to 'fill the gap.' This often leads to addictions."

In lieu of creativity, we may fill our lives instead with alcohol, drugs, or food, with "busy-ness" or "things" or addictive relationships in order to medicate the sense of loss we feel over the straying of our creative gifts and dreams. We use all of these to block our sense of loss, to block our awareness there has even been a loss. The shaming words remain lodged in our consciousness while the gifts they negate remain locked beyond our reach.

"Am I really a bossy bitch?" wonders my friend Alice—who is not!

"Am I really a sissy?" wonders my friend John—who is not!

No matter that Alice is an effervescent and generous woman who is a delight to be around, full of playful ideas. Whenever she gets scared, she hears her Milquetoast ex-husband who was passive except with his wounding words.

No matter that John is a solid and loving man who might better be characterized as a "man's man" than a sissy. He was a bookish boy and when he is under siege emotionally, the words he hears are those of his military father: "Get out of your room. Get out on the ball field. What are you? Some kind of *sissy?*"

Most of these assessments have never been reevaluated in light of our own values and beliefs. Because they were used to shame us, we—ashamed—keep them hidden from ourselves and from the world. It often takes the glare of success to cast them into horrifying visibility.

Into the void of self-worth we insert the words we've been taught to use for ourselves. Our emotional or intellectual Achilles heel starts to throb as the old wound acts up again. In working with the Narrative Time Lines of many, many students, I've discovered that most creative people carry litanies of self-abuse, descriptions that were used for them—or more accurately, against them—in childhood.

It is astonishing the number of words, phrases, and actual insults used to tamp down our creativity. When I teach a creativity work-

Originality has nothing to do with priority. An image is like a musical key; just because someone used G-minor before doesn't make Mozart a copycat.

STEPHEN MITCHELL

The art just wants to be made. It pushes through the vehicle (the person) into manifest form.
VICKI NOBLE

Openness, patience, receptivity, solitude is everything.
RAINER MARIA RILKE

shop, one of my favorite and most cathartic exercises is having the class call out the words used to control them as children. Often we come up with a list of derogative words numbering nearly a hundred! Let me give you a few choice epithets here:

Dreamer

Dilettante

Head in the clouds

Impractical

Irresponsible

Crazy

Lazy

Weird

Flake

Eccentric

Too sensitive

Too intense

Unrealistic

Childish

Wishful thinker

Grandiose

Arrogant

Selfish

Foolish

Silly

Stuck up

Deluded

Out of your mind

Obsessed

Procrastinator

Dilly-dallier

Conceited

Not feminine enough

Not masculine enough

Not American

Not focused

Not disciplined

Not in reality

You may have a dozen other words that have been hurled at you. Please note that they are often contradictory. You may simultaneously stand accused of being too much of one thing and not enough of another. Unexpressed, unacknowledged, unesteemed, our disowned gifts become shadow versions of themselves. Our good points become our bad points. Whatever it is that you were or are—it's wrong. *You're wrong.*

Wait a minute. Maybe *they're* wrong.

The challenge, then, is to be the creative myth-maker that we are, to consciously choose our myth, lest it be chosen for us by the collective mind.

MARY ELIZABETH MARLOW

⁓ Task: Alchemy—Converting Dross to Gold. ⁓

Many of us are plagued by the words used to describe us as children. Many of us fail to realize that these words are often the ore that we can alchemize into nuggets of gold. Go back through your Narrative Time Line and look for any damning or daunting words. Let's look at you and your childhood epithets differently.

In mystical tradition, alchemy was the process by which grosser metals had their vibration lifted until they were transformed into gold. This "lifting" process was a closely guarded secret. Magic words and secret ingredients were involved. As a result of your work with this essay, we've got them.

We will use alchemical techniques to convert your childhood wound-words into gold. All we will need is the words themselves and the power of your imagination. Then a pinch of compassion as the conversion catalyst. In other words, you are asked to look at your past and transform it through acceptance. Claim the word-wounds and work *with* them. While this may sound like you are being asked for sainthood, it is actually a very pragmatic piece of personal house-cleaning.

In this exercise, you are asked to take ten childhood negatives and look at them closely, searching for the silver linings that will turn them into gold.

Very often the things described to you as your weaknesses are the strengths which will serve you well in your creative endeavors. Use imagination and compassion to make the transformation. Here are a few examples:

Dilettante	converts to	*interested in many things.*
Dreamer	converts to	*powerfully imaginative.*
Impractical	converts to	*visionary thinker.*
Eccentric	converts to	*original.*

1. _____.

2. _____.

3. _____.

4. _____.

5. _____.

6. _____.

7. _____.

8. _____.

9. _____.

10. _____.

⌇ Task: Post Your Golden Words ⌇ Where You Can See Them.

There are several ways to do this task, all equally valid. Some of you may wish to cull and clip your words from magazines. Some of you may wish to use the fancier print fonts on your computers. Others might want to buy some good rough paper and a felt-tipped calligraphy pen. Whatever you choose to use, take each of your newly converted words and make a Post-it version of the word. (You may wish to make several of each). Decorate that Post-it. Gild it. Glitter it. Illustrate it. Illuminate it. Above all, consecrate it: you are the new word, not the old.

"Original" . . ."Passionate" . . ."Exciting" . . ."Imaginative" . . ."Festive" . . ."Humorous" . . ."Generous" . . ."Adventurous."

Post these descriptions of yourself on mirrors, above workstations, inside your closet, or on the door so that you see them every time you leave the house, allowing you to carry a positive sense of yourself into the world.

Additionally, you may wish to record these words so that you can play them to yourself as you drive. Try recording them in the first, second, and third person:

"I, Tom, am inventive, shrewd, focused . . ."

"You, Tom, are inventive, shrewd, focused . . ."

"Tom—he is inventive, shrewd, focused . . ."

You might want to keep the full list of them next to your bed so that you can read them to yourself before sleeping or use them as your morning wake-up call.

∼∽ Task: Kill a Creative Monster. ∼∽

All of us have Creative Monsters. Our monsters shamed us around our creative personalities and work. Because the part of us that creates is an inner child, a playful, sensitive, and vulnerable creature, a Creative Monster is a real ogre. Ogres, of course, belong in Fairy Tales, and that is where we are going to put them.

In order to do this task, you must go back into your Narrative Time Line, select a Creative Monster, and lop off its head. The death need not be literal. Sometimes, a punishment seems even more delicious. I am thinking now of a Fairy Tale written by one of my students to deal with a former teacher called the Grammar Monster. No matter how brilliantly the student wrote (and she did write brilliantly), all the teacher could ever find to comment on were fine

Most contemporary therapists who work in depth with their patients know that behind the rigid top-heavy posture of most contemporary men is a little child with years of stored-up tears and fears.

STEPHEN LARSEN

*What the people of the city
do not realize is that the
roots of all living things are
tied together.*

CHAN K'IN VIEJO
quoted by Joan Halifax. He is a La-
candon shaman.

points of grammar—some of them so fine you would need a micro-scope to discover them.

"With grammar like yours, you will never be a *real* writer," roared the Grammar Monster. (She was wrong.) Nonetheless, her re-marks were destructive and lingered like thorns in the confidence of the victim who had, as it happened, very fine grammar indeed.

Enter the Fairy Tale. (For a detailed example of one, sneak a peek ahead to the next task and read "The Wizard Of Words.") Did my student kill the Grammar Monster? Death at the stake? No. She did something much more satisfactory. Death by *mistake*. With the simple stroke of her pen, she struck the Grammar Monster alive and well and incapable of speaking grammatically. Every time the Gram-mar Monster spoke or wrote, it came out grammatically wrong. Destined to live a long and miserable life while "dying of embarrass-ment," the Grammar Monster was finally expunged, expelled, and exiled from my student's consciousness. That is what Fairy Tales do.

I have often been criticized for devising this tool, so I hope you have an excellent time using it! I have been told that this tool is sim-ply too bloody-minded and that it makes us really rotten people to use it. I don't believe that. I believe that negative memories hold enormous amounts of power—power that is rightfully ours. It is the purpose of this exercise to reclaim that power. Try it and you will find that you do.

Select a Creative Monster and mete out a terrible fate.

～ Task: Celebrate a Creative Champion. ～

All of us need Creative Champions. Our champions encourage and support our personalities and work. Some of us are lucky enough to have had real life champions. (Sister Julia Clare taught me to believe in myself as a writer.) Others of us have found such support hard to come by. All of us can always use more, and creating more is what you are about to do.

Using the same fairy tale mind-set that you employed in the task above, please create for yourself a Creative Champion. Yours might be like Merlin or perhaps the Lady of the Lake. It might be a fairy godmother or a masterful magician. Create the figure that appeals to your own imagination. Now, write a brief story in which your Creative Child seeks—and receives—that figure's creative blessing. For example:

THE WIZARD OF WORDS

I am a small child who wants to be a writer. I have written a story down and I have it with me, scrolled up into a roll. I know that not far from my house, in a tall, magical wood, there lives a powerful Word Wizard whose words can create miracles and wonders. With the blessing of this Wizard, my words can do the same. Although everyone warns me that the woods are dark and scary, I set off to find the Wizard—that's how much I want to be a writer.

I walk and I walk. Morning comes and goes. Afternoon comes and goes. Twilight descends and I begin to grow apprehensive. Just as it begins to grow dark, I see ahead of me a glowing golden square set in the forest floor. When I reach that square, I see that it is actually a glass door and through it I can see a tunnel. The tunnel is lit by torches. It could be salvation or it could be a trap.

I open the door and enter the tunnel. I know I might meet a dragon, but then again, I might meet the Wizard of Words. . . . By the flickering light of the torches, I walk for a very long time. The tunnel leads deeper and deeper into the earth. I clutch my scroll of words close to my side. It is the best story I have ever written—at least it's the one I wrote that day—and I am hoping it will win the Wizard's blessing.

Finally, the tunnel ends in a large, round cave. The walls are covered in wine-colored leather and they are lined with books in many languages. Where, I wonder, is the Wizard of Words? In the center of the room, I notice a tall mirror. Maybe he is hiding in the mirror, I think—wizards frequently do that.

Cautious but determined, I look in the mirror. Yes! A Wizard is there!

"Show me your manuscript," the Wizard directs, reaching out with a jewel-encrusted sword. I unroll my story and allow him to read it, touching each word with the tip of his sword. To

A Bushman child will be carried a distance of 4,900 miles before he begins to walk on his own. Since, during this rhythmic phase, he will be forever naming the contents of his territory, it is impossible he will not become a poet.

BRUCE CHATWIN

The mystics believe the ideal man shall walk himself to a "right death."

BRUCE CHATWIN

*I've always felt the hunter
was an image of the artist.
The artist is a hunter, and
God is a hunter, hunting us.
We are always being looked
at by God, by the hunter. In
my studio, I am in the eye of
the hunter.*

MEINRAD CRAIGHEAD

my astonishment, every time he touches a word, a vibrant jewel falls to the floor of the cave.

"Do you want your treasure?" I ask the Wizard when he has finished reading, and a heap of jewels lies on the floor by my feet.

"Foolish child!" the Wizard roars. "The treasure is yours! Such is the value of your words!"

With that, the Wizard vanishes and I find myself staring back at me from the mirror. True, I do look a little like a Wizard. Also true, the jewels still lie scattered at my feet, waiting for me to claim them. I stuff the jewels into my pockets and carefully place my story under my shirt, next to my heart. (It is far more valuable than I had realized.)

Newly rich, I retrace my steps through the tunnel, open the sealed-glass door, and climb into the forest clearing where I find a crowd of villagers awaiting me.

"Who goes there?" they shout.

"It is I," I announce, "the Wizard of Words."

Secret Selves

The town I live in is blessed with extraordinarily beautiful natural light and, therefore, an extraordinarily high artist count. This, among many things, means that the town often takes on a playful character—most particularly at Halloween. For days before and after, all sorts of dress-up characters can be encountered anywhere—in the grocery store, at Walmart, servicing your car. (Yes, the kids get to dress up, too, but it is the adults who really do it up.)

Not only do we let our child selves out of the bag on Halloween, we let the cat out of the bag as well. Our costumes often reflect our secret, hidden aspects that we don't reveal in everyday life. For example, an editor friend of mine is an upstanding community figure and the soul of grace and integrity—married, monogamous, and happily so by all accounts. Nonetheless, on Halloween, he appears as his alter ego, a skeletal Don Juan, black caped, mustachioed, a smooth and seductive dancer. This archetype is one of his "Secret Selves" and he clearly enjoys letting it have its day.

Each of us, as Whitman writes, does "contain multitudes." Contacting the jostling crowd of inner selves, giving them a chance to speak and to act, can greatly enrich our lives. You have been working with your Narrative Time Line and many forgotten or misplaced parts of you have by now come into clearer focus. You may have remembered with great clarity the you that delighted in building

> *...Art is not just ornamental, an enhancement of life, but a path in itself, a way out of the predictable and conventional, a map to self-discovery.*
>
> GABRIELLE ROTH

I am closer to the work than to anything on earth. That's the marriage.

LOUISE NEVELSON

model aircraft carriers or the you that was a Brownie scout and learned to press leaves between wax paper and preserve their fall colors year to year.

Each of these historical selves forms the root system for your adult Secret Selves. Let me cite an example.

One of my Secret Selves is Mother Abbess. She is the product of my sixteen years of Catholic education, the years spent in long, drab, gray-and-blue jumpers. As you might expect, Mother Abbess has some very firm opinions about what is proper and what is not. Dresses, for example, should be ankle length, flowing or formless rather than form-fitting. This is especially true for a teacher, the Abbess insists. And so, my teaching clothes are just as the Abbess dictates . . . although I have negotiated the leeway of having them designed by Jo Dean Tipton so that they more closely resemble fairy-godmother garb than a nun's robes.

Vying for a voice next to Mother Abbess is another Secret Self whom I call Bon Bon. Bob Bon is a giddy blonde. (The grown-up version of my cheerleader self from St. Joseph's Catholic School.) She and Mother Abbess are at polar extremes from each other and have really had to work at a dialogue. Bon Bon loves vintage convertibles and fire-engine red lingerie. She likes froufrou in all its forms, and her idea of a great dress is something slinky. Mother Abbess does not approve!

Mediating between these two selves can be a little tricky—and yet, mediating between the two is also critical. Left in the sway of Mother Abbess, I would be leading a secular life of poverty, chastity, and obedience. Ruled by Bon Bon, I would be a high-living bon vivant whose work output was nil. Juggling input from each of them, I manage a life that is both festive and productive. There are many days when, under my Mother Abbess exterior, I am wearing Bon Bon's red lace. There are other days when, despite Bon Bon's play-and-more-play agenda, I accomplish my writing, teaching, and service work.

Each of these selves is important to me. Each of them contributes important pieces to my identity and each is a voice I must listen to in order to remain in harmony. One way to think of this is to think of each of us less as a singular musical instrument than as an entire orchestra. Each of our Secret Selves has a particular timbre that enriches the song of our life.

Of course, men as well as women harbor a multitude of Secret Selves and can benefit greatly by making their existence a conscious part of their self-image. I am thinking now of Patrick, a world-class entrepreneur, whose Secret Selves included a folksinger and a mountaineer. Among the first fruits of his creative recovery were restringing his guitar and taking a climbing trip to Italy. (This after a full decade in which his only mountain climbing involved the stacks of paper on his heavily trafficked desk!)

My longtime friend and partner, Mark Bryan, has a Secret Self that we called Geekley. His Geekley wears Coke-bottle glasses and would be perfectly happy forever buried in a stack of books sending out an occasional communiqué via E-mail.

Now, to see Mark in his usual Public Persona—tall, dark, and handsome—you might not dream of Geekley's existence. Yet it was Mark's bookish, intellectual side that first drew us to work together through his love—and gift—for writing.

Unacknowledged and unaccepted, some of our Secret Selves can be very difficult to live with—particularly if we keep them locked in the closet so that they can spring out only occasionally and scare us to death. "Where did that come from!" we often exclaim when a disowned Secret Self suddenly puts in an appearance.

I am thinking now of a kind and tenderhearted man, who hides this Secret Self under a show of bristling bravura. (His presenting persona is Hip Harry.) A devoted father, he recently underwent an intense bout of depression. Yes, he had undergone a rotten divorce and was living separated from his children, but he had a new girlfriend and . . .

And since she resented his involvement with his children, he had temporarily misplaced the Doting Dad Secret Self and was living almost entirely out of his charismatic Hip Harry persona. Hip Harry had places to go, people to see, and deals to make. He got along fine without his kids, but Doting Dad did not. It was only when this man got the two selves into dialogue with each other that he was able to

To be at peace with ourselves, we need to know ourselves.

CAITLIN MATTHEWS

What you do instead of your work is your real work.

ROGER EBERT

find his center of balance and stop the mood swings that had begun to dominate and destroy his life.

Some of you may be thinking, "Oh, dear. This sounds like therapy." Yes, it does, because among its many other functions, art *is* therapy. Discovering and uncovering your Secret Selves actually allow you to begin functioning in a more conscious and creative way.

You may discover, for example, that your Public Persona is one of the least enjoyable of your many selves. Hoping to buy approval, you may be doing Martyred Mary or Dutiful Dan. With a little excavation, you may find you have repressed a self that is far more vital and much closer to the you you would prefer living. In other words, you may have a dominant self clamped down tight as a lid on a Secret Self—or Selves—who is bubbling with energy and gifts for you.

I remember teaching a workshop in Michigan where Mark's and my "students" were actually college professors. The minute we turned to Secret Selves, a particularly prim and proper young woman suddenly burst out, "Chloe the Bitch!"

The room rocked with laughs of recognition. There were quite a few "Chloes" lurking about. And Chloes can be very helpful, if we let them.

When we allow our Secret Selves to weigh in with their opinions and votes, we often get a far more balanced view of the situations that we are in. For example, your Public Persona may operate along the lines of, "Oh, Sally, be charitable." This thinking doesn't serve you well in a highly charged professional situation where skullduggery and sabotage are at hand. While Sally is thinking, "She/he couldn't possibly have meant to take credit for my idea . . . ," Chloe the Bitch might be thinking—*and saying*—"Wait a minute. That's *my* concept. Let's give credit where credit is due!"

Becoming acquainted with our Secret Selves puts us in the position of traffic controller. We can signal the appropriate self to the fore. A friend of mine, baffled by social graces, learned the trick of asking himself, "What would Cary Grant do in this situation?" He would then do *that*.

Convening your Secret Selves like a board of directors is a very effective way to tap their collective wisdom. This can be done very

As a rule, it was the pleasure-haters who became unjust.

W. H. AUDEN

Is it, I have wondered, that the archetypal subsoil of the North American continent invites the personal vision quest?

STEPHEN LARSEN

simply by taking a sheet of paper, asking a question, and then letting each of your Secret Selves weigh in with an opinion or a plan of action. Accepting each voice as valid and worth listening to is often a key to far greater self-acceptance—and self-comfort.

My beloved friend Laura has a Secret Self that I have nicknamed Vampy Vanessa. As you may recall, Laura is a kindergarten teacher and her daytime persona radiates bright goodwill. However, she is also a tall, willowy blonde and her nighttime clothes reflect Vampy Vanessa's fondness for something that suits a real femme fatale: black lace, the gleam of something gold . . .

Vampy Vanessa is as much a part of my beloved friend as her sugar-and-spice Miss Very Nice teacher's self. If Laura doesn't let Vampy Vanessa go out dancing, Miss Very Nice tends to get a little bit grumpy. It is all a matter of balance.

As we acknowledge and accept our Secret Selves, our decisions can be formed more holistically. Our lives take on the shapes and colors of our multifaceted personality.

Another Secret Self of mine is a persona whom I call Violet. Violet is my shy, bookish intellectual. She is the part of me who writes and reads poetry. She is the Secret Self responsible for the delicate flower wreaths in my writing room, for the handmade lace curtains and pale lilac walls in the room where I work on my musicals.

Please allow yourself to undertake the following tasks in the spirit of Halloween play. We are inviting our Secret Selves out into our conscious minds so that their input can have some *play* in our imagination and in our lives.

A wise man never loses anything if he have himself.
MONTAIGNE

Nothing worse could happen to one than to be completely understood.   C. G. JUNG

～ Task: Name Five Secret Selves. ～

Choose a particularly playful piece of music. Light a scented candle or a stick of incense. (If you don't have either of those, use a whiff of vanilla, lemon extract, or aftershave on a piece of cotton ball.) What you are after is a combination of sound and scent that takes you out of your everyday self and lets you explore.

Now list five Secret Selves. Resistance may rear its head along the lines of, "If I know about them, how can they be secret?"

*The ground of the soul
is dark.*
MEISTER ECKHART

Don't be so literal. What we are going for here is catching sight of ourselves in some of the guises we may not often wear. If this feels difficult for you, think back along your Narrative Time Line. Was there a Secret Self from your adolescence who is still with you? (My Bon Bon appeared in eighth grade, when I was unexpectedly elected to the cheerleading squad.) What about your twenties? Did any Secret Self surface there? That's when my friend poet James Navé found he had a traveler self, an American Marco Polo who had him crisscrossing the continent, thumb outstretched. That self is with him still, years later, as he logs his frequent flyer miles for trips to exotic locales.

If you still find yourself stuck, list twenty things that you love and ask yourself which part of you loves them. That should suffice to provoke a name or two.

∼ Name Those Selves: ∼

1. _____

2. _____

3. _____

4. _____

5. _____

∼ Task: What's in Those Closets? ∼

For this task, imagine that you are walking into the closet of each one of your Secret Selves. List five things you find in each closet. Be very specific. For example:

1. Martyred Mary: sensible plain pumps, a blue gabardine city suit, a modest floral dress with a lace collar, a terry-cloth robe, terry-cloth slippers. Lots of plain white undies.

2. Bon Bon: red stiletto high heels, a midnight black lace peignoir set, a red silk evening dress, a pair of

silk "men's" lounging pajamas, a non—politically correct fur coat.

3. Reliable Ralph: a half dozen shirts, plain white and plain blue, two suits, one navy and one tan, sensible lace shoes, a raincoat, a plain black umbrella. Ah, yes, slip-on galoshes.

4. Dashing David: a black pullover sweater, a black silk shirt, a white linen collarless shirt, a gray "nubbly" raw silk sweater, two pair of Italian designer pants, a white silk scarf, a black cashmere overcoat, driving gloves.

~ Task: What Would Your Life Be Like? ~

In this task, you are asked to imagine what your life would be like if it were led by each of your Secret Selves. I like to begin by picking your most "wet-blanket" self, the one who is really very little fun. Take five minutes and write about life under the regime of this self. Not much fun, is it?

Next, take your most fun Secret Self. What would your life be like if this merry rascal were running it? Would Steve the Sailor have you island-hopping aboard a sloop? (Maybe you do need to take sailing lessons.) Again, write for about five minutes.

Now work with those selves that fall in between the two poles. Let each of them have a shot at running the show. You will discover, by now, that each of your Secret Selves has both pros and cons. You may need a Cautious Catherine as much as you need a Reckless Ruth.

As an artist, it is easy to become habituated to expressing one of your Secret Selves to the relative exclusion of others. You may think of your work as "cheery" or "dark." Learning to accept and appreciate selves that are *other* than your presenting self allows you to explore arenas of work that do not fall into your usual bailiwick.

Timothy Nero is a painter and sculptor whose work is extremely powerful and often quite dark. At Christmas of last year, he was among a group of artists asked by a prestigious gallery to do "angels." Needless to say, Tim's angel was not a fluffy little concoction, but was

I welcome all creatures of the world with grace.

HILDEGARD OF BINGEN

Life is not a problem to be solved, but a mystery to be lived.

THOMAS MERTON

rather a great skew-winged creature that appeared to achieve transcendence despite itself. This made it deeply moving and far more interesting than the many angels that were all sweetness and light. The assignment to "do an angel" allowed Tim to explore the Secret Self who just might believe in them.

Cinema Self

Some of you may be familiar with an old Danny Kaye movie, *The Secret Life Of Walter Mitty.* In the film, Kaye plays a Milquetoast son, dominated by an overbearing mother. His lackluster life is enlivened only by his persistent creative fantasies—in which he, Walter Mitty, is secretly a hero.

This outsize, spiffed-up, heroic version of him is what I would call a "Cinema Self." Very often, while it seems like a pipe dream, our Cinema Self is really an expression of our vein of gold—a mock-up version of a larger, grander self that is straining to be born. I once had the opportunity to watch two people whom I knew be transformed before my very eyes into Cinema Selves.

Art enables us to find ourselves and lose ourselves at the same time.
THOMAS MERTON

In my twenties, when I was working at the *Washington Post* during Watergate, I knew both Carl Bernstein and Bob Woodward. We all knew them. They were these two nice guys who were just a little *obsessed.*

"Carl and Bob," the newsroom thinking went, "those two are a little bit crazy."

A little bit later, the thinking went, "Carl and Bob. Those two are a little bit crazy . . . but they *might be right.*"

Still later, the thinking went, "Carl and Bob . . . those two are right!"

*There are no mistakes. What
happens during the process
of making something is
sacred and organic.*
VICKI NOBLE

Still, nothing quite prepared the newsroom for, "Carl and Bob . . . those two are *Dustin Hoffman* and *Robert Redford?*"

From their everyday reportorial selves, they were suddenly glamorized into Cinema Selves. I remember the day that Robert Redford first came to the newsroom. It is a good thing there was no fast-breaking news crisis because the telephone operators were very "busy"—busy gawking at Mr. Redford, the glamorized "cinema" version of Bob Woodward.

After the cameras quit rolling, after the office was back to the clack and grind of a daily newspaper, a little cinematic magic still clung to Carl and Bob. If they weren't exactly movie stars themselves, they were more definitively star reporters. Their Cinema Selves had lent some indelible ink to them, after all.

All of us have a self that we live with as our normal, everyday self. That self is probably bigger than it used to be and smaller than we wish it would be. In other words, there are many days when we wish we could be larger than we currently are. Like Alice with the magic mushrooms (our moods), we keep getting larger and smaller. One day we are "up to" making a very tough phone call. Another day, we "shrink" from the task.

It's all relative, we say. On the days when we feel relatively large, we take risks to expand our lives. On the days when we feel relatively small, we retreat to the safety of a smaller version of ourselves. Like Walter Mitty, we daydream about what our lives would be like if only we were able to live as our larger, more cinematic selves. Here you are asked to play with what I call Cinema Self.

Cinema Self is a larger-than-life, idealized version of you. The kind of you that looms from the silver screen. It is a glossier, more daring, more glamorous than you are, but it is based on *you* as you actually are. You are the prototype from which this character is drawn.

You might want to think of this in terms of what seminal creativity teacher Barbara Sher (her best-selling book *Wishcraft* is a classic self-actualization tool) calls a "style search." The questions are designed to let you think about what constitutes glamour and expansion *to you*.

~~ Task: Cinema Self. ~~

Please fill in the following:

1. What kind of car does Cinema Self drive? Perhaps several? Is it a classic Mercedes convertible sedan, a vintage Volkswagen bug, a '65 Chevy truck?

2. What is Cinema Self's "signature" article of clothing? A bomber jacket? Carole Lombard pajamas?

3. Where does Cinema Self live? Town? Country? Both?

4. What is Cinema Self's spiritual practice? Tai Chi? Retreats at Christ of the Desert? A goddess circle?

5. What three places has Cinema Self loved visiting that you haven't been to yet? Tibet? Texas? The Costa del Sol?

6. What is the title of Cinema Self's memoirs? *Travels with a Restless Mind, Adventures of a Peaceful Heart, Reflections of an Avid Angler*?

7. What is Cinema Self's relationship to animals? None, thank you? Approximately the same as the San Diego Zoo's?

8. What three adjectives are usually used to describe Cinema Self? Charismatic, childlike, adventuresome?

9. What is Cinema Self's relationship to friends? A wide-ranging circle of acquaintances? A tight cluster of intimates? What you might call a loner?

10. Who plays Cinema Self in the movie? One star or several for different ages? Yourself or an established cinema presence?

What if we smashed the mirrors
And saw our true face?

ELSA GIDLOW

The Vein of Gold

By now, you should know yourself far better than you did at the be-ginning—especially if you have finished your Narrative Time Line and done some work with Cups.

What we are going to do now is play a game. It's a rather de-manding game, but we have been working up to it and we are ready. The trick in working with this game is to remember to *play* with it as well. The game is called "The Vein of Gold."

Before we go any further, I'd like to say a word about the title: I stole it. It was my privilege on two occasions to have lengthy dia-logues with the late film director Martin Ritt, nearly unparalleled as an "actor's director" who elicited brilliant, star-making perfor-mances from his actors.

It was a young Martin Ritt who directed young Paul Newman and Patricia Neal in *Hud.* It was Ritt who made Cicely Tyson a star with *Sounder* and who directed *Norma Rae,* the film that changed our impression of Sally Field from Gidget to an actress of depth and stature.

Ritt had a theory about actors and brilliance. He called it the vein of gold.

A grizzled, curmudgeonly man with the wrinkled mug of a prize shar-pei dog, Ritt sat with me for hours in a hotel suite in Chicago and later in a church basement in Canada, detailing his views. Even as we were talking, I felt as though he were handing me a creative Rosetta Stone, making me an initiate in some mystery school of the arts. He would probably find such a dramatic description so much hooey, but he broke a code for me and handed me the key to a decade of further work. This was the nub of his skills, his directing secret.

"All actors have a certain territory, a certain range, they were born to play. I call that range their 'vein of gold.' If you cast an actor within that vein, he will *always* give you a brilliant performance. Of course, you can always cast an actor outside his vein of gold. If you do, the actor can use craft and technique to give you a very fine, a very creditable performance, *but never a performance as brilliant as when he is working in his vein of gold.*"

I thought of Robert De Niro and his brilliance in roles centering on the themes of male bonding, loyalties and betrayals. Brilliant as he was always, did his roles requiring the love of a woman ever have the same resonance?

I thought of Kevin Kline and his solid performances as a dramatic actor. Didn't they pale next to his wicked comedic skills? Wasn't comedy his vein of gold?

Meryl Streep, an actress who adores comedy and plays it every turn she gets, snares us more surely in roles requiring high drama—and high-end drama, at that. Her blue-collar heroines never capture us quite as surely as her blue bloods do. We love her a little foreign and very much in jeopardy, longing for a man, not for justice.

With Jodie Foster, we believe her blue-collar heroines when they thirst to find justice. Or the killer. We have less conviction, as she does, that her finding the right man is the answer.

None of this is to say that actors shouldn't act just as they choose in whatever they choose. It is simply to say that Ritt was onto something when he noticed the vein of gold.

As a writer-director myself, for years after that conversation, I found my mind circling back to Ritt and his theory. Once he had placed in my head the concept of a creative vein of gold, I saw evidence of its validity everywhere, and not just among actors. I saw ev-

For a creative writer possession of the "truth" is less important than emotional sincerity.

GEORGE ORWELL

idence in those all around me that there were themes in life and in work that were simply more resonant and rewarding than others.

My brother, Christopher, a composer, is a piano player's piano player, but when he sets sail on an old Hammond organ . . . His rendering of "Amazing Grace" is truly a spiritual experience, his vein of gold.

Among my photographer friends, Mitchell Canoff is the wizard of the candid black-and-white street portrait. Aloma excels at timeless studio portraiture. Writer-photographer John Nichols strikes gold with color landscapes. Each has a vein of gold.

"What should I make art about?" people often ask. The answer, put most simply, is "What you care about; what you think about."

Most people, although they may not be aware of it, have certain trains of thought that are their favored routes through a day. Asking yourself, "What do I mull about? What do I think about when I'm not thinking about anything else?" can yield some pretty interesting results.

Some people think about sex. Some people think about money. Some people think about the murder they read about, and read about still, in installments in the daily paper. Other people wonder about UFOs, out-of-body experiences, ESP, what God is like, if there is a God, if there is an afterlife, if truth is always relative, what the market's going to do. . . . Some of us think about welfare mothers, teen pregnancies, class privileges, the power of the media, and yes, the lifestyles of the rich and famous.

You may say, correctly, that all of us think about all of these things, and that may well be true. It remains true that some of these topics are more fun for you than others. (Say "more absorbing" if it is hard to admit that reading about grisly murders or celebrity sex scandals is just plain fun for you.) Those habitual lines of thought, those areas of speculation that we rake over again and again, are an excellent guide to what we should write about, paint about, dance about, make movies about, collage about, knit about, etc.

It is very important to make art about what we are *really* interested in, not what we *should* be interested in. All too often, we aim at writing a script we *should* write, and when it's done with, that's exactly how it reads—like a noble effort, well meant but somehow hollow. The same holds true for dutiful paintings, meals, poems, letters, even curtains.

Listen to what Michell Cassou and Stewart Cubley write in *Life, Paint and Passion:*

> To create is to move into the unknown—to move into the mystery of yourself, to have feeling, to awaken buried perceptions, to be alive and free without worrying about the result. But the mind is conditioned to think it wants a nice painting, a nice tree, beautiful scenery. No! Maybe you want monsters. Maybe you want chaos, maybe you want a mess. Maybe it will feel really good to paint an ugly painting. Maybe that would open your being much more than a masterpiece. . . .

All of us have had the experience of watching a movie or episodic television that felt like an exercise in paint-by-numbers. Similarly, all of us have seen performances by great actors that were technically brilliant but oddly uninhabited. What went wrong? we wonder. On paper the premise sounded right enough. The formula sounded good.

But art is not about formula.

Look again at director Martin Ritt's theory about this. Remember? He called it the "vein of gold." We are going to be looking for that in us all, but for the moment let's look at how it functions in a public forum—our most public art form, the movies.

Think again of Robert De Niro. He excels at playing loners or men who bond intensely with other men. We have loved De Niro in *Taxi Driver, The Godfather Part II, The Deer Hunter, GoodFellas,* and many other films where he played into his strength as a man's man. Male-female films are somehow beside the point for him. Romantic love is simply *not* De Niro's vein of gold—but male bonding is.

Having mentioned Streep, let us look at her multi-striped career and how much we enjoy her when she is playing a larger-than-life heroine with upper-class problems, a foreign accent, and a noble, tormented heart. She herself loves doing comedy, but we have not made

The artist is a receptacle for emotions that come from all over the place: from the sky, from the earth, from a scrap of paper, from a passing shape, from a spider's web.

PABLO PICASSO

A creative writer can do his best only with what lies within the range and character of his deepest sympathies.

WILLA CATHER

her a beloved comedienne. As fine as her work has been in her turns as a blue-collar worker and mother (*Silkwood* and *The River Wild*), she was unforgettable as Isak Dinesen in *Out of Africa* and Sophie in *Sophie's Choice.*

Sophie's Choice brings us back to another brilliant actor, Kevin Kline. A truly great comic actor, for years he languished in romantic leads, playing very sincere, even syrupy nice guys. Remember him as Sissy Spacek's husband in *Violets Are Blue?* Perhaps not. Those nice-guy roles, and those movies, never quite jelled. Despite his impeccable technique, the camera never quite loved him as the simple nice guy. Kline may be many things—and a technically marvelous actor is one of them—but uncomplicated nice is not his vein of gold.

As his Otto in *A Fish Called Wanda* made clear, wicked humor is Kline's forte. He is smart, shrewd, and great—especially at the very difficult art of physical comedy. Now that Kline is mining his vein of gold, his career has taken off and acquired some appropriate altitude.

"Dying is easy. Comedy is hard," the old actor's joke runs, and Kline is able to turn his vein of gold to good avail even when the material is less than golden. It was Kline's glittering comic gift as well as Meg Ryan's heart of gold that made even *French Kiss* a film we can recall with affection.

Writers, painters, potters, photographers, all of us have our vein of gold. Most often, what we enjoy making art about is what we enjoy seeing once it's made—which is about what we enjoy mulling over, whether it's in a news story or a movie, a magazine or a conversation. If you think about a theme a lot, chances are good it's in your vein of gold.

How do I know what I think about? you might ask. It is true that we are sometimes so busy thinking about our favorite somethings that we don't even know what they are. What follows is a set of sleuthing techniques for nosing out your vein of gold.

Technique One: Favorite Films. Name five favorite films. They can be any films at all—good films, bad films, childhood films, grown-up films, recent, classic, or vintage films. Just pick five of them. *Any* five.

Here's a sample list, mine:

1. *The Ghost and Mrs. Muir.* An old British film about fated love. The lovers come from differing circumstances. . . . One lover is alive and well. The other is a ghost.

2. *I Know Where I'm Going.* Another British classic by director Michael Powell. Another love story about "fated love." This time one lover is a city girl and the other is a country man.

3. *Holiday.* Yes, another love story about lovers from differing circumstances. This time she's an heiress and he's a striver who is set to marry the "wrong" sister.

4. *Always.* Steven Spielberg's "officially" unsuccessful film about—you did guess it—fated love. This time about love surviving past the veil of death.

5. *Blithe Spirit.* It's another film of love surviving death.

That's my list, and yours might be very different. The point is to take whatever five films you arrived at off the top of your head and to do a little looking at the list. What are some of the common denominators involved in these films?

One way or another, each of my movies is a period piece—obviously, I like movies set in another time, another place, and featuring some aspect of being an outsider that forces another way of looking at things. Many of the films center on a belief in the supernatural having a hand in human affairs. Fate and death figure largely in all of them.

And there are more common denominators. All of my films involve mystery—theological, technological, or psychological. All involve matters of life and death. (Yet another favorite film of mine is a different Michael Powell classic, *A Matter of Life and Death*, featuring, yes, fated lovers, the supernatural, and, yes, matters of life and death.) Another theme common to my films is that they all involve questions of conventionally held beliefs. Off the top of my head, I

One day, it was suddenly revealed to me that everything is pure spirit.

RAMAKRISHNA

*Belief consists in accepting
the affirmations of the soul;
unbelief, in denying them.*

RALPH WALDO EMERSON

might equally well have come up with an entirely different list of favorites:

1. *Topper*

2. *A Guy Named Joe* (The "source" for *Always.*)

3. *Splash*

4. *The State of the Union* (And any number of Hepburn/Tracy films, featuring mismatched, perfectly matched lovers.)

5. *The Thin Man*

Does this list negate my first one? Not at all. It amplifies and confirms it. Again, these films are all centered on fated love, lovers from differing circumstances, mystery—and again on death. Sex and death are intertwined—as are questions about fate and the afterlife. Even *Splash* is not so far removed as it might seem. It, like *Blithe Spirit*, concerns fated love.

What do I glean from all this? I learn that I am interested in love and death, and the fateful combining of the two. Looking back over my own body of work, which includes four full-length plays as well as a dozen screenplays, I see this amply borne out.

My first play, *Public Lives*, is a tragicomedy about the afterlife. The hero dies in scene one. In scene two, he sits up on his bier, lights a cigarette, and the show goes on. My first film as writer-director, *God's Will*, opens with the death of the protagonists and then follows their career as theatrical ghosts.

The list goes on. There is *Twinkle*, billed by my Hollywood agent as a sort of "*Splash* who fell to earth." There is *Star-Crossed*, a comedy about ill-fated lovers who repeatedly try—and fail—lifetime to lifetime to solve the same hand-me-down mystery. Comedy or tragedy, the themes remain the same. In *A Mile Straight Down*, a beloved deceased wife is found to be very much alive and well and living with another man, in another country.

In short, time after time, in many different guises, I have enjoyed writing about the very things I enjoy watching and reading about. I am not alone in this. For the past decade, I have taught screenwriting.

It is my experience as a teacher that the best scripts always come from those topics closest to the heart.

Let me give another list of favorite films, Mark's, for you to practice with:

1. *Rocky*

2. *An Officer and a Gentleman*

3. *It's a Wonderful Life*

4. *Ikiru* (Often called Kurosawa's *It's a Wonderful Life.*)

5. *The Grapes of Wrath*

What themes do you see in common? There's social injustice, the "haves" versus the "have-nots." There's the everyman hero who must overcome his past and his lowly station to save the day. Look closely and you will also see other subthemes: the true love found *only* by being true to oneself. You get the idea. Now, not all of the movies will clearly articulate all of the themes but there will be noticeable, repeating patterns—and these repeated patterns are the gleam of the vein of gold.

"All of my movies are really my own story," Mark says. This is true for all of us if we look closely enough. Remember, one more time: we are the "origin" in "original."

"I put in my pictures everything I like," Picasso said. If you read every story written about child abuse, that is a topic for you. If money-laundering stories are your regular reading material, they will yield you a lively story on financial shenanigans. If you enjoy looking at lilies and want to paint, paint lilies!

What follows is another task to help you *begin* looking for your vein of gold. Sometimes it helps to enlist a sharp-eyed friend in this procedure. Often, our own themes are so close to us that we may miss them when we look for them.

I think, to a poet, the human community is like the community of birds to a bird, singing to each other. Love is one of the reasons we are singing to one another, love of language itself, love of sound, love of singing itself, and love of the other birds.

SHARON OLDS

~ Task: The Vein of Gold Quiz. ~

1. Name five favorite movies. (Any five loved films will do. They can be current or oldies but goldies. Do not

*Disciplined activity and
heightened sensitivity can
reveal a spiritual path for the
artist which can lead to
a private spring of
magic waters.*
RICHARD NEWMAN

consider this list to be set in stone, just write it out
quickly, off the top of your head.)

2. Name your favorite childhood book. (This book
should probably be from *your* childhood, not one of
the books you read to your kids.)

3. Name three characters you loved.

4. Name three characters you would love to play.

5. Name three topics you think about.

6. Name three topics you read about.

7. What was your childhood book about?

8. What are your movies about?

9. Do your movies and books have anything in common?

10. Do your characters, your reading, and your thinking
connect up somehow with your movies and your
childhood book?

Sometimes this quiz can be a little tricky to self-administer. You
may want to have several friends from your cluster list tell you what
common denominators they see in your lists. (You may want to get
together as a group and plan a party around this chapter.) By the time
you are finished working with this book, this quiz will be more
meaningful and resonant to you. Think of this as playing an elaborate game of Clue with yourself.

You may also want to look through your quiz for what I call the
"Karmic Question." This is an issue, a question, or a concern that you
and your favorite characters are working on "solving."

For example, one film student came up with a film list that involved both *The Godfather* and *The Godfather, Part II* plus *Apocalypse Now* and *Lord of the Flies* and *A Clockwork Orange*. This
student's Karmic Question involved the proper use of power. He was
concerned with issues of cruelty, domination, strength, and weakness.

∼ Task: Binge Reading. ∼

This technique involves something delightful for most creatives—binge reading.

Before you begin, quickly jot down five topics you frequently read on. (Include the topics you secretly read on.)

1. _____

2. _____

3. _____

4. _____

5. _____

Now, proceed directly to the supermarket checkout counter and acquire at least three "rags" you would not be caught dead reading. I believe in buying the *Enquirer,* the *Star,* the *Globe.* (These papers involve stories where the stakes are hilariously or tragically high: "Mother Marries Son—Twice!") If you must, also buy the *New York Times, Newsweek, Time* and *People.* Take them all home, lock yourself in your bedroom with a pair of scissors and a red pen, and mark, clip, and save *any* story you find remotely interesting. This should, after a week of bingeing, yield you quite a collection.

Now start sorting. Look for the common denominators in your stories. Sex. Medicine. Money. Tragedy. Science. Look for the psychological common denominators, too: triumph against all odds, betrayal by best friends, victory through perseverance, etc. In short, divide, if you can, into topic and theme.

This process, done carefully, should yield you a fairly good idea of what it is that strikes you as interesting—and it need strike only *you* that way. There is no point, ever, in worrying about whether something will interest only you. *If you find it interesting, so will somebody else.*

This process may well strike some of you as silly—too random to be revelatory. Believe what you will, but try it. Then try it again.

~ Task: Grab-Bag Collage. ~

Working as rapidly as you can, pull twenty to thirty images from a stack of magazines. Glue these images to a poster board in whatever way feels enjoyable to you. The images do not need to—and often don't or won't—make sense. They are intended to be very free-form, spontaneous, and top-of-the-mind. You don't need to know why an image appeals to you. It can be a "dark" image or a "light" image. Just yank and paste. Do not overthink this exercise and do not read ahead to the next one until you have completed this task!

~ Task: Matching. ~

(Note: Do not read these instructions until you have completed Task Three. You will wreck the game for yourself!)

If your Grab-Bag Collage is finished, sit down with that and your Vein of Gold Quiz. Look for image matchups. (It was Mark Bryan who first focused me on this phenomenon. He was right!)

Do you see an image from your favorite childhood book? Could that train be from *The Little Engine That Could*? Is that Nancy Drew's shiny roadster?

Do you see any images from your movies? What about those lions and palm trees? Isn't *Out of Africa* on your list?

Look at all those children in the center of your collage. Wasn't education something that you read about?

Again, enlist the help of a sharp-eyed friend. Very often a friend can spot images and themes that we ourselves might miss. For example, your friend might say, "All of your films were about social justice. Look at this cluster of images here, the Third World children . . ." Or, alternatively, "We must have missed a theme somewhere. There's a lot of romance in this collage. Where is it in your films?" In this way we can both see what is obvious to us and about us and chip away at our denial around what is not. You may be softer-hearted or tougher-minded than you have cared to admit. By spotting our vein of gold and owning it, we begin to be able to mine it for the riches that may differ from those we imagined we would find.

Unconditional acceptance of feeling then allows the person maximum learning, evolvement, and attunement.

CEANNE DEROHAN

Learn to see, and then you'll know that there is no end to the new worlds for our vision.

CARLOS CASTANEDA

～ Task: Write Up Your Findings. ～

Set a timer for one hour. Cue up music that "expands" you. (I use Tim Wheater's *Green Dream*.) Pen in hand, sit down and write out what you have learned about yourself from your work with the vein of gold. Try to think of this as a field report. You may even want to describe yourself in the third person:

ROBERT'S FIELD REPORT

I discovered that Robert had an interest since childhood in the welfare of his community as a whole. This was reflected in his film list by his choice of Frank Capra and Sidney Lumet movies, two directors whose themes center on social injustice. In his reading choices, he centered on social issues and world events, with a concentration on the underprivileged. In his collage, this same concern was shown in a cluster of images involving Third World countries, UNICEF children, and refugee camps.

Be sure to write for one full hour or even longer. Allow yourself to really "talk" about what surprised you, what dismayed you, what intrigued you. Be sure to include whatever recognitions indicate you may need a change of direction. Take time to speculate on what form that change of direction might take.

Creativity is a different quality of spiritual life than humility and asceticism; it is a revelation of the god-like nature of humanity.
NIKOLAI BERDYAEV

The Meaning of Life is to see.   HUI NENG

Breaking Camp

"When you begin to listen to your own story, you will be amazed at how interesting your life is," writer-teacher Mandy Aftel tells us. It is my hope that this is precisely what your work with the Kingdom of Story has begun to convince you. As you exit this kingdom, pause for a moment and survey all that you have done:

Your Narrative Time Line has wrung from your life events a cohesive form that you yourself can recognize and validate. Your work with "Cups" (so named for the tool "cupel," a porous cup used in assaying gold and silver) has allowed you to excavate rich pockets of autobiographical material. Your Fairy Tales have shown you the cathartic power of the imagination at play with your life events. Your Secret Selves and Cinema Selves have fleshed out the cast of characters—and the sense of character—that you yourself contain. Your Vein of Gold Quiz has given you a sense of the thematic concerns that thread through your life and merit your attention.

Good work! Give yourself the satisfaction of knowing that you have covered a great deal of territory as well as having gained the spiritual stamina necessary for moving ahead. You will find that the tools of the Kingdom of Sight build upon the work you have already accomplished. Allow yourself to appreciate the spiritual masonry of your foundation.

The Kingdom of Sight

Beauty is in the eye of the beholder," we say, but we must consciously focus on beauty to take it in. Think of an automobile ride through magnificent scenery. If you are going too fast or are too self-preoccupied, the scenery whizzes past unnoticed. The same is true with our lives. In this kingdom, we will be exploring our lives through the sense of sight. We will *look* at our lives visually to *see* what they look like. This means that we will consciously *focus* our perceptions on the information that can be gleaned from visual sources.

"Merely *looking* at the world around us is immensely different from seeing it," says artist Frederick Franck.

For those of us who are highly intellectual in the ways we process information, turning from words to pictures can be both a shock and a relief. When we read, we actively grasp for information. It is an appetite-driven acquisitive process, a.k.a. "a thirst for knowledge." When we approach images, we must learn to open and receive information holistically instead. We glean impressions, intuitions, and feelings as well as information. The experience is multisensory, although it may be intellectual as well. Do not be surprised if your Skeptic resists. Your Skeptic likes "control." "One picture is worth a thousand words." That bromide can become an actual experience. We incorporate information differently, perhaps at greater depth, when it comes to us visually. Persevere and you will gain creative range.

Sight

The local painters were my idols. . . . These artists, too, were grown-ups, but they were grown-ups who could still see! Their eye was still in love! Like mine!"

FREDERICK FRANCK

Joan Didion tells us writing is the act of saying, "I, I, I." I'm sure it sometimes is, but to me, it is more often, "Eye, eye, eye." We write about what we see, about what we are trying to see clearly. We write, and write some more, because language is slippery, and truth is. We write because the light we have to see by is always shifting.

For example, I am writing this essay in a hotel room on the western coast of Oahu. Outside my window, the Pacific is, well, *pacific*. It stretches calm and nearly flat and nearly endless beyond my view. Trying to see it clearly, I note bands of blue tinged with both gray and green. On my balcony, a tiny bird pecks at the AstroTurf carpet strip hunting for crumbs. The act of looking brings me into focus.

What a mixed bag this hotel is: air conditioners grinding out the roar of the surf; waves patiently breaking as they did long before electricity came to this island. I am impatient with the hubbub I hoped to escape here, and yet I am writing on a tiny, high-powered laptop computer. I have not left civilization behind me, either. Writing, I see that. I weigh my own ambivalence, my mixed values. I know myself just a little better.

"Our own life is the instrument with which we experiment with Truth," Thich Nhat Hanh tells us.

Writing is one way we examine our reality. It is one form in which we can explore and express it. Writing, like all forms of expression, demands that we look at things. In the face of our denial, at the risk of our comfort, it demands that we see. When we can write clearly about a person or event, it is because we have the willingness or the clarity to see it. Seeing it, we can name it. Naming it gives us a sense of possession, at least of our own experience.

But there are many things that resist being named with words, and that is why we do more than write. Sometimes the lantern of language is not enough. In order to *see*, we must look at things differently, using different tools.

"Images communicate more truth, in a certain way, than language," Vicki Noble remarks. I believe she is right about this.

When we work visually instead of verbally, we often make deep intuitive connections. As Frederick Franck says, "When the eye wakes up to see again, it suddenly stops taking anything for granted."

If seeing is believing, it is also understanding. Let me give you an example. I'd worked for years as a writer with the material of my early childhood. I knew I was the obstreperous "Avis child," always trying harder, in my birth position as second daughter second best, a sort of genetic ellipsis between my parents' firstborn and first son. To hear me tell it (ay! ay! ay!), I wore hand-me-down clothes, lived in the shadow of my older sister's glory, and held a dim candle to my towheaded brother Jaimie's light.

This was before I took to heart Rod Stewart's dictum, "Every picture tells a story, don't it?" When I began to work visually as well as verbally with the material of my life, my understanding deepened and expanded.

Working with old family photographs and magazines, I collaged my childhood between one and five. At first I thought I knew what I was looking for and what I would find. I wanted a zebra, a horse, and a donkey—for my three beloved stuffed animals, Zeebie, Reddie, and Donk-Donk. I wanted that donkey to do double duty, collaging my mother's scathing words, "You make a wonderful donkey, Julie, but a terrible lapdog." According to my mother and my well-burnished resentment, I just wasn't as holdable, huggable, or cuddly as a small person might be. Yes, going into my collage, I knew what a paste-up of horrors it should be.

Imagine my surprise when I looked at what I *saw* instead of only

To become truly immortal, a work of art must escape all human limits: Logic and common sense will only interfere. But once these barriers are broken, it will enter the regions of childhood visions and dreams.

GIORGIO DE CHIRICO

It is looking at things for a long time that ripens you and gives you a deeper understanding.

VINCENT VAN GOGH

According to one critic, my works looked like scraped billboards. I went to look at billboards and decided that more billboards should be scraped.

MARK TOBEY

seeing what I was looking for. Yes, there was the famous picture of me wreathed in mud and sucking a garden hose as if it were a hookah. But what was this? Who were these young, fragile, hopeful lovers looking at each other with such hope? My mother's sticklike, slender legs . . . my father's racy porkpie . . . the gleam in their eyes, in their shared smiles over the heads of their three little angels—all these details were news to me. My parents were lovers—young lovers, crazy about each other, stretching fingertips and smiles to connect with each other. So in love, so busy, who had time to torment their second-born? Who had the inclination?

If seeing is believing, it is also understanding. My parents were too young, too busy, too wrapped up in each other to indulge in malice. At worst, I suffered from distraction, *not* destruction.

Working with images in collage, it is often our random juxtaposition of two disparate images that decodes the belief we carry in our heart.

Q: Why did I put that picture of Matthew next to a bulldog?

A: He always bullies me!

Q: Why did I pick Goldie Hawn spread-eagled on a bull's-eye as an image?

A: I feel like a target myself!

Several years ago, when I sought to understand a troublesome love affair, I collaged it and found I depended on the turbulence it provided me with as a sort of ersatz fuel. My creative self was dead center in the middle of my collage—a girl-child in a magician's cap—but the man I was in love with showed up as a cluster of images underneath. He was lifting me like Samson, pushing me up like a volcano. Looking at this, I was shocked: I used my lover and my anger at him as a propellant and didn't trust a gentler fuel to give me a creative liftoff! Viewed this way, I owed him a thank-you and myself an apology. A gentler creativity soon followed.

When words fail me, I turn to pictures. Most specifically, I turn to collage. I keep the ground rules very simple for myself: set a time frame and topic, then tear through magazines, free-associating.

When life is very complicated, this simple act of selection immediately calms and focuses me. I don't overthink my choices. I just hold my subject loosely in my mind and then pull whatever images appeal, whether they seem to be appropriate or not. I am less after art than I am after artifact, or even art-as-fact. My collage is a sort of time capsule: I felt this way then about that. For me, the phrase "make sense" is quite literal, and the sense I often need to use for insight is my sense of sight.

"What do you *see* yourself doing in five years?"

"What part do you *see* yourself playing in the breakup?"

"What do you *see* as the areas of conflict between the two of you?"

Questions like these are excellent questions for collage work. Pose them and then pull images rapidly. Very often we will let ourselves choose images that speak our truth before we are able to use language to do so. Setting such images on the page, listening to the answers they supply for our questions, is often deeply transformational, but whether you actively pose a question or not, collage work is a tool of transformation.

I am not alone in being surprised by the "I" my eye revealed. Set to make a general life collage, one in which images deliberately reflect autobiography and affections, a student of mine chose image after image of the sea. Water was everywhere in the pictures he chose. Meanwhile, he was landlocked in the Midwest and, more than that, landlocked in a rigid nine-to-five job and highly structured, safe, serious, stratified, and predictable life. What he yearned for on all levels, physical and metaphysical, was not just water but *flow*.

"Maybe I'm thirsty," he joked, but he was—thirsty for change and what might be called the living water of a soulful life.

Because collage bypasses language, you do not need to abstract symbols into words to absorb their meanings. A vibrant woman who felt herself trapped in a deadened marriage collaged masses of flowers trapped amid urban structures—bricked in, encased, enclosed, cemented over, but blooming wildly at heart. Her collage taught her both how she *saw* her marriage and that while *it* was dead, she herself was alive and well and nearly ready to make changes.

In working with collage for transformation, it is tempting to take

To paint is to love again, and to love is to live to the fullest.
HENRY MILLER

As an artist, it is central to be unsatisfied! This isn't greed, though it be appetite.
LAWRENCE CALCAGNO

Once the art of seeing is lost,
Meaning is lost and life itself
seems ever more
meaningless.
FREDERICK FRANCK

The creative mind doesn't
require logical transitions
from one thought to another.
It skips, jumps, doubles back,
circles, and dives from one
idea to the next.
BONNI GOLDBERG

the often-piercing insights we gain and then use them as knives on ourselves. "See? You hate your marriage. Get out of it, then. Can't do it? You coward, you liar, you . . ." Easy does it. Lay off.

What we are is human beings, not human *do*ings. Insight may point the way to change, but often being able to read the signs is a huge change in itself. Without deliberately cultivated compassion for ourselves, spiritual and creative growth becomes a forced march through the hostile territory of our own judgments.

Although collage means ripping, tearing, and shredding, it also involves paste, glue, and the mending art of making something from the pieces. Perhaps the most important piece of collage work is its real goal: the peace we can make with parts of ourselves.

Framing a simple question like, "What's in my future?" and then tearing images as a sort of ragtag reading can be very powerful and revealing. You may see yourself having moved from town to country, from fat to thin, from married to single, or vice versa. A dream of traveling may emerge, or a plan for higher education. You do not have to be a trained artist or a trained art therapist to find collage making both artistic and therapeutic. Often, talking over a collage with a friend can yield new insights. Their interpretations may reinforce or differ from your own.

About fifteen years ago, I made a collage as part of a therapist-facilitated women's group. At the top and right of my collage was a cluster of images relating to stars, space, energy, and beams of light.

"What are these?" the therapist asked.

"They have to do with Star People," I heard myself answer, wondering what I could possibly mean by *that*, knowing that I did mean something very real to me, just elusive. The therapist, knowing my Hollywood past, interpreted the collage cluster as relating to my first husband, a film director, and the continuing bond I felt to him.

Maybe the cluster did relate to that *for her,* but it didn't feel that way to me. Taken collectively, all of the images expressed for me an intense spiritual longing, a desire for connection with what might be called higher consciousness, higher guiding forces. When I tried explaining this to the therapist, she balked. While she may have believed in a spiritual component to life, she hardly saw it as having the same magnitude as interpersonal relationships. *I did.*

The more we talked about my collage, the more the rift widened between me and the therapist, me and the group. On the other hand, the more we talked—and the more I looked at my collage—the stronger a sense I had that a great rift in my own consciousness was healing. I did believe in the guiding influence of higher forces. Before I could put it into words, I could put it into images: spiritual growth was my personal priority. Spiritual solutions, not therapeutic ones, spoke to my consciousness.

Although I had not undertaken the collage as a ritual of closure for my life in therapy, that is what it became. From that day to this, therapy has been a component available to my spiritual life rather than vice versa. If seeing is believing, I saw that I believed. My sources of change and transformation have differed ever since.

Memory is a net.

OLIVER WENDELL HOLMES,
SR.

～ Task: Time Capsule Collage. ～

From whatever source—magazines, newspapers, catalogs, cereal boxes, old photo collections—collect and save twenty images that in some way resonate with your memories, associations, and life experiences from years one to five.

Do not be too literal with yourself. If your dominant memory of your toddler's bedroom is the great green leafy tree outside the window, you can use a picture of the rain forest or even a salad if that green works for you in conjuring the association. Remember, you are both the "I" and the "eye" in this exercise. It is not necessary to know *why* an image speaks to you. The fact that it does is connection enough.

Take about twenty minutes and swiftly lay the images down on poster board. I prefer working with old-fashioned Elmer's glue, although there are those who swear by glue sticks. Feel free to add words or glitter, to outline with Magic Marker or dabble with paints. This is your collage and it is meant to reflect your child-self. Try to let yourself go back to that child and remember.

Just as you worked with the Narrative Time Line, dividing your life into five-year increments, using the Time Capsule Collage as a parallel tool is very powerful and cathartic, and something I would strongly suggest. You may want to set aside time each day for a week to move another five years further with your Time Capsule Collage. You may also want to hang these collages for a while. A hallway hung with a row of them becomes a visual Narrative Time Line, not unlike a home movie.

~ Task: Create a Treasure Map. ~

When we create something, we always create it first in a thought form.
SHAKTI GAWAIN

As sharply and subtly as images can reveal our subconscious fears and pressures, they can also, potently and persuasively, speak to—and for—our dreaming heart.

For Doris, the act of making a collage was very frightening. Moving through that fear, selecting her images, and putting them out in plain sight taught her that it was "safe to put my insides out where other people could see them."

Married for many years to an Italian, Doris saw her collage held Italy and her love of that culture. A recent grandmother, Doris saw her collage held the image that conveyed a young man holding an infant son. Beyond these domestic images, it held images that conveyed her yearning for a thinner, more girlish figure as well. Not coincidentally, that is a wish that has subsequently come true.

Because images speak directly to the subconscious mind, they are a very potent form of wishing. Collages that aim specifically at a desired outcome are often called "Treasure Maps," and they can be used to galvanize the spiritual world to produce desired material results.

Motivational sales managers will often goad their team to higher sales with images of bonus perks like luxury trips, high-powered cars, and dream TVs or stereos. These "Treasure Maps" aim at material goods, but maps can be made for accomplishments as well.

When I dreamed of shooting a feature film and was afraid to do it, I collaged myself shooting one. True, I had to graft my girlish head of curls onto the manly body behind the Panavision camera I found in an old issue of *American Film*. True, the hermaphroditic result looked a little silly. Still, I felt a little silly aspiring to this dream. (Girls from Libertyville, Illinois, did not do things like that.) My collage showed me doing it, silly or not. Silly or not, I soon did it.

Please design for yourself a Treasure Map. It can focus on material things you would like to gain, accomplishments you dream of succeeding at, or even of qualities you wish to embody more fully. The definition of "treasure" is up to you. Follow the same general guidelines that you did above. Work rapidly and without any demand that you create "Art." Remember that this is a spiritual tool and that you can open your work with it by formally asking for spiritual guidance:

> O Great Creator, please guide me in my choices. Please inspire me in my selection and my goals. Please let me be open to my own Highest Wisdom. Let images speak to my highest and most secret heart, calling forth my truest self into manifestation and expansion on behalf of myself and my fellows.

When you have completed it, post your Treasure Map in a prominent place. Be sure to remember that this tool—like many of the tools in this book—can be used more than one time. You may wish to set aside one afternoon every month or so to redo your Treasure Map or to map out your treasure in a different area—work, relationship, possessions, achievements, emotional ideal.

The idea is like a blueprint; it creates an image of the form, which then magnetizes and guides the physical energy to flow into that form and eventually manifests it on the physical plane.

SHAKTI GAWAIN

When you start a painting, it is somewhat outside you. At the conclusion, you seem to move inside the painting.

FERNANDO BOTERO

Color

Creation is interested in the unborn. The painter is like a gardener, handling the seeds, not producing them or making them perfect.

MICHELL CASSOU AND
STEWART CUBLEY

In my town lives a tiny, silver-haired sprite named Rhonda Flemming—no, not the actress, although Rhonda is highly theatrical. Dressed at all times in shades of purple, violet, lavender, lilac, and mauve, she is frequently stopped on the street by total strangers, tourists from all over the country, who want to know if she is what she looks like to them: a metaphysical teacher. Yes, she is.

So magical, bewitching, and colorful is Rhonda's playful appearance that many of these strangers screw up their courage to ask her if she knows anything about some of those exotic things they've heard so much about that they have even come to Taos hoping to learn more: tarot, perhaps, or astrology, numerology, crystal healing . . . The list goes on. Yes, she does know about "it"—whatever the "it" is.

In all the years that I've known her, I have yet to discover a spiritual system in which Rhonda is not well versed, if not an adroit practitioner. She is, for example, a yoga teacher. And an astrologer. And an Egyptologist, a numerologist, and color therapist. It's the color therapy I want to talk about here.

It is commonplace to remark of great artists, "What a colorful life!" We seldom stop to realize that this can be a literal phrase. I remember reading as a young woman that Anaïs Nin had painted every room of her Paris home a different, contrasting color. How magical!

I thought then. (How magical! I think now—when every room of my adult home is painted a different and wonderful color.)

One of the things that *will* happen to you as you work with the tools of this book is that your color sense will shift and become far more acute. Some colors that you have always worn will no longer appeal to you. Other colors, ones you've "never looked at twice," will suddenly catch your eye. Why is this?

Color, like sound, is made of vibration. *Everything is*—even those things that appear to be solid, or relatively solid, like ourselves. All of us use the expression, or at least have heard the expression, "He's really got bad vibes." Well, colors have good or bad vibes as well—depending on how compatible their wavelength is with our own.

Please do not think that I am speaking metaphorically or even merely metaphysically here. I am speaking the literal, *physical* scientific truth. Red, yellow, blue, green, orange, purple—each vibrates at a certain signature frequency. Each sends out a certain length of wave, measured in angstroms.

Some colors are more visible than others. These have longer wavelengths and a lower frequency, or intensity, what you might want to think of as the color equivalent of deep musical pitch. Orange, for example, is more easily visible than blue. It is a color "bass note" capable of being seen ("heard") at a great distance. This is why we put it on crossing guards and on children's safety clothes.

Just as certain colors "go together," other colors do not. They argue, or clash like a dissonant chord. Another, useful way to think of color is as visible sound. When we work with colors, we are in effect building visual chords or symphonies.

"I try to apply colors like words that shape poems, like notes that shape music," said Joan Miró. When Rhonda wears purple, she is striking a high note, wearing the color associated with the highest rays of spiritual healing.

Shortly before Mark and I married—and long before we amicably divorced—we moved into a rental house. The walls were painted a hip, "neutral" gray—very chic, very emotionally draining.

"Mark, I can't live with this color," I told him. "I'd be a lot happier if we painted these rooms yellow."

A color vibration is sensed not only through vision, but in many other ways. Every color vibration has an impact on all physical systems and organs of the body, which respond to these frequencies.

CHARLES KLOTSCHE

Fields of energy react with each other in a stimulating, equalizing, or sedating way. We can experience this upon entering a room filled with people, quickly sensing whether that room is permeated with vibrations that are harmonious or discordant.

CHARLES KLOTSCHE

Easy is right. Begin right and you are easy. Continue easy and you are right.

CHUANG TSU

"Yellow?"

Mark was dubious, but willing, provided I find a "good" yellow. I found a wonderful, buttery Chinese yellow and he set to work. (I painted, too, but so inexpertly he got exasperated and sent me back to writing.)

Within days, the house glowed with wonderful golden yellow light. Once the fumes cleared, both Mark and I felt worlds better living there. Why? Did we just "like" yellow?

Well, yes and no.

I do *like* yellow, but I also consciously *use* yellow. In terms of color healing, yellow is used as an antidepressant. It stimulates the intellect and raises the mood. This is why so many Swedish homes are painted with tones of yellow and trimmed in blue, its complement. Sweden is so dark during such a large portion of the year that suicidal depression is a very real variable. (Sweden has the world's highest suicide rate.) Yellow is an effective deterrent to the dark moods brought on by short days and northern latitudes. Chicago, where Mark and I were living, also is notoriously gray and dark during the winter. Our sunny yellow counteracted the gloom.

Although color healing may be a new concept to some of you, it is, in fact, an ancient tradition and an integral part of most spiritual paths. In the Judeo-Christian tradition, we see the colors of the priest's vestments used to signify the "tone" of the Mass he is celebrating. For joyous holidays, we see white and gold. (In Eastern tradition, these colors are associated with God energy.) In Western political terms, purple is the color of royalty. (In Eastern spiritual tradition, it is associated with the highest human energies.)

We need not know any of these associations to begin experimenting with color and its impact on our well-being. Remember to bring home paint chips. Take them out and look at them closely. Which colors "speak" to you? What do they say? Because color is a "silent sound," it does speak to us.

How many times have we talked about "cheery yellow"? What about a "dash of red"? (That's a literal term there. Red is a stimulant.) What about a "soothing blue"? (That's another literal term. Blue is a sedative color, with a cooling effect.) Next consider green.

We speak of a "handsome" green—as if the very sight of it speaks to our heart. (Green does, in fact, speak to the heart.)

"What about black?" you may ask. Why do so many artists favor black? What does that color do?

Actually, black is not a color. It is the absence of color. It is, therefore, the "color" of potential, of mystery. Black goes with everything. In clothing terms, this is why it is so easy to accessorize and can be worn so many different ways. Artists may favor it not because it is hip but because it is so nondistracting.

And white? White is the color that encompasses all other colors. This is why it is the color of spiritual mastery, implying as it does that the other colors (levels of consciousness) have already been attained and embodied, perfected.

In working with this book, you will find yourself becoming more and more sensitive to color and its impact on your life, your environment, and your mood. By working with color consciously and creatively, you will find that you can, in fact, create a more colorful life.

My writing room is painted lilac. It has a high, ethereal energy that invites me to think expansively. My business office, the room I call "the cockpit," is a vibrant pumpkin orange. This color is earthy and grounding—as alert as I need to be on financial calls.

On a practical level, color can have an enormous impact on you, your creativity, and your energy level. The tasks that follow invite you to begin experimenting with this.

Color is directly connected to a particular vibration that, when used properly, will connect the brain almost instantly to that which it seeks to know. JOSEPH RAEL

Body of earth, don't talk of earth.
Tell the story of pure mirrors.
The Creator has given you this splendor.
Why talk of anything else?
RUMI

∼ Task: "Fabricate" a More Colorful Life. ∼

In order to experience a solid dose of "pure" color, there are few ways as concrete as going to a good, large fabric store and working with the bolts of silk and rayon and light, gauzy cotton. Take a few down. Unwrap enough to see what "works" for you and what doesn't. Very often you will have a strong and immediate emotional response to a color. You may want to invite a newly discovered "positive" color into your life.

Fabric can be a stunningly inexpensive way to alter your environment. I am thinking now of the year I lived in a rental white

I try to apply colors like words that shape poems, like notes that shape music.

JOAN MIRÓ

As human beings we live in a world of colors. Each color is part of a whole. It is disharmony within this whole that leads to spiritual and physical dissonances within us, and ultimately to illness.

INGRID S. VON ROHR

apartment. It had high, wonderful windows and beautiful light, but it felt cold and impersonal until I took down its snowy white rental curtains and put up some gauzy sky blue ones that abruptly transformed the room into a piece of heaven (or a piece of an Aegean isle, depending on your association). Because curtain material can and often should be light in weight, it can be light in price as well. I have time and again used curtains to declare "Curtains!" to a dour room or work space.

Task: Speculate on a Different Spectrum: Try On Colors You "Never" Wear.

Very often we have a few colors that we think of as "our" colors, those that look good or feel good on us. We have other colors that we view with suspicion, indifference, or even hostility. We may have inherited associations with them that are not even our own. Red may be too "racy." Purple may be "tacky." Orange may be "loud." And so we never try those colors on to see how they actually look, feel, and sit with us. The impact can be physiological as well as psychological: red clothing raises blood pressure; blue clothing lowers it.

Try those colors on. Go to a store and deliberately try on the colors you are "sure" aren't your own. Do any of them, in fact, work for you? I had never owned *anything* purple in my life until dress designer Jo Dean Tipton surprised me with a purple dress and overrobe. I tried it on with hesitation and looked at myself in astonishment. I *loved* purple.

"That's really your color," Jo Dean remarked.

Up until that moment, it hadn't been.

Doll

It was my dubious privilege, not many years ago, to teach at a prestigious university, a revered research institution. I was a member of a
distinguished faculty (a word that means "gift" or "ability," lest we
forget) that specialized in deconstructionist theory. In other words, to
a man (and woman), they knew a great deal about how to take something apart, but precious little about how to construct anything.

Become as little children.
JESUS

Working there broke my heart. Gifted students had their rough
but promising early work dismembered, taken apart before it had a
chance to come together. The faculty had a gift for quashing anything that felt too raw and full of life. Over and over, I had to remind
myself, "They're just sad about their own creative selves. They're just
out of touch with their own creative joy and don't know it."

Our main building was a gothic glory bedecked with ivy tatters
and reeking of academia. It looked like a remnant of Camelot, and I
myself initially undertook my job with visions of higher learning as
a sort of secular Holy Grail. This particular quest was quickly dis-
pelled.

I remember one incident vividly.

Late one autumn afternoon, as golden but fading light was
streaming in through the upper windows, I quite literally bumped
into a colleague of mine as he and I were going up—and down—the
same staircase. We collided at a landing.

One learns by doing a thing;
for though you think you
know it, you have no cer-
tainty until you try.
SOPHOCLES

"I hear you're into creativity!" he exclaimed. "Whose?"

"Whose?" I wasn't sure I'd heard him correctly.

"Whose theories?" he asked. "I'm into creativity, too. I was wondering whose theories you enjoy?"

The stairwell echoed with a moment of cavernous silence while I racked my brain for the name of any creativity theorists. Finally I blurted, "There's a misunderstanding here. I do it!"

"Do it?"

"I make things. Create them. You know. Films, plays, books. All sorts of toys, really."

"Oh. Oh, dear. Well, lovely to meet you."

"And you."

And we went our separate ways.

In a sense, those who build things and those who take things apart are always going their two separate ways. The energy of construction and the energy of deconstruction feel very different, although both are energies of discernment, although both ask the same question, "What if . . . ?"

When we are engaged in the act of making something, we are involved in making something up. In a sense it is quite true that every picture tells a story, and the picture is one that we are developing as our vision becomes more and more clear to us.

In this book we are building, and building on, our vein of gold. This means we look to the past to develop the future. The "negative" of the past may yet develop into a positive—and we can quite literally take a hand in this.

I would disagree with those who say we cannot change the past. We can heal it, transform it, utilize it, build on it—any number of creative things. Why do I mention this now? Because we are about to engage in a particularly childish task, and one I believe to be most powerful. We are going to make dolls.

I think it's quite possible you will need a bribe to execute this chapter. Please bribe yourself. In my experience as a teacher, this assignment meets with the most resistance and results in the most reward. Resistance rears its head because perfectionism is lurking in the wings. (Who wants to make a "bad" doll?) Sexism usually can be found there as well. Women may feel like this is too much like "old-lady crafts." (And what's wrong with them?) Men may feel just a little unmanned. . . . A *doll*? (Think of it as a totem if that helps.)

Perfectionism, sexism, a nasty feeling that now is the time to rebel . . . If any of these are eddying through your consciousness, join the club.

There is something about making a doll that is just so childish.

There is something about making a doll that is just so threatening.

We want to say it's a stupid idea. We want to say it's a terrible idea. What we don't want to say, but intuitively know, is that it is a *powerful* idea.

According to doll-making legend, the original word for doll was "idol." We have just lopped off the "I." When we make dolls, we are invoking godlike powers. Doll-making is a very powerful form of magic. Because we are working directly with the human figure in a form that appeals to our child-self, we are talking directly to our creative consciousness, which in turn speaks directly to our Higher Self, or Deep Self.

Theologian Starhawk phrases it this way: "Younger Self . . . wants to be *shown*. To arouse its interest, we must seduce it with pretty pictures and pleasurable sensations—take it out dining and dancing, as it were. Only in this way can Deep Self be reached."

Of course, few things could enchant a Younger Self more than a doll. Dolls "capture the imagination," and the imagination, once captured, can be channeled toward desired ends. Knowing this, it is easy to see why certain religions have barred the use of images, as well as why other religions have used such images to great political effect.

As doll-maker Elinor Peace Bailey writes,

> What is there about the representation of the human form, however whimsical, that makes people want to possess it? What magic is transferred into that form which gives it power over so many?
>
> The question is not easily answered. Many doll collectors find in them a genteel reminder of their childhoods. All kinds of fantasies can be aroused by dolls. Sometimes divine powers

Let the beauty we love be what we do.   RUMI

An essential portion of any artist's labor is not creation so much as invocation.

LEWIS HYDE

can be invoked through a doll, and it can be seen as a benediction on the households of those who have the faith to receive it. Since his earliest history, man has changed the abstract into simple forms and given them the power to heal and enlighten.

I live in New Mexico, where many of the churches contain *santos,* astonishingly powerful, hand-carved icons—doll-Virgins dressed in handmade clothes, doll-saints, and Christs that speak directly to the heart, doing far more to unify the congregations than a wordy sermon can.

The Great Way is not difficult just avoid choosing.
SEN-T'SANG

Writes artist-writer-healer Vicki Noble, "Doll-making is an elaborate version of creating a fetish. It is more complex and powerful." No wonder those *santos* cast a powerful spell over the churchgoers' hearts.

In Hawaiian Kuna religion, this connection to our subconscious child-self is called contacting our "ku." Without such contact, our rational mind stays too much in the middle, in control, and our prayers, invocations, and desires for manifestation do not reach our Higher Selves.

In Western creativity theory, this is what Rollo May was talking about when he said that creative insights came in periods of release *after* intense mental effort to solve a problem.

In twelve-step language, this is what is meant by the expression, "Let go and let God."

Doll-making is a very potent form of turning it over to God. Therefore, dolls are extremely potent tools for manifestation. (It is no accident that dolls are used in voodoo.) But if dolls can be—and have been—used negatively, they also can be used positively, and that is what we will be doing here.

Just as we have seen that words can be used to call into our life the qualities that we wish to attract and embody, so, too, dolls can be used to manifest our wishes and dreams. Let us say that you have an area of yourself or your life that feels lacking: making a doll can help to manifest the change that you desire.

Sometimes, the "me" that the doll expresses is a previously unacknowledged self, larger and more expansive, more potent and more daring than we had let ourselves feel.

I am thinking now of David and the work he did making a "Creativity Doll." (I put the words in quotes because his creation was not what you might think of as a doll, although that was its starting point.)

David's doll was more of a mobile. It consisted of:

- A flat piece of flagstone ("My grandmother. She is dead but my mother is still bound to her and drags her with her into everything.")

- A "mother doll" (tied, indeed, to the flagstone grandmother)

- Two paper airplanes ("My sister and me, tied to my mother, who is still tied to her mother.")

- A knife ("I don't really know what the knife is doing but I had to put it in.")

David demonstrated how neither he nor his sister could really fly, even though they had wings and were designed for flying. He threw his plane into the air but the string that bound him to his mother cut short the flight and his airplane crashed abruptly.

"David, the knife is there for you to cut yourself free," I told him.

"Oh, yeah," he said, considering the possibility.

"Freedom! Freedom! Freedom!" the class took up the chant. "Freedom! Freedom! Freedom!"

For a long moment, David stood stock-still and looked at the evidence of what his art revealed to him. Then he grabbed the knife and cut loose the airplane that was David. Like a javelin thrower, he sent it sailing across the room, grinning jubilantly.

For David, the act of doll-making was one both of self-disclosure and self-emancipation. For his applauding classmates, it was an empowering example. They stamped, cheered, and whistled.

"I was determined to hate this exercise," he told me. "I was very resistant."

He was also very brave.

Remember Carolyn, the beautiful woman who never knew she was one? When I suggested to Carolyn she might want to try a Cre-

The unfolding of the unexpected becomes the energy that drives you. You discover how thirsty you are for exploration without analysis. You feel strangely at home in a place you can't define. You are truly creating.

MICHELL CASSOU AND
STEWART CUBLEY

Listen. Make a way for
   yourself
inside yourself
Stop looking
in the other way of looking.

RUMI

Creativity is a spiritual action in which a person forgets about himself, moves outside of himself in the creative act, absorbed by his task.

NIKOLAI BERDYAEV

ativity Doll–making project around her two images, Egghead and Bombshell, her eyes grew very round and she furiously blinked back tears.

"How did you know I never had dolls?"

I hadn't known that, but it did fit with her being denied knowledge of her feminine appeal.

"I'd like to make a feminine doll," Carolyn confessed. "At least I think I would."

"Doll-making is fun even if you have had dolls," I assured her. "Your doll doesn't even have to look like a real doll. You can make it of whatever you want to make it from, and you can make it say whatever you want it to say. The materials and the subject matter are really up to you."

When Carolyn made her Creativity Doll, she began by hauling out a huge box of fabric scraps. Was she a turquoise-and-orange-striped Gypsy doll? Was she the femme fatale in black velvet going to opening night? What about the scarlet swirled-silk moire? All of them were lovely, but . . . From the bottom of her scrap box Carolyn hauled out a swathe of beautiful old lace. The minute her hands touched it, she knew that this was her fabric.

Carolyn set to work on her doll. The head was fashioned from white sheeting, then stuffed with the heart-shaped shield of an old shoulder pad. The body was sheeting, stuffed with silk scraps and then swathed in lace. An ornate black-and-gold renaissance ribbon demarcated the waist. A streamered, roseate-headed old horse-show ribbon—golden, like Carolyn's hair—became the hair.

On her heart, Carolyn placed a five-pointed amethyst earring. "I am a star," Carolyn caught herself thinking, "I just didn't know it." From one ear she hung an amethyst-and-amber earring. A flowered shawl made from an old kitchen curtain completed the doll. Carolyn used a photo of herself to draw on the face, using indelible markers to fill in big blue eyes and pink lips and cheeks. When she was finished, Carolyn gave her doll a place of honor on the mantel.

"Making the doll felt wonderful," Carolyn told me. "As if I were claiming myself—my *beautiful* self." In the next few months, Carolyn's looks did indeed soften as she took on a new glow of feminine confidence. To cast it colloquially, she began to look like the "doll" she really was.

For Richard, doll-making was an even more assertive act. A mild-mannered man who was actually a very powerful artist, Richard spoke softly and often seemed to view himself as something less than the spiritual warrior he might have wished. In all disputes he was the mediator—a thankless job, he sometimes felt. In fact, it was sometimes a real drag being dependable, reliable, *sweet* Richard.

Richard needed to flex his muscles a little bit and become Yang Man. His Creativity Doll took a totem form. Out walking, he came upon a dog skull, which he carried home, along with a strong, gnarled stick. Working with felt-tipped pens, he painted the skull. The left-hand side of the skull had red dots. The right hand had black dots. The background on the left-hand side was black. On the right-hand side it was red, except across the eyes, where he used a harlequin pattern of black-on-black and red-on-red. Using strong red twine and baling wire, Richard bound the skull to one end of the stick. The totem was potent.

"It was all material that was at hand. It was very offhand, easy, and natural, the way that it all came together," Richard says. "I did have to boil the skull before I applied the pigment," he adds, laughing like a naughty young boy. "It feels a little bit like a talisman. I don't feel precious about it, like it is spooky or mysterious. To me it feels playful, but I always like there to be a slight bit of danger in creativity."

To the eye of this observer there was something else apparent in Richard's doll, and that was a sense of authority. Sure enough, that is what manifested in his life within a few months of his making the doll.

∼ Task: Make a Creativity Doll. ∼

Using whatever materials you choose to, allow yourself to make a Creativity Doll. Dolls have been made from sugar and spice and everything nice as well as from dog skulls and snails and pinecones and tire irons. It is *your* doll.

When you see each leaf as a separate thing, you can see the tree, you can see the spirit of the tree, you can talk to it, and maybe you can begin to learn something.
WILLIAM J. BAUSCH

Why is it that dexterity, knowledge of art, and taste do not necessarily add up to what we seek in art?
PETER LONDON

Remember, you can make a doll to call forward a gift or situation. Angela, a woman who moved to Chicago only to be jilted, made a bride doll for herself. Shortly after, she met the man she "really" wanted to marry. I'm not saying the doll caused him to propose, but it certainly opened her to bridal energy and she had a wonderful time visualizing herself walking happily down the aisle.

June, who felt her sexuality had been misplaced in the wake of a devastating divorce, reclaimed it for herself by making a series of small erotic clay goddess figures.

Those who have worked with The Artist's Way and built an Artist's Altar often find that to be the ideal home for their new creations. Others find they ensconce their doll on the mantel, in a bookshelf, or next to their computer. If you have focused your doll around a particular quality which you wish to invite into your life, you may want to choose the doll's resting place accordingly. June's erotic goddesses inhabit her bedroom and bath.

Task: Make a Creativity Monster.

Again, choosing whatever materials spring to mind, let yourself create an image that speaks to you about artist bashing. I have seen robotic monsters, booze-bottle monsters, monsters made from movie-magazine images. You can use a shoe box, a tin can—even, as one man in New York did, a vibrator, "Which represents my metallic sexuality where I have channeled my creative impulses wrongly."

In one of my New Mexico classes, Liz made a Creativity Monster that looked like a classic hag—or one of the Skectics from the movie *The Dark Crystal.* Withered and bent, formed from a piece of wood with shaggy bark, the monster had red, beady eyes and a golden dagger to stab creativity with. Written all over its body were killer words: "not good enough," "could have," "should have," "too old," "not talented enough." The monster was mounted on a slab of wood covered with more words, the graffiti of the unconscious: "You can't," "It's too late," "Who do you think you are?"

"This is my Creativity Monster," Liz told her classmates. "And I plan for us to burn it!"

If you do not burn or otherwise demolish your monster, you may wish to give it a place in your home or office. Students have been known to hang tiny Out of Work signs around their monsters' necks and perch them right in their work area. Often the act of making a monster so minimizes the block it represents that the resulting creation becomes a kind of mascot.

Basic Black:
The Mystique–and Mistake–
of the Suffering Artist

*Art history is, after all,
someone else's story about
someone else's adventures.*

PETER LONDON

In our art-toxic culture, we have pernicious myths that darken our views on artists and on art. Chief among these myths is that of the suffering artist. Mark Bryan refers to this as the Edgar Allan Poe school of artistry: "Get drunk, die broke in the gutter."

Yesterday I spoke with a wonderful writer whose work I have long admired. We were both knee deep in drafts—I myself in this one; the other writer in a novel.

"You know how it is, Julia," the writer said to me. "You have to suffer. Hemingway, all those guys. Everybody has always had to suffer for art, right?"

"I don't know," I ventured. "Some of my best stuff has seemed to come through pretty easily and fully formed. What about you?"

"Well—even when it's easy, it's still hard," the writer insisted, and we quickly got off the phone.

In America, we have traditionally confused the progression of alcoholism with the depressive arc of many an artistic career. Alcohol is a depressive drug. Many of our most revered writers and painters have suffered from serious alcoholism, and the darkening depression endemic to the progression of their disease has colored both their careers and our views about what makes "serious art."

Alcoholism is often linked to suicide, and yet we act as if it were Hemingway's artistry that pulled the trigger on that shotgun. Alcoholism is a common precipitant of fatal car crashes, and yet we talk about Jackson Pollock's death as though it were his art that bedeviled him.

A great many lives, only some of them artists', have been ruined in pursuit of alcohol, drugs, and promiscuous sex. In our culture we often confuse the darkening progression of alcoholism with the progression of a "serious" artistic career. We act as if writing caused F. Scott Fitzgerald's fragility.

It is my belief that we are in the middle of a quiet revolution. With the advent of twelve-step groups, we have learned, as a nation, the novelty of a non-hierarchical spirituality—one based on experience, not theory. In other words, people are no longer believing in "God as told to them by." Their "vision" of God is lightening.

Since art making is an act of faith, the new autonomy many people feel is beginning to show up in a new kind of art: lighter-hearted, and less depressive—to be blunt, less alcoholic. The old adage "There are no second acts in American lives" no longer rings true. (And it was only true in the first place because so many of our great writers were too drunk to write them.) Newly wealthy in sober artists, we have a generation of sober writers, filmmakers, actors, and painters. We are enjoying solo albums by artists who are working in sobriety. And they are playing a different tune.

The myth of the suffering artist needs to be dismantled. It makes everything a big deal, a high jump. There's no place for trying things out, baby steps, a flyer or two—not if everything is so ego-based, not if everything is about how serious we *look*.

So pervasive is our mythology about the suffering artist that it is a common artistic posture, a badge of honor worn to prove the seriousness of our creative expression. What no one is admitting in all of this is that making things is fun. A working artist is a playing artist. As Carl Jung says, "The creative mind plays with the objects it loves."

Artist Timothy Nero is blunt: "The whole suffering artist thing is hogwash. Art is made from life. That means it's made from joy. It's

Art as process is a meditative activity. True painting is prayer; it happens when everything inside and outside joins in one action.

MICHELL CASSOU AND
STEWART CUBLEY

made from pain. It's made from *whatever* the artist is going through."

True, that "whatever" is sometimes a spiritual discontent, but not always, and very often the act of making art so alleviates that discontent that what is felt in the act of creation is not agony but something a lot closer to ecstasy.

Dress designer Jo Dean Tipton, who creates by painting on silk, describes it this way: "When I am working, time goes away. My surroundings disappear. If music is playing, I no longer even hear it. I am completely in the world of what I am making . . . and it's wonderful."

As it happens, I love words, and I have been a poet for thirty years. I have participated in some readings and some poetry "slams" (the poetic equivalent of boxing matches), and I have noticed that depressive poems very often are deemed somehow more roadworthy than better-crafted, lighter ones.

Of course, we have long observed that comedies are slighted in the race for Oscar. Weepy, serious films tend to carry the day—*The Lion King* being a recent, long-overdue exception.

The mythology surrounding "serious art" is a real problem for many creative artists. When a note of levity or hope creeps in, so can a fear of no longer being taken seriously. Not only does this make artists into poseurs and channel their work along acceptably serious lines, it can make the prospect of creating any art at all seem daunting.

"We have to suffer for our art, right?" my writer friend asked me.

I believe that if we believe that, we surely will suffer. We may not even notice when we are not. In my experience, it is not the act of making art that is painful. It is the desire to make something and not acting on it that causes pain. When we are engaged in our creativity, we are in love with our process. Yes, there may be stretches where the going gets rough, but that happens in any love affair. To my eye, what is really painful is *not* practicing our creativity. That, to me, smacks of unrequited love: the wishing, the yearning, and the inability to engage.

If this sounds like too much idealism for you, I would ask you to experiment a little the next time you are depressed. When the blues hit, make something. Make anything: a cake, cookies, curtains, a new bookcase, a nasty little ditty about whatever is bedeviling you.

The minute we are engaged in creating something, the something of our choice, we are back in our own power and no longer at the mercy of the powers that be. (Whoever we conceive them to be.)

This is probably as good a place as any to talk about the fact that the blues is not the only mood that can be used as fuel for creative expression. In fact, "mood" need not be used at all. There is a persistent notion that we must "wait for the muse to strike," as though creativity were so mysterious and capricious that we can, at best, hope to snare it as we would a rare butterfly.

The reality is just the reverse. We are the ones who are capricious. We are the ones who do not show up. We are the ones who disappear for long periods of time. Creative energy is a constant and we can *always* tap into it.

Consider these words of Douglas Anderson in *The Planet of Waters:* "Rivers course through the oceans of earth. You call them 'streams' or 'currents.' In just the same way, great streams of living music wander the universe. All the universe is an ocean of music. . . ."

Listen, too, to the wisdom of theologian Dr. Ernest Holmes: "Out of the limitless creativity of God, I accept the flow of new ideas. . . . The Divine Spirit is flowing through me in an individual way and I accept the genius of my own being. All the Presence there is, is flowing through me in an original manner. I accept Its right action, Its new ideas. . . ."

Too often, however, we resist such openness. We only want to tap in when we feel an intense mood and hope we are "guaranteed" a "quickie" masterpiece instead of an experience of a less-exalted variety.

Creativity involves process, and process involves change. The truism we often hear is that we often resist change because change is difficult or change is painful. This is not quite accurate. It is the *resistance* to change that is difficult or painful. In the same way, *it is the resistance to our creativity that causes us to equate it with suffering. It is important to remember that "effort" and "suffering" are two different things.*

We can make art, letting the voice of the goddess—the oracle—speak through us in healing words and images.

DOROTHY MACLEAN

We must embrace pain and burn it as fuel for our journey.
KENJI MIYAZAWA

Creativity is our species' natural response to the challenges of human experience.
ADRIANA DIAZ

Creativity requires energy, sustained creative energy. Sustained energy requires two things: stamina and openness. When we are open, our creative energies, which are the energies of the Universe, are able to flow through us with minimal wear and tear on our own systems. When we are closed—and we are closed or blocked when we have belief systems that hamper the flow—we will experience our creative energy as a bumpy and dangerous ride.

Creativity gets a bad rap. It is widely considered dangerous, out-of-control, crazy. It is considered these things because, like electricity, it contains voltage, spiritual voltage, and should be worked with as a smooth flow rather than in huge electrical storms or bursts. Because many of us are frightened of being out of control, we don't know how to be in control and creative at the same time. We either shut down our creative flow to a trickle or we turn the dial wide open without regard for keeping our feet on the ground through simple, sensible self-care. In other words, we either abstain from our creativity or we indulge in it as binges. Neither extreme is a right use of our powers.

Listen for a moment again to Dr. Ernest Holmes from his 1934 pamphlet "Creative Ideas":

> Every scientist knows that he takes power out of life that he doesn't put it in. And so it is in dealing with that more subtle energy and power we call Mind or Spirit.
>
> One of the first things to do is to learn to accept, and to expect this Power to flow through everything that we do. We must combine our belief in this Power with the conscious use of it for definite purposes. We have greater abilities and resources than we have yet realized.

The main purpose of this book is to help you contact your flow of universal energy, recognize it as both your own and universal, and help you to use it with more ease. In other words, this book is about being both open to creative current *and* safely grounded.

Fine. So how do we do that?

All of us have had the experience of being effortlessly creative—just not in our own behalf. When we are working on someone else's behalf, baking a birthday cake for someone we love, just helping out or troubleshooting where someone else is stuck on a project, we often feel great ease and come up with solutions that are natural *and* inspired. This is because our belief system is in accord with our actions. We believe it is good to help people, and so our creativity can flow unimpeded straight through us and into the job at hand. It is only when the spotlight returns to our self and the well-conditioned, culturally formed mythology around creativity that the process becomes a bit more bumpy.

"So who do you think you are?" the Censor hisses. (And most of the time the answer to that is *not,* "A wonderful artist, thank you.")

Whenever the Censor enters the creative dance, it is like trying to dance while being pelted by rocks. You never know quite what angle the hailstorm of abuse will come at you from, but come it will. We all know how the process goes. We get a word or a brushstroke down and the Censor announces, "That's wrong. Stupid. Where are you going to go from there?"

How many times have you helped a friend word a proposal or résumé only to find yourself speechless on your own behalf? If the Censor can trick us into looking ahead into the future ("Where are you going to go from there? . . . What will they ever think of that?"), then the Censor can put doubts onto your creative path like a series of hurdles that your creative energies must leap over for you to do your work.

Picture your energy as a flow, or if you like, a beautiful golden horse. Now, this horse is quite capable of smoothly leaping all obstacles in its path, but if you think the horse is crazy and dangerous and out of control, if you are hanging on for dear life, begging it to stop, or kicking it frantically as if it doesn't want to jump—is it any wonder your creativity feels a bit like a bucking bronco?

All of us are intended to conduct creative energy. All of us *can* create once we allow ourselves to do it. It is the allowing bit that is tricky. If we still believe that being creative is selfish, isolationist, could make us broke—who wants to do it then? No wonder our creative projects look impossible. No wonder they feel impossible. A few simple guidelines can help to ease this:

Approach your creative projects gently. Begin by taking a look at

The soul, among all creatures, is generative, like God is.

MEISTER ECKHART

the jumps (blocks) that your belief system has constructed as an obstacle course. An excellent way to do this is by simply listing *on paper* every fear and anger and resentment you have about the project at hand. For example:

- I'll do all this work and the book won't be taken anyhow.

- I'll turn in this project and the whole team will see how limited my ideas really are.

- I'll do a great job and someone else (_____) will steal all the credit, as usual.

- I'll work on this painting for weeks and botch it at the last minute.

In a general sense, all artists are shamans, insomuch as they are channeling images or concepts on behalf of the collective.
VICKI NOBLE

Often, this simple bit of housekeeping can clear away our resistance to entering the creative flow. In this regard, learning to think of creativity as a long-term relationship is very helpful. There will be good days and bad days. That's the nature of a long-term union and a far healthier level of expectation, one that is far more accurate, than demanding it provide honeymoon peak experiences every time.

"But still it must take such discipline," I am frequently told.

Actually, no. It doesn't. I love words. I love playing with them. I love seeing what I can do with them and what they can do with me. A day when I write is a happy day. A day when I don't write is less happy. This is not discipline. It is affection, enthusiasm, adventure— any number of other words besides discipline.

Now, I know that this is heresy. I know that this is proof positive that I'm rather lowbrow or airy-fairy or anti-intellectual. That's all right with me. I am an artist, and I am the one who defines myself that way. It's a little like Rumpelstiltskin: if we wait for someone else to come along and wave a magic wand, naming us an artist, ("Ah-hah! You there! You are an artist!"), we may wait a terribly long time.

I am a writer. Writers write. Painters paint. Sculptors sculpt. It is the act of engaging in an art form that names us potter, poet, actor. Of course, it is only human to yearn to be a published writer, a galleried painter, an employed actor, but if we are writing, painting, acting, that act validates us as an artist, and despite the mythology to the contrary, that act will give us joy.

Many of us do a number of these things, and we do them quite well. It is at this point that the dread word "dilettante" enters the conversation.

A second extremely destructive American myth about artists is the notion, doubtless borrowed from the assembly line, that we should do just one thing. I call this the "lug-bolt mentality." It goes something like this.

Anthony, a gifted painter, gets an itch to sculpt. His painter friends are horrified. He's a good painter. If he starts "fooling around" with sculpting, he won't look serious anymore.

All too often, in the name of looking serious, an artist scuttles a promising new avenue of exploration. God forbid we be seen as a dilettante. No, no, we must be seen as serious, even driven.

Notice I said "we must be seen as." Here is yet another pernicious aspect of our mythology: you are not a "serious artist" unless you are *perceived, recognized, acknowledged* as a serious artist. This takes the power away from the artist and puts it in the eye of the beholder. One more time, the artist is reduced to a poseur instead of having the dignity of a self-determined life. In other words, we are *acting* the role of artist rather than inhabiting the identity of artist as it suits us.

Bette Midler once remarked to me that if she had the right shoes she could play anything. I knew what she meant. Being able to "dress the part" often allows us to recognize that something is a "part" and not the whole of ourselves or a situation. For this reason, I have included the following two tasks, which appear to be very lighthearted and non-serious but which can actually create important inner shifts.

Art doesn't transform. It just plain forms.

ROY LICHTENSTEIN

When you lose simplicity, you lose drama.

ANDREW WYETH

～ Task: Dress as a Serious Artist. ～

Drag out all of your basic black. Rip a few holes. Smudge some dark circles under your eyes. Grease your hair back in some patently unattractive dork hairdo. Sprinkle your shoes with specks of white. Scuff them. Do not wear a belt. Go to a coffee house. Act dour. Grimace and scribble furiously, cursing quietly under your breath. Finally, announce, "Screw it!" and stalk out.

Painting isn't an aesthetic operation; it's a form of magic.

PABLO PICASSO

Unless a capacity to dream and fantasize is there, derivative things will be made.

PETER LONDON

You may wish to undertake this role-playing with a friend. Go to a coffee shop together. You may wish to invent a fictional project you are working on, one involving only the most dour and existential themes. Additionally, you may wish to give your dramatic character all of the character traits associated with the most clichéd version of a suffering artist: let it be known you have a serious drinking problem, you are promiscuous, you can't earn a living, you sponge off your friends, you are neurotic, self-centered, miserable, contemplating suicide. . . .

It is your friend's job, as you reveal all of this, to treat you with the utmost care, as if you are indeed some volatile, otherworldly creature. Carry on this posture as long as you can. Be very careful not to laugh in the middle or you will destroy the effect.

As with doll-making, this is a deceptively playful exercise, and one which may startle you by what it reveals. For those of you who have considered yourself too "straight" to be a real artist, it may be a revelation to discover that you can "pass." For those of you who have been acting out some version of this already, it may break the code and allow you to look pretty in pink someday if that's what appeals to you.

Task: Dress Like You Might Be Having Fun.

Take a plain white T-shirt. Using an indelible Magic Marker or regular acrylic paint or Versatex fabric paint or oil-based ballpoint fabric pens, doodle a design that says you are a non-serious artist.

In the days when he was teaching art, painter Tim Nero would teach color theory by asking his students to come to class one day in what he termed "disposable whites." He would then arm them with squirt guns filled with liquefied acrylic paint, inviting them to "lighten" up and explore, perhaps even change the spectrum of their artistic behavior—and their art—to something more playful.

Cracking

One of the most difficult aspects of creative emergence is a process I call "cracking." We crack an egg. We crack a nut. We crack a shell. We crack a mystery or a book. In a sense, we are all of the above, and as we begin to explore the contours of our psyche, putting more and more internal pressure to bear on the shell that both defines and limits our self-image, we often experience a sense of *crack-up*. Tiny fissures, hairline cracks, appear in our previous reality: our facade is cracking. We are growing, and that can make us feel very fragile.

Because cracking can feel a lot like cracking up, it is valid to say that going sane feels just like going crazy. When we are cracking the encasement of our personal histories in order to reorder ourselves in a new, larger, and more fluid form, we may act and react differently. Catching sight of ourselves in the mirror, we may even look different. This is because our lens is changing and we are seeing more through our own eyes and less through the eyes of others and our culture.

Candace, who had always thought of herself in disparaging terms such as pudgy, suddenly and delightedly thought, "I'm voluptuous. Somebody out there ought to appreciate a good Rubens!"

One of the primary symptoms of the cracking stage is figure-ground reversal. Many people are familiar with the famous example of the face and the vase: viewed one way, it is a classical urn; viewed

Being an artist means: not numbering and counting, but ripening like a tree, which doesn't force its sap, and stands confidently in the storms of spring, not afraid that afterward summer may not come.

RAINER MARIA RILKE

You should keep on painting no matter how difficult it is . . . unless it kills you, and then you know you have gone too far.
ALICE NEEL

The true artist, the artist-within, is the one who is really moved by the myo, *the as-is-ness, of things, of their intrinsic, unhallowed sacredness.*
FREDERICK FRANCK

the other, it is a woman's profile. That is what is meant by figure-ground reversal. Events and people that have always looked one way to us suddenly look another.

We see the gift in a difficult situation. Looking back on a troubled childhood, we suddenly realize the hostile parent was actually terrified himself. We feel a sweep of compassion, and a lifetime's resentment washes away.

Conversely, the officially happy childhood that was really a construction of denial begins to reveal its grimmer aspects as a family history of alcoholism comes into reluctant focus. As the denial cracks, rage hisses and bubbles though the fissures. A life of internalized anger is being released.

The process of creative emergence is a process of energy expansion. Wherever our energy is blocked by denial, the buried emotions and information need to be allowed to surface. Our original self seeks to break free so that our creative energies can move into expression. We are *not* cracking up under the pressure of self-exploration. Instead, we are cracking open a self-concept that has become confining and claustrophobic to our spirit.

"The crack in the egg has opened up to the wonderland of myself," one student phrased it.

Still, we have an awful lot of mythology about artists being crazy, and many of us have a deep-seated fear that if we really allow ourselves to move into our creativity, we will find ourselves to be exactly that. And so, we tamp down our creativity and wonder why it makes us so uneasy.

It makes us so uneasy *because* we tamp it down.

"I just took the energy it takes to pout and wrote some blues," said Duke Ellington.

The King of Swing knew a thing or two not only about music, but also about human nature. Depression is often an unfaced anger. That anger, acknowledged and used productively, can be a great source of creative fuel.

Often, we hide from our angers because we do sense that they contain energy, and that frightens us. We talk of "seeing red," as though anger were a nuclear bomb that goes off just behind our eyelids. It can feel that way. The surge of adrenaline can be very powerful, coursing through our system and leaving us first energized and then exhausted. The amount of counter-energy that it takes to block our anger can leave us feeling sullen and depressed. That is precisely how Catherine found herself feeling in the wake of her divorce— sullen, depressed, unwanted, unloved, unhappy . . .

Catherine, a born dancer, a woman who loves to dance, never lets herself go dancing. She misses dancing. She misses the part of herself that dancing lets out, but that part of her is her sexual side, and she is not really comfortable with letting that energy show. What she *is* comfortable doing is bemoaning her lack of suitors. Recently, as part of a workshop I was teaching, Catherine let herself dance.

"God, Catherine," exclaimed the man she was dancing near. "You're a great dancer. You're so sexy!"

Catherine blushed scarlet to the roots, but she has cherished that compliment ever since and has even made a pact with the man that the two of them would go out dancing "very soon."

"The depths of our beings are not all sunlit; to see clearly, we must be willing to dive into the dark, inner abyss and acknowledge the creatures we may find there," theologian-artist Starhawk tells us.

Some of these creatures—and creations—may startle us. *But they will not hurt us.*

Creativity is safe. We don't need a license to practice it. Experts are lovely and know an enormous amount about theory and are very good in their place, but we are all created equal, and the operative word there is "created." God is the Great Creator, and we are all safe when we are practicing our spiritual inheritance.

We are not meant to think of our creativity as some wild and savage beast caged in our subconscious. That's part of the cultural mythology that has robbed us of our birthright as creative beings. No, the idea of being an artist isn't an act of ego. In our culture, it's an act of surrender: "Okay, okay, I'll risk it." The ego wants us *not* to write or paint or dance or act—or to do that thing *perfectly*. That, of course, is impossible, and so often we are afraid to do it all.

Our creativity is a normal and natural part of us. We are meant to sing, dance, draw, and doodle poems. Art lives in the *heart*, and we all have one.

Creativity is an act of survival. It organizes and gives voice to ex-

Freeing the body inevitably leads to freeing the heart.

GABRIELLE ROTH

Science and taboo-type reactions actually should be mutually exclusive, because science should be characterized by openness.

JOACHIM-ERNST BERENDT

To walk a sacred path is to know and trust that there is guidance to help us live our lives on this planet.
DR. LAUREN ARTRESS

Our creativity does not consist in being right all the time, but in making of all our experiences, including the apparently mistaken and imperfect ones, a holy whole.
MATTHEW FOX

The act of painting is a spiritual covenant between the maker and the higher powers.
AUDREY FLACK

perience. For creative beings (and we are all creative beings), experience is only half of an experience. We experience life and then digest it by making something out of our experience. Creativity makes life useful to us. It also makes us useful to life.

As Michell Cassou and Stewart Cubley write: "All repressed feelings accumulate inside and become more and more threatening as time goes on. The error is to ignore them. They may be huge, bloodthirsty, and glow in the dark but they are cardboard demons and they lose their power as soon as they have been painted."

Or written.

Or drawn.

Or danced.

Or sculpted.

Or sewn.

Or sung.

Or . . .

This act of creative exploration is what begins to crack the mask we have worn between ourself and our Self. Cracking the mask is exciting, but it is also frightening. We may sense, correctly, that we do not know what we will see when we look into the mirror that our work affords us. Is that so terrible? How much more terrible to always know exactly what to expect!

"We generally don't know the whole story of what we make. Art communicates and the channel for communication is sometimes the last to know the details," healer-artist-shaman Vicki Noble writes ruefully.

So what? Why do we need to know the whole story before we start writing? Why do we need to make a lovely painting, dance a "beautiful" dance? We may, in fact, need to do just the opposite. In fact, it is very helpful to think in terms of opposites.

Earlier in the book, we worked with Secret Selves. A glance at your Secret Selves list may show you that many of them are opposites—or near opposites. In much the same way, our official desires and our secret wishes may be quite opposite to one another—a scrap of self-knowledge we often seek to avoid.

Once we begin to embrace it instead, once we begin to allow the mask to crack a little, adventure can set in. These adventures can be small but very rewarding. A woman I know is an inveterate "lady." Secretly, however, she harbors an itch to be just a little bit wilder.

"Go try on great leather jackets," I urged her. "Price and sit on great motorcycles."

"I couldn't!" she exclaimed . . . but she did.

Last weekend she arrived on my doorstep looking very, very pleased with herself—and with her new leather bomber jacket!

Once we acknowledge our inner polarity, we can begin to play with it. Once we begin to play with it, we can work *with* it instead of having *it* work against us, creating that "terrible" sense that something "terrible" is about to happen.

Task: Look At It This Way—On the One Hand . . . On the Other . . .

This is a writing exercise and it is intended to be done as quickly as possible. First, number a piece of paper from one to twenty. Then fill out the sentence, "On the one hand, I'd love to _____; on the other hand, I'd love to _____." Twenty times.

Do you feel the stretching of your consciousness as you embrace apparent opposites? Can you see that you can encompass more emotional range than you may have realized?

Now number the paper again. This time draw a line down the middle and label one side "Officially" and the other side "Secretly." Now finish the phrase "I am _____" twenty times in each column.

Do you notice a little tingle of excitement in the meeting of your "official" and "secret" selves? Very often the mere act of mutual acknowledgment is enough to start change-provoking dialogue.

Task: Mirror, Mirror: Apply a Facial Mask.

For this task you can use a commercial product (my favorite is a mint green mask my mother used to use) or you can make a do-it-yourself mask mixing oatmeal and egg whites or water. Whichever you choose, apply a nice, generous coat of it and allow it to dry. Now go to a mirror, stretch your face a little, and experience the "cracking." Notice how liberating it feels to go through your "monster phase," in

First thoughts have tremendous energy. It is the way the mind first flashes on something.

NATALIE GOLDBERG

The truth dazzles gradually, or else the world would be blind.

EMILY DICKINSON

Perhaps all the dragons of our lives are princesses who are only waiting to see us once beautiful and brave. Perhaps everything terrible is in its deepest being something helpless that wants help from us.

RAINER MARIA RILKE

which your oatmeal self looks just the way you feel on a bad day. Now scrub the mask off and step back. See the brighter, more alive self that emerges?

This exercise is the physical embodiment of what I call "creative molting." Use this experiment to remind yourself that the "cracking" feeling you may often feel when undergoing spiritual change is actually a symptom of greater impending health.

Task: Face It: Make a Power Mask.

(If you are claustrophobic, don't do this task. It may frighten you.) For this task you will need to buy hospital bandages, the starch-soaked kind that harden to form casts. You will need a good mirror, a small bowl of water, scissors, and petroleum jelly. You also may want a headband to keep hair from your face and, if you choose, a friend to apply your bandage strips, as it can be tricky doing this by yourself.

First, cut the bandages into six- to eight-inch strips—a *lot* of them! Next, apply petroleum jelly all around your hairline and, for good measure, over your eyebrows and around or just beneath your lower lashes in a narrow band. Now dip several strips into water and begin building your mask. Most people prefer building across the brow and down the cheeks first. You will leave holes for the nostrils and may or may not choose to cover the lips. Apply enough strips that your entire face is thoroughly plastered. A tingling sensation will occur as the mask starts to set. Don't be alarmed by this.

Allow the mask to dry firmly, and then very carefully pry it loose. Rinse your face gently. If it's reddened, remind yourself that it will calm down. These are hospital bandages and have been used by thousands of people.

Once your mask is really dry, poke two holes for ribbons in the upper edges. Now, set to work to decorate it. Acrylic paints, sequins, glitter, feathers, ribbons—remember, your mask does not need to be "pretty"! It can express other aspects of yourself as well. If it would "feel better" to make a monster mask, do exactly that.

Art does not reproduce the invisible; rather, it makes visible.

PAUL KLEE

The mask is revered as an apparition of the mythical being that it represents, yet everyone knows that a man made the mask and that a man is wearing it . . . and the logic is that of "make believe."

STEPHEN LARSEN

Breaking Camp

"In a dark time, the eye begins to see," poet Theodore Roethke told us. For many of us, the work we have done within the Kingdom of Sight required considerable courage. Pause here and consider what you have accomplished:

With your Time Capsule Collages, you have allowed yourself a deep, non-linear perspective on your life. For your Treasure Map, you found the courage to name a dream and reach for it in your mind's eye. Seeking a more colorful self, you experimented with a spectrum beyond your normal comfort range. Making your Creativity Doll, you invoked your right to incorporate your own creative powers. Making your Creativity Monster, you miniaturized your antagonists. Dressing as a "serious artist" and "like you might be having fun," you allowed yourself to actively enter into ways you can wear your creative persona. ("It's all in the playing . . .") Exploring the shifting perspectives within "Cracking," you allowed yourself to consciously undergo the process of metamorphosis.

Armed with the tools of two kingdoms, you now move into a third, the Kingdom of Sound. As before, the tools of this kingdom build upon the work that you have already done. The insights that you carry forward with you now will be integrated and greatly expanded by your use of the tools of sound.

The
Kingdom
of Sound

As we move into this kingdom you might want to imagine that you have been blindfolded and now need to proceed solely by auditory cues. In this heightened state of awareness, you would find yourself acutely aware of the nuances and impact of sound.

We gather far more information by sound than we normally realize. Very often the "tone" of a conversation tells us far more than the words themselves. In a larger sense, the "tone" of our life may be harmonious or discordant. Sound can be used to create a more melodic flow in our daily lives and in our relationship to ourself. Unlike verbal or visual communications, sound works directly on our emotional state. The visionary Rudolf Steiner postulated that this was true because music had its archetype in the divine realm, whereas the other arts were more worldly.

Although we seldom think of it as a literal phrase, in this kingdom, we will be working with sound in order to make lives that are quite literally *more sound*. Although we seldom think of it in this way, our voice is an instrument—the most powerful of the many instruments on this planet. It is worth noting thar we commonly use the word *instrument* in two primary arenas: music and medicine. This is not coincidence. Music *is* medicine. The human voice and our conscious use of it as instrument is the scalpel of healing our diseased planet profoundly needs.

Sound

It was six A.M. on a California morning. Against my better judgment,
I was awake and committed to teach a roomful of people in Beverly
Hills. Their energy was terrible—or at least it felt that way to me.
"I'm wonderful, don't you think?" they seemed to me to be saying to
one another. "I'm wonderful, and I'm certainly more wonderful than
you are. . . ."

Was it just me? I took my notebook and retreated to a lobby
wingback chair to find out. Moving my hand across the page, I
watched my fears and resentments trot into view.

"It's too early."

"I'm too tired."

"They're too hip."

"I'm not hip enough."

Blah, blah, blah . . .

In the nearby dining room, the early risers were chatting each
other up. My brain was doing a fine job all by itself: "Look at those
plastic (porcelain) smiles. Listen to those screechy voices. This whole
thing feels so artificial, so ritualized. Can't anybody talk in a normal
voice range? Must everyone be so busily fabulous all the time?"

To say that I was negative is an understatement.

Enter a tall, bald man with lovely, loping energy.

"Who's that?" I paused in my griping long enough to wonder. "He looks . . . fun."

As it turned out, he was supposed to be fun. An internationally noted composer, virtuoso flautist, and sound healer, his name was Tim Wheater, and he was billed as our morning's entertainment. I was supposed to teach and then he was supposed to entertain us. I was the main course. He was the dessert. We were both intellectual breakfast.

As luck would have it, we were seated at the same table. This felt like a blessing. I leaned across to him and asked, "Would you mind toning for me, for them, before I teach? I'd like for them to be able to hear."

"Why . . . certainly," a startled Wheater replied.

Unbeknownst to either of us, we were tinkering with a highly ritualized form. Having the entertainment before the main course was a little like suggesting we put the communion before the offertory in a High Mass. Needless to say, our master of ceremonies was less than thrilled by our tinkering. Fortunately, he still went along with it.

"We can be, ah, flexible here, can't we?" he importuned the audience. "Julia and Tim have asked . . . We can let them, can't we?" And so, Wheater got up to tone.

If you have not heard toning, you should know that it is an ancient spiritual technique that is very centering. Done vocally, it creates harmonics that calm the spirit and still the mind. A friend of mine compares it to "listening to wind in a cave." This is an extremely apt image. The mouth *is* that cave and the breath and control that create sound *is* that wind.

Ducking to the stage, harmonium under one arm, Wheater settled in to tone. He was genial but quietly authoritative.

"Good morning, everybody. I've been asked to tone for you. Obviously somebody here has a notion of what it is I do. . . ."

What Mr. Wheater did then was build a cathedral of sound in which to teach. Working his hand harmonium, which set up a low drone, he began vocalizing. The sounds produced were intense, hypnotic, and oddly piercing. Comprised of deep, clear fundamentals and

The universal vibratory energies were called by the ancient Egyptians the Word or Words of their gods; to the Pythagoreans of Greece they were the Music of the Spheres; and the ancient Chinese knew them to be the celestial energies of perfect harmony. DAVID TAME

Your voice takes you to your heart. GABRIELLE ROTH

. . . there has probably not been any desert waste or migratory horde that did not possess its own songs. As an animal species, the human being is a singing creature . . . .

WILHELM VON HUMBOLDT

"Toning" is the use of the
voice as an instrument
for healing.
JONATHAN GOLDMAN

All passionate language does
of itself become musical—
with no finer music than the
mere accent; the speech of
man, even in zealous anger,
becomes a chant, a song.
THOMAS CARLYLE

their higher harmonic overtones, the sounds retain the flavor of their Tibetan and Mongolian monastic origins.

"There is no mystery about toning. It can be understood through material science, physiology, and psychology as well as the most ancient concepts of man's relationship to his God," writes sound healer Laurel Elizabeth Keyes. Still, toning *sounds* mysterious.

Within seconds, the chaotic room stilled to a hush, and then to something deeper than that—a calm. Wheater toned until a profound shift could be felt in the room's atmosphere. No longer was it a room full of social selves, armored for daily interactions. It was now a room full of souls, opened to an experience of the eternal.

"Ah . . . thanks, Tim," our emcee managed to croak.

"Thank you, Mr. Wheater," I echoed. I got up to teach before a centered, receptive audience. I was centered myself.

Sound had made the difference.

"Sound bypasses the intellect and has the inherent ability to trigger the emotions," sound healer Joy Gardner-Gordon tells us.

"There is nothing better than music as a means for the upliftment of the soul," wrote Sufi master Hazrat Inayat Khan.

"When the human being hears music, he has a sense of well-being, because these tones harmonize with what he has experienced in the world of his spiritual home," taught visionary Rudolf Steiner.

"Everything is sound," taught the ancient wisdom traditions.

"*Nada Brahma,*" states Indian spiritual tradition.

Joachim-Ernst Berendt explains the phrase this way: "*Nada Brahma* means not only: God, the Creator, is sound; but also (and above all): Creation, the cosmos, the world, is sound. And: Sound is the world."

It can be said more simply.

"The earth sets some music going in us and dance we must," wrote Edgar Lee Masters in the *Spoon River Anthology.*

Dance we must!

A friend of mine, Gerard, lives in midtown Manhattan, in the midst of a high-decibel cacophony. It is, he claims, music to his ears—a long-grown-accustomed-to urban lullaby, as soothing as the sound of water. When I visit him, my sleep is pierced by sirens. My wake-up call is the sound of jackhammers tapping out a salute.

"How do you do it?" I sometimes whine.

"Oh, I love it," he assures me. And he does. To Gerard's city ear, the noise of traffic is the sound of music. Without its accompaniment, he feels displaced.

I live at 7,500 feet above sea level, on a mountain range where coyotes are my nocturnal sirens and neighboring roosters my reveille. An occasional stiff wind is as loud as it gets, except for the showy *perididdle* of hail during freakish off-season ice storms. I like a life soft and full as a heartbeat. I listen for birds and the throbbing slough of water pulsing through my asequia. Perhaps because of this, I live my life to the sound of drums, pipes, and rattles.

It is, of course, a staple of shamanic traditions to "journey" using drums or flutes. Many of us have done it unconsciously for years using rock and roll to move our energies up and out, using Gregorian chant, Pachelbel's "Canon," or pieces written in pentatonic scales to deepen and center ourselves.

Long before I became conscious of how it functioned spiritually, I used drum and flute music to alter and expand my consciousness. Whenever a blow to my creativity left me confused or disabled, I healed myself sonically—not that I would have ever put it in those terms. What I knew, all I knew, or needed to know, was that in times of trouble or difficult creative passages I would play the same piece of music over and over until my dilemma was resolved, first in my consciousness and later in my life.

What I was doing, of course, was washing myself in sound. I was playing lullabies, comforting and cajoling my creative child, coaxing her with the promise of both safety and adventure, to come back out and play. For many years, it wasn't obvious to me or my intimates just what I was up to. What they saw and heard was a woman in the grip of a musical obsession.

"Mom! That music is giving me nosebleeds!" my daughter would wail. "Do we have to hear it *again?* How about something with lyrics?"

Unfortunately, for the most part, lyrics were out of the question for me. When I was out of sorts, music had *sounds,* not words, to soothe the savage beast. I was relieved when I found Hazrat Inayat Khan's explanation of this: ". . . health is a condition of rhythm and

In the beginning was the Word and the Word was sound.

DON G. CAMPBELL

In fact, the word enchant *comes from the Latin* incantare, *meaning "to sing or chant magical words or sounds."*

JONATHAN GOLDMAN

Men vent great passions by breaking into song, as we observe in the most griefstricken and the most joyful.

GIAMBATTISTA VICO

The peace for which every soul strives and which is the true nature of God and the utmost goal of a man is but the outcome of harmony.

HAZRAT INAYAT KHAN

Work with sound until you are absolutely amazed that you can produce such a sound and it seems to you that you are just the instrument to which the divine pied piper blows the whisper of the incantations of his magic spell.

VILAYAT INAYAT KHAN

If the sound generated by the vocal cords into the vibratory network of the universe has the faculty of tuning one, it is because it links one with the cosmic symphony.

VILAYAT INAYAT KHAN

tone. And what is music? Music is rhythm and tone. When the health is out of order, it means the music is out of order."

Although I didn't know it—although I wouldn't know it until a decade and a half after I began practicing it—I was working with rudimentary forms of sound healing. For me, this progressed first from listening to healing music and later to making it myself.

It is no accident we call it a heart*beat.* Music is the heart's native language. We speak it in bliss and in grief. We speak it intuitively and unconsciously. For many of us, sound is a natural tool. What do we do when a baby fusses? We croon to it.

"Every child is a musical instrument," insisted Rudolf Steiner, who founded the Waldorf schools to put his educational theories in practice.

No matter how sophisticated our lives may be, we need to think of ourselves as creative children. We need to remember a child's openness: "Make believe you're brave /And the trick will take you far/You may be as brave /As you make believe you are . . ."

As these creative children, we are each of us not only an instrument but also a note, even a song. When we open our hearts and sing to and with each other, we quite literally create harmony. If we are going to heal the world's maladies, those larger versions of our own, music is the balm, the medicine, with which we will be able to do it.

In my mind's eye, I see healing circles of sound—large, amphitheater-size circles—in which we gather to hold flickering candles and tone together. (More on toning in just a little bit.)

"Use the scale of overtones as a Jacob's ladder to climb," advises Vilayat Inayat Khan.

If the concept of toning feels daunting, you can begin with something very simple, either a lullaby or a "Spirit Song."

Composer and sound healer Shawna Carol maintains that singing *is* natural medicine. Teaching a process she calls "Spirit Songs," she works with people to release their emotional and creative blocks through singing them out. Spirit Songs are extemporaneous heart songs, shaped by emotional expression, not lyric content. You pick a topic that you sense you need to work with, and then you wordlessly vocalize to release it. (This is an extremely powerful technique.) Working with Shawna, I began to "sing" my dead mother, whom I miss but seldom weep for. Within minutes, tears were rolling freely down my face. I was contacting and healing a grief that I had carried, frozen, for a decade and a half.

Perhaps more than any sense except smell, sound bypasses our rational mind to move us at a primal level. During my first marriage, I worked with my husband on a documentary music film called *The Last Waltz*. It was a terrible time for us. We were young, volatile, heartbroken, and driven. Forces beyond us seemed to be driving us apart. And yet . . . and still . . . I remember looking up at him as we sat in an office at the old MGM, exhausted after a long, torturous shoot during which we heard Robbie Robertson's "Last Waltz" theme over and over for days.

"I cannot remember being this happy," I remember saying. "I know everything is terrible, but something here is *so* right."

The something, of course, was Robertson's music. Built on waltz time, it had a cradling effect that worked energetically to open the heart. I knew none of that then.

Music speaks to the wounds we have no words for. It heals where all else fails. Just as all of us are creative, all of us intuitively possess the power to heal. We have proved it over and over, just rarely given ourselves credit. Further, many of us have intuitively reached for sound as our healing tool but not recognized that was what we were up to.

"To listen deeply within is to awaken the musician," sound healer Don G. Campbell assures us. I have seen this in my own life.

Dorothy Caroline, my mother, the mother of seven, would turn to her piano whenever she felt overwhelmed. Sitting at the keys, she would play the "Blue Danube" waltz over and over until her mood adjusted its level to match the tranquility of the music.

A friend of mine, an overworked divorce attorney, walks through the door to her high-rise apartment and goes directly to the stereo. The punch of a finger takes her directly to Rio, where her spirit enjoys an alter ego as a Latin dancer. Within five minutes, she bears a closer resemblance to the girl from Ipanema than she does to "Counselor, about this motion . . ."

Think of the times you have watched a friend rise from the ashes of heartbreak, shedding weight, depression, and self-defeating pat-

Music has the capacity to touch the innermost reaches of the soul and music gives flight to the imagination.

PLATO

Toning is the process of making vocal sounds for the purpose of balance. . . . Toning sounds are sounds of expression and do not have a precise meaning.

JOHN BEAULIEU

"Toning" is an ancient method of healing. . . . The idea is simply to restore people to their harmonic patterns.

LAUREL ELIZABETH KEYES

As we chant our physical bodies into finer attunement, the people living on the earth and the living earth itself will find peace.
JOSEPH RAEL

The Chinese believed that this Primal Sound was, though inaudible, present everywhere as a divine Vibration.
DAVID TAME

FREQUENCY + INTENTION = HEALING.
JONATHAN GOLDMAN

terns. Recently, I watched a beloved girlfriend mend from a depressive, claustrophobic marriage by setting herself a regime that involved six nights a week out dancing.

"That sounds exhausting," I told her, thinking, "and compulsive, too."

"Mmmm. Maybe. But it's fun," my friend replied. "I *love* music."

Fully expecting I would later think of this as her "manic" phase, I settled to wait for my friend to calm down. She didn't do that. Instead, she cheered up. Despite my judgments, despite my well-meaning but negative opinion, she pursued her dancing path and passion. After a few months, even I had to admit her plan was working. Her calls were full of cheer, new plans, and new self-worth. Of course, all that dancing aerobicized her as well, gifting her with a more svelte shape as well as spirit, but when she picked up the phone, I would catch her humming to herself. It was music as much as muscle tone that was the real variable. She was singing the body electric, and it had turned on the lights for her.

Three months into her dance marathon, my friend acquired a Casio keyboard, "just to fool around with a little." After four months, she progressed to writing "just little things." After five and six months, time at the keys was a regular part of her day. Home from work, she would unwind by letting her fingers do the walking. Relaxed, if not rested, she'd head back out the door to go dancing. Do I need to tell you that she now loves a dancer as well?

My friend had healed her heart by listening to its delight. "What would I *love* to do?" she asked herself, not "What *should* I do?" Sound healing is simply using sound consciously. It is perceiving sound for what it is: energy. It is using that energy to heal whatever bad energy our body is holding or experiencing. Bad energy makes itself felt first as a sense of dis-ease, and later as disease.

Although we may prefer to phrase it differently, all of us have had our experiences with good and bad energy.

"What's eating him?" we may ask of a colleague whose "bad vibe" puts us off.

"Did I walk into the middle of something? Is this a bad time?" we may query, entering a room where the tension is palpable.

The point is, our bodies know bad energy when they feel it, and they know good energy, too. Someone's tone of voice can either set us on edge or set us at ease. Our own voice, used therapeutically, can heal what ails us and others. I would like to share a dramatic case in point.

It was nine o'clock on a Thursday evening later in that same week when I had first enlisted Wheater's help with my teaching. I had been told that I would be working with sound healing, but I still knew very little about it. I hoped to find out more but didn't expect to experience more quite so directly.

After a long dinner talking about our work, Wheater and I had stopped at a bottle store in Venice, California, to buy water and continue our long conversation. Leaving the store, we were accosted by a young, charismatic, and very drunk beggar. Something about the young man stopped me in my tracks. I plucked Wheater by the arm. We became an audience.

Off on a sudden and still-dazzling improv riff—a stomach full of booze, a head full of songs, and a heart full of pain can be a pretty potent combination—the young drunk got our attention and our empathy.

"Give me a couple of bucks, let me give you a couple of songs," his jive began. "Dough for Do. Do, re, mi—you see?"

His rhymes were fast and facile, but his eyes were dull—the empty eyes of a life whose occupant has moved out.

"So much talent, so much waste," I was thinking, seeing my young, alcoholic artist self in the rearview mirror. I wanted to tell the man, "Quit the booze. It will kill you and your creativity." He would never have heard me. Words are too righteous sometimes. They divide us when we mean to connect.

Clearly this was an artist and an artist-to-artist connection I was feeling. If I couldn't share my story, what could I offer? How to connect to this man?

That's when I one more time pressed Wheater unexpectedly into service.

"Please tone for him," I entreated. "Please."

Graceful even under pressure, perhaps sensing I was going nowhere until he *did* tone for the man, Wheater stepped quietly to the man's side.

Since it is very rare in our society to be personally sung to, this experience usually awakens the soul and speaks to the heart, helping that person to hear and sing their own song.

CAITLIN MATTHEWS

The basic attunement for harnessing the will in healing with sound is the intoning of a single pitch on an open vowel sound.

SARMAD BRODY

Since time began, priests, healers, shamans, mystics, medicine men, and magicians of all persuasions have been aware of the power of specified verbal formulae, spoken or sung out loud, or intoned silently within.

BRIAN AND ESTHER
CROWLEY

"Can I show you something, man?" he asked.

Startled, the man gave a nod yes.

With that, Wheater drew the man's head close to his chest, cradled his arm around his shoulders, and began toning into his ear.

The toning went on for a few minutes, maybe more. As I watched and listened, the drunken vagrant shifted in his body. His eyes cleared as his soul came back into them. His gaze was still pained, but now clear and focused as Wheater finished his toning. They stepped apart.

"Thanks, man. I love you, too." The vagrant now spoke clearly. "That's what you told me, isn't it?"

It was Wheater's turn to nod yes. Using sound as the bridge, he had met our fellow traveler in that world where souls recognize and embrace each other. More than dollars had exchanged hands. To watch Wheater was to get a sense of Merlin conjuring the power of sound.

"Clearly, we should all become sound healers," I said a moment later as we were back in the car and driving away.

Wheater gently explained to me, "We all already are."

It is my hope that by consciously working with sound, you will recognize and heal yourself. The following tasks are heart steps in that direction.

∼ Task: Sing a Spirit Song. ∼

Pick a topic on which you sense you have deeply felt, "stuck" emotions. Take a minute to center yourself through deep and steady breathing, then allow yourself to begin singing sounds related to your feelings. (Save words for later.) Continue this until you feel you have cleared the energy. This may take anything from a few minutes to half an hour. Take time to calm and center at song's end as well.

∼ Task: Lullaby. ∼

For five minutes each day (five private minutes), hum or sing or lullaby to yourself. You may remember a favorite childhood lullaby—

"Turra Lurra Lurra" or "Hushabye"—or you may want to borrow or invent one. After a few days of this—sooner, if you want to—sit down and write yourself an "official" lullaby. One of my invented lullabies ran:

> *Just trust your heart.*
> *Trust where it's taking you.*
> *Just trust your heart.*
> *Trust what it's making you.*
> *Just trust your heart.*
> *Trust that it's taking you home. . . .*

A little later, the lullaby evolved:

> *Just trust your song.*
> *Trust what it's bringing you.*
> *Just trust your song.*
> *Trust that it's ringing true.*
> *Just trust your song.*
> *Trust that it's bringing you home.*

Songs are thoughts, sung with the breath when people are moved by great forces and ordinary speech no longer suffices.

ORPINGALIK

But then, a sensitive is not always walking about with his head in the clouds. The meaning of mediumship is balance—balance between two worlds—and you are the balance wheel in the middle.

ENA TWIGG

Man cannot live without mystery. He has a great need of it. LAME DEER

In devising your lullaby, be liberal with yourself, not literal. You may begin to hear your own music or you may find yourself borrowing someone else's. The point is soul-soothing and certain music, your own or others', will do that for you. "Amazing Grace" makes a fine lullaby. So does "Oh, Mary, we crown thee with blossoms today . . ." So does "Over the Rainbow." I have used "Take the A Train," and you certainly may use whatever you please—whatever pleases you. Some people shower and sing. Others lie on the floor or in the bath. Still others sing as they walk, run, or drive. My current routine involves a walkabout pace and monosyllabic toning. The routine changes as I change and my needs change. Experiment to see what suits you. Remember, you are not to sing *well;* you are simply to sing.

"Do, re, mi, fa, sol, la, ti, do," is a surprisingly soothing and effective lullaby. The alphabet works, too. ("A-B-C-D-E-F-G, I can sing me back to me!") Many students enjoy borrowing Sanskrit "seed sounds" or the famed Buddhist mantra: *"Om-mani-padme-hum."* (The bibliography of this book contains a number of books on sound and sound healing that you may want to explore.)

While officially we have no English-language mantras, they can be easily devised:

I will to do thy will.

Open my heart and show me my part.

Light up my life and let me end strife.

Give me the grace to walk in your ways.

Give me the love, below as above.

Both the words "heart" and "home" can be soothing and centering when repeated over and over. Both work sonically to open the heart, as can be felt by the deep vibration in your breastbone when you repeat them in a low register. Of course, I like to hear the "art" in "heart" and the "om" in "home."

~ Task: Washing with Sound. ~

All of us know that after a busy, stress-filled day at the office, a shower can be refreshing. What many of us do not know is that we also can shower using sound. This can be done in two ways, one externally and one internally.

First let us talk about the external method. Let us say you come home from a stress-filled day at the office, have a fight with your friend or spouse, or find a sense of tension lingering in the house after houseguests who overstayed their welcome leave. Cuing up your sound system, you can use sound to clear the static from both you and your environment.

Just as in safety music, all people will have their own taste in Wash It Out music. For some, it is literally the sound of waves. They will put on an environmental album and let the steady and repetitive drone of waves wash their rooms and their consciousness. For others, a little more propulsion seems to be required. (Ever notice how teens

... sing the wandering soul back home.
CAITLIN MATTHEWS

What will nurture the creative vision necessary to turn around a world possibly heading towards its own destruction? Music.
LORIN HOLLANDER

I now use my "artist voice" to celebrate myself as much as a larger being.
RICHARD NEWMAN

I believe that music, sound, and auditory vibration make up a critical factor in the graceful path to the next stage of revolution.
BARBARA MARX HUBBARD

like to crank up the heavy bass to banish how "we" have "made" them feel?)

While your tastes may not run to heavy metal, you may find yourself attracted to a propulsive drum. Don't be surprised if the drums move you into dancing out some of the anger as well. Allowing yourself to do this little banishing ritual can be a lot more fun than trying to sleep that night with tension twisting between your shoulder blades or gnawing at your stomach.

Do not let any of your tastes in Wash It Out music alarm you. There are people who play the *Messiah*. There are people who play bossa nova. There are people who play the Boss. What is important here is simply remembering that units of sound are named waves for a reason, and that waves can and will wash us clean of our angers and anxieties.

When we begin to use sound *consciously* we begin to be able to fashion a tool kit that is both versatile and portable. The next method, internal sound clearing, is so portable that all it requires is you.

Okay, we are back to those angry, anxious feelings. This time, you are going to generate the Wash It Out sounds by making them yourself. Start with whatever seems appropriate—maybe a low growl of rage over having boundaries violated. Maybe a howl of pain. Maybe a threatening hiss. Pick the sound that feels cathartic to you. You may growl, howl, hiss, stomp, chomp—the choice is yours. Use any or all of your sound vocabulary. You may want to match up your body language as well.

Having done some banishing sounds, you may now wish to try some comforting little clucks or hums—yes, the same sort of soothing sounds you might make to baby someone—in this case, you!

~ Task: Forming a Sound Round. ~

Many of us have happy memories of caroling at Christmas. Some of us have happy memories of singing in a chorus as a child. Yet relatively few of us sing in groups as adults. We just don't feel our voice is good enough to merit that kind of commitment, even though we

Rhythmic stimulation, not only from sound but from other factors, influences consciousness.

HOLGER KALWEIT

The man that hath no music in himself
Nor is not moved with concord of sweet sounds
Is fit for treasons, stratagems, and spoils
The motions of his spirit are dull as night
And his affections dark as Erebus
Let no such man be trusted.

WILLIAM SHAKESPEARE

The circle is an old and universal symbol, having power and motion in both the physical and spiritual realms. It is the archetypal symbol for wholeness.

TED ANDREWS

The human being is essentially sound, vibrations, and melody. . . .

HOLGER KALWEIT

The goal of the musician was to manifest within the medium of audible sound a music which expressed accordance with celestial order.

DAVID TAME

If the body can respond so decisively to music, it must in some sense be music.

DON G. CAMPBELL

do enjoy singing whenever we let ourselves do it. Forming a sound circle, what I like to call a Sound Round, is one way to let ourselves do it again.

What is a Sound Round? It's a circle of people who sing or tone together. It is a way of working collectively to raise one another's spirits—or, if you prefer, one another's vibrations. Rather than focusing on songs, the simplest way to build a Sound Round is to focus on thinking of the group as an instrument, a vocal instrument, which can make simple, clear, and powerful sounds. Doing this is called "toning." The technique is ancient and best learned by doing.

Mystic traditions teach that each vowel corresponds to an energy center within the body that is opened and energized by sounding the vowel that is its "seed sound." This process is called toning because, quite literally, it tones us up.

While toning is an art and a practice that can be developed with more and more mastery, it is also a spiritual tool that can be taught gently and easily, without a lot of unnecessary hokum. As a rule of thumb, the voice opens with the heart. If you want to open your singing voice, focus on opening your heart to a more loving vibration, and the voice will open and clear as well.

Both our bodies and our hearing alter as we begin working with sounding the vowels. At first, we will tend to hear just one "fundamental" note at a time. Eventually, we will hear shadow notes, or harmonics, that occur as we sing each fundamental. Over time, we will be able to generate these harmonics more and more distinctly and deliberately. This process is then called "overtoning" to emphasize the higher harmonics.

I don't like to make any of this very mysterious because I don't think it needs to be. Groups can begin very simply by singing the vowels starting at middle C and going up to G.

"A, E, I, O, U." (Ascending.)

After the circle has sung the vowels a few moments, the same sequence should be followed with the mouth closed. Immediately, a vibration will be felt. The mouth has now become a "sound cave," a portable spiritual site that resonates.

By moving the tongue forward and backward, closer and further from the roof of the mouth and opening the lips slightly, a shift occurs that begins to allow us to move and change the sound. We can project it up into our nasal cavities, creating a humming or buzzing sound. We can project it out through our lips like a rounded kiss, making a sound that closely resembles whale calls. When we keep our lips closed and hum the sounds, we can feel the vibration in our chest cavity cradling our heart, but that is not the only part of the body in which the sounds effect a shift.

Any work with these techniques rapidly opens the body. The energy centers—"chakras," or wheels in Sanskrit—begin to function with more clarity and balance. It is important to remember that sound is powerful and that each of the energy centers has a "job" and a vowel, or "seed sound," which calls to it to do that job more forcefully. For this reason, it is important not to work dominantly with any one vowel to the exclusion of others. It is also important to end the Sound Round with a safe and gentle landing. I like to do this using the alphabet song.

The alphabet song!

Yes, the simple A-B-C song you learned in kindergarten. Embedded in that simple song are two things: the vowels with which we are working and a set of tones that soothe us both because of their familiar associations and the ways in which they work sonically on the body.

Other safe landings for group work include the repeated sounding of "Amen." The point is to discover what works *for you*. Many Sound Rounds close with the sound "Om," usually repeated three times.

There are a number of very good—fascinating—books on sound healing, many of which are mentioned in the bibliography. Additionally, I have included a discography because sometimes hearing, like seeing, is believing.

～ Task: Songlines ～

My brother and several of my close friends are composers. Several years ago, I realized that my habit of writing Morning Pages and their habit of writing notes were essentially the same thing: two different ways of leaving the tracks of our consciousness. I took notes and they wrote notes—simple as that!

Music is the answer to the mystery of life; it is the most profound of all the arts; it expresses the deepest thoughts of life and being; a simple language which nonetheless cannot be translated.

ARTHUR SCHOPENHAUER

No man, however civilized, can listen for very long to African drumming, or Indian chanting, or Welsh hymn singing, and retain intact his critical and self-conscious personality.

ALDOUS HUXLEY

By exposing ourselves to more amenable noises— melodious music, the sounds of nature, a running stream, the sea, birds singing, and the like, we can repair at least some of the damage done by unwanted noise.

BRIAN AND ESTHER
CROWLEY

Just as writing leaps from word to word by a series of choices, music leaps from note to note. We "write" music. "Words" and "notes" are really statements of position, little trail markers along a route of consciousness that we might call a song, a book, or a letter. Another way to think of them is as "footprints."

When we want to blaze a new trail of consciousness, we can use our feet to help us do it. I establish a pace that is not really a walk and not really a run, more of a glide. With each footfall, I use the rhythm to *vocally* affirm my sense of direction and aim toward my desired destination:

> *Power and wisdom come to me/*
> *Support and opportunity . . .*
> *Power and wisdom come to me/*
> *Support and opportunity . . .*

In my experience, use of a rhythmic glide very often moves the recited affirmation into the arena of song. In fact, when I am writing music, long gliding excursions are my technique for "catching" melodies and lyrics. So effective is this trick, I sometimes run with a tape recorder. Sound healer Don Campbell explains this phenomenon this way:

> The basic power of music is in the rhythms of the physical body. Walking, running, breathing, and the ever-present roar of our pulse create the underlying beats that underlie the sonic world. . . . If a movement is repeated many times, a melody, a word chant, or some tonal activity begins to emerge.

I'll say! This spontaneous or deliberate vocalizing can be used to enormous good effect. It is the most potent form of prayer that I have ever found; the most powerful conduit to an expanded sense of possibility; the most direct route to the Imagic-Nation or, as some might put it, the Causal Plane, where our focused desires, energies, and intentions create results.

The combination of motion and chanting is extremely powerful. We tattoo the earth with our feet as we move, and this tattooing drums thoughts into our consciousness as well. Both movement and chanting lift consciousness and create carrying power. For this reason, wishes and prayers made verbally while the body is in motion have an extremely strong carrying wave for manifestation.

Sound healer Jonathan Goldman has devised a formula:

$$\text{Visualization} + \text{Vocalization} = \text{Manifestation}$$

That has certainly been my personal experience, but I have amended his formula slightly:

$$\text{Visualization} + \text{Vocalization} + \text{Motion} = \text{Manifestation}$$

Before I compose a piece, I walk around it several times, accompanied by myself.

ERIK SATIE

Silence

*The true human is someone
who is aware, someone who
is, moment by moment, to-
tally and completely merged
with life. . . . Out of that capacity of inner and outer
listening comes the quality
of humility.*
JOSEPH RAEL

Most of us lead busy lives. Such lives are often noisy—too noisy, we
say, for us to hear ourselves think.

This phrase is a literal warning. We need to hear ourselves think.
We need to *listen* to our thinking.

Our technological society has convinced us to stay in touch, but
not with ourselves. We use car phones, cellular phones, faxes. We use
our time to keep others constantly apprised of our whereabouts and
our current thinking. And that thinking, often high in voltage and
velocity, is flowing very fast.

As a culture, we are in the rapids. There are no quiet pools where
we dally for a day or two in silence, using our time to fish more deeply
for the questions and answers we harbor within ourselves. In other
words, we live a swift and buffeting life where our deeper selves are
often battered against the rocks (and roll) of our existence.

"I need to slow down. I need to catch my breath," we say, but we
don't do it. We don't do it because we don't really know how.

One way we can do it is through Morning Pages. Another way we
do it is through walking meditation. A third way to do it is through
the conscious practice of silence.

Silence is how we catch our breath. Silence is how we hear ourselves think, and also how we can hear the still, small voice speaking
within us. As creative beings, we need silence. We need it or we cre-

ate chaotic art rooted only in the reflection of what is around us, un-grounded in the deeper earth of ourselves.

The deep earth of self is what theologian Paul Tillich calls "the ground of being," his synonym for God. We don't need to think of God when we think of the ground that silence brings us to, but often we do. More accurately, we may suddenly feel that God is thinking of us. In silence, great swathes of our life may suddenly begin to make sense to us.

"So that's why that happened!" we may suddenly think—meaning our job change, our marriage or divorce, the shift in a friendship with a formerly close friend.

Thinking of God, even if that thinking is simply mulling over "Is there or isn't there?", opens the mind to a new flow of possibilities. This flow of possibilities is the stream of inspiration all of us are seeking. Remember that inspiration means "the drawing in of breath." We inhale inspiration when we are quiet enough to note it. We are always breathing, but silence allows us to focus our attention on the breath and what it is telling us. "A moment's insight is sometimes worth a life's experience," remarked Oliver Wendell Holmes.

In silence, those insights come to us.

"Silence makes the secretions of the mind visible," writes Joan Halifax, her tone making clear that she doesn't consider the mind our loftiest component. She adds, "I believe it is through stillness and silence that the door opens."

Silence allows us to hear the opening of that door. In fact, we open it ourselves as we breathe deeply, center ourselves, and allow the chatter of our unquiet minds to grow still.

All great spiritual traditions focus on breath work. Shamans draw in what they need from the spirit world. Masters ride their breath to a center where they rest in the indivisibility of the All. As artists, we need to catch our breath by declaring time-outs from the noisy world around us.

Trappist monk Thomas Merton put it this way:

> When we are alone on a starlit night; when by chance we see the migrating birds in autumn descending on a grove of junipers to rest and eat; when we see children in a moment when

It is only in the intentional silence of vigil and meditation, or in the quiet places of nature, that we encounter the song of the universe. Like the wind through the telegraph wires, this song echoes along the pathways of the cosmic web: it includes the celestial spinning of the planets, as well as the hum of insects and the dancing song of the grass; it includes the song of all the ancestors and spirits as well as the beating of our own hearts.

CAITLIN MATTHEWS

Nothing in all creation is so like God as stillness.

MEISTER ECKHART

they are really children; when we know love in our own hearts; or when, like the Japanese poet Basho, we hear an old frog land in a quiet pond with a solitary splash—at such times the awakening, the turning inside out of all values, the "newness," the emptiness and the purity of vision that makes themselves evident, provide a glimpse of the cosmic dance.

And silence, like a
poultice comes
To heal the blows of sound.
OLIVER WENDELL
HOLMES, SR.

~ Task: Silence. ~

Do this task as you devise it. There will be a specified form of it later in the book.

Safety

*"The problem is how to be open enough and
safe enough at the same time."*

W. A. MATHIEU, *The Listening Book*

Creativity is risky business—or at least it feels that way. Like anything risky, it is also enlivening. It makes us feel. Without creativity
our lives quickly go flat. Numb to our feelings and impulses, we go
through the motions of life but we avoid living. Sometimes it simply
feels too scary to face what we are feeling. Sometimes it feels too
scary to face what we are thinking. At times like these, we need to be
cradled, encouraged, and accompanied. For me, the most effective
way to do this is through music.

When I am looking at a large risk, I turn to music, most particularly the music of composer Michael Hoppé. (I often use his music
and Wheater's when I teach.) Perhaps Hoppé's most familiar work is
The Yearning, winner of 1993's CD of the Year. Composed and performed by Hoppé on keyboards with Wheater playing an impeccably
pure alto flute, it cracked open my heart the first time I heard it.

I had gone to Los Angeles to teach but got very sick with abscessed teeth, which needed root canal operations. Really hurting, I
could not sleep. I lay on my sickbed listening to Hoppé's music.

*One can now say that in musical experience man experienced himself as being at
one with the world. He experienced himself neither
within nor outside himself.*

RUDOLF STEINER

*It is the wrong rhythm, the
chaotic rhythm, that brings
about chaotic results.*

HAZRAT INAYAT KHAN

I want to sing like birds sing
Not worrying who hears or
what they think.

RUMI

Music is essential to the
modern shamanic journey. It
is the inspiration, the guide,
the calling. It holds our sto-
ries, our myths, our hearts
and souls. It speaks to the
spirit of our times.

GABRIELLE ROTH

What song did the great fire-
ball sing? What tune accom-
panied the formation of the
galaxies? The music that
ushered in the cosmos played
on, inside us and around us.

BRIAN SWIMME

Abruptly I started sobbing and then, astonishingly to me and to Re-becca Clemons, the woman who was nursing me, I burst into song.

Forget the abscessed teeth! Forget the sore and swollen jaw! I sang and sang and sang. Weeping and singing. Singing and weeping. (As sound healer Joy Gardner-Gordon notes, "Sound can be used as a form of deep tissue work, to release old programs and pain.") Tears and fears moved through me for most of a long, fever-racked night.

Every half hour or so, I would go and get into a cool tub, trying to break my fever. When I did that, words and phrases would come to me, firmly and insistently: "Body of sound, body of light. Body of sound, body of light."

Back in bed, unable to sleep, I was given to understand that I was being taught, that the phrase I was hearing was instruction. If I—or we—wanted to bring in more light, sound was the way to do it. We had been doing it backward, focusing on the light when sound was what would get us there. *Sound made light.*

In the hours before dawn, I "saw" huge auditoriums filled with flickering light from which rose the sound of toning and chanting. I "understood" that we could create an enormous planetary change by raising our consciousness through sound. Not only could we do this, I saw we *would* do this, and that we would do it on a global scale. I would be very much involved.

The next morning my fever subsided and I went out to teach from a deep and quiet place that was new to me. From that day to this, sound has been central to my own spiritual path and to what I try to teach others. In an unfolding series of sonic adventures, I have continued to have new understandings centering on sound and have been excited to find these confirmed by others who have seen or heard the same things. For example, my image of amphitheaters filled with flickering lights and huge crowds of people toning for world harmony—others have "seen" this, too.

I was very excited to read Jonathan Goldman's account of toning inside the pitch black inner sanctum of Palenque, the Mexican ruin, and seeing light appear. I had seen a similar phenomenon myself and was happy to have some companionship even on the printed page. I feel it is very important we share what we learn and, if possible, where we learned it. My most consistent teacher is personal experience, but corroborating it is a comfort that stabilizes experience into fact: it *did* happen.

When I hear *The Yearning* it still cradles my heart, which is one of the reasons I use it when I work. It gives me, and my students, safety. Frightened to write about something, I may cue up *The Yearning* and let it move with me into the dark woods I am exploring. (Other people might use Brahms's "Lullaby" the same way.)

I am not alone in using *The Yearning* this way. A nurse named Christy Flory wrote to Hoppé recently:

> I bought the CD and listened to it at home and promptly went out and purchased at least fifteen copies . . . baby gifts, wedding gifts, Christmas gifts, rocking my niece to sleep. . . . Recently one of my favorite patients died of AIDS. For his last birthday I gave him a copy. *The Yearning* played in his room as the family sat with him at his time of death. . . .

I know people who use Gregorian chant or Native American flute music the same way. For me it is essential that the music be both deep enough and safe enough at the same time. In other words, for me, it must contain both passion and purity to feel both safe and open, as Mathieu says.

In addition to Safety Music, I also look for Expansion Music. This is music that encourages the listener to quest in response to its movements. For example, when I teach, I will often cue up the B-side of Wheater's album *Green Dream* and play it while I ask people to write about their "Ideal Day" in the life they currently have and their "Ideal Ideal Day" in a life they must stretch to imagine. The music, with its Celtic quest and spirit of pilgrimage, pushes them further than they can easily go when writing without it. Vangelis's "Chariots of Fire" is another wonderful piece of Expansion Music for many— but remember, *you* are the one who chooses the music that is expansive *to you*.

I have been an active artist for twenty-five years. In those years I have had periods where my work was less frightening than others, but very often my best work came to me as I stretched to reach it. It is this stretching, this sense of being drawn out beyond one's bound-

Since people are made of sound, listening is important. . . . A true human is a listener who is constantly attuned by working with everything that is happening.

JOSEPH RAEL

I began to hear music differently. I began to hear something in bare sound I had never heard before to experience in the very act of hearing an upward intention, as if some current were drawing us toward it.

W. A. MATHIEU

Sound bypasses the intellect and has the inherent ability to trigger the emotions.
JOY GARDNER-GORDON

Through vibration, harmony, tone, melody and meaning, music stimulates within us direct experience of expanded reality.
BARBARA MARX HUBBARD

aries or capacities, that led me to look for companions to travel with—musical forms, companion spirits, objects that spoke to me of a world beyond my fears. Often a beautiful leaf or stone rested where I wrote; one year a row of crystal Christmas ornaments hung above my desk in mid-July.

As we journey within to find our own voice, creativity both isolates and connects. Because of this we must find the courage to voice our True Note to ourselves and to share it with others. To find that courage, I sometimes bring emblems of my most accepting friends into my work space with me. For example, some years ago, when a shattered love left me muted and ashamed, I received a letter from my beloved friend Laura.

"Just a quick note to say—do not chide yourself, berate yourself, belittle yourself for having fallen in love with someone who did not receive your love with the care and grace it deserves. . . . I know you grieve. Just don't beat yourself up for having loved. . . ."

As Laura had intuited, that was exactly what I had been doing, and it made it very hard for me to trust myself about anything, perhaps especially writing, which is an act of revelation not unlike making love. And so, I kept Laura's letter folded on top of my computer, kept my Safety Music playing, and I grieved *through* writing until I felt that, yes, I was glad that I had loved, glad that I had risked.

It is not coincidence that I have talked about creativity and love and risk in the same essay. Creativity is an act of love, an act of connection, a sharing. Creativity requires risk just as loving does. We very often confuse creativity with intellectualism, but they are not the same.

Rumi writes:

> *Lovers and men of intellect cannot mix:*
> *How can you mix the broken with the unbroken?*
> *Cautious men of intellect shrink back from a dead ant:*
> *Lovers, completely carefree, trample down dragons.*
>
> *The intellect says: "The six directions are limits: there is no*
> *   way out."*

Love says: "There is a way: I have traveled it thousands of
times."
The intellect saw a market and started to haggle:
Love saw thousands of markets beyond that market.

It is that last line I'd like to talk about: "Love saw thousands of
markets beyond that market." Too often, when we think about creativity we are like lovers who are afraid to love. "Where is this going?" we ask. Or, "Where will this get me?" We want our creativity
to be linear. We want it to take us somewhere . . . successful. In other
words, we want to love without risk. We see the market and we want
to haggle.

"Will this sell?" and "Will he/she marry me?" are two very goal-
oriented ways to approach what is meant to be a process, not merely
an end result. When we are able to open to process, we often find that
the end result, while not what we intended, is better than what we
might have planned.

I want to tell you this about the heart that I had broken open by
that blasted love. I got thirty songs from that love. I got a play from
that love. Arguably, I got a new me from that love. Who is to say that
man didn't love me very well, refusing to love me? As Hazrat Inayat
Khan wrote, "If anyone strikes my heart, it does not break, but it
bursts, and the flame coming out of it becomes a torch on my path."

All artists are tempered two ways. The first firing is by our external experience. We travel, explore, test, compare notes, and tell stories. This is our visible journey. The second tempering is internal. It
is the soul travel undertaken as we test the truth of our external experience against our own inner landscape. This invisible journey is an
experience of resonance.

Everything is tested internally, sifted, and sorted, gold from
dross. This is what is meant, ultimately, by an artist having a body of
work. Our work is the body of our experience. It is also, ultimately,
the body of evidence we offer to our fellow travelers that proves we
have done the work and that doing the work is possible. Living and
learning with an ear cocked for the sound of the True Note, we literally come to embody our truth.

There is nothing better than
music as a means for uplift-
ment of the soul.
HAZRAT INAYAT KHAN

When I am afraid of my own creativity (which may be to say when I am afraid of my own passion), I turn to the passion and creativity of others whose hearts have burst into music and I let them light the way for me.

∼∼ Task: Building a Sound Shield. ∼∼

In New Age circles, there has been a great deal of teaching around using light as a means of self-protection when in negative environments. For example, we are often told to imagine ourselves surrounded by white light (the Tibetans use blue) or to imagine ourselves covered with outward-facing mirrors that bounce negativity back to the sender. My own experience is that sound, the use of an internal song, is a far more effective barrier and allows me to climb when I need a little more spiritual altitude to avoid a crash with "enemy" aircraft.

It is probably worth noting at this point that another way to think of light is simply as solidified sound, so all we are really talking about here is starting at the source and letting sound *light*en our load.

When I am feeling challenged, I take a cue from Rodgers and Hammerstein and, instead of whistling, I take some little ditty and use it to rhyme my way out of trouble:

> *You can't make me angry.*
> *You can't make me mad.*
> *You can't even cause me*
> *To feel bad or sad.*
> *You can pout like crazy.*
> *You can hurl abuse.*
> *I won't feel I'm lazy.*
> *Chuck your slurs, they're just no use.*

Rhymes like these are astoundingly easy to construct once you set up a rhythm for them. You may want to practice this technique a little bit at home. The song you use to rhyme to doesn't even need to be one of your own.

We are created equal, but we are born into each lifetime with different temperaments, personalities, and inclinations to harmonize.
HAL A. LINGERMAN

. . . the shaman utilizes the drum to gain access into the mythical realm of reality. Through the drum's rhythms he or she transcends time and space to reestablish communication between the spiritual and the physical realms.
MICHAEL DRAKE

What you are doing, of course, is creating a personalized mantra that functions as an effective barrier to toxic vibrations. Because many of the rhymes that spring to mind are humorous, the sonic shield has the added advantage of lightening our mood and taking our focus off the perceived adversary. Because anytime we think in adversarial terms we are locked into the other person's energy level, this is another reason that I prefer the use of sound as a shield.

Task: A Sense of Safety.

Find one piece of music that brings to your heart an absolute sense of safety. For me, this piece of music has often been Michael Hoppé's *The Yearning,* which features Tim Wheater's incomparable flute. Hoppé himself listens to Mozart for safety because "Mozart always takes you out for the adventure and always brings you home." Another beloved musical piece of mine is composer Harold Moses' work, *Edges of the Soul.*

Please be careful not to judge yourself for what your Safety Music may be. My generation grew up with Rodgers and Hammerstein's tune:

> *Make believe you're brave*
> *And the trick will take you far*
> *You may be as brave*
> *As you make believe you are. . . .*

Do not be surprised if that or something similar surfaces! You may well use a childhood song. My mother crooned "Turra Lurra Lurra" to us when we were upset. That Irish lullaby still soothes me. Christmas carols, with all of their joyous associations, may work for some of you. Others may find themselves comforted by music with no familiar cultural associations. When I was living in London, I came across an extraordinary group, Tuu, who worked with Tibetan bowls and Chinese percussion instruments, and their work gave me a great sense of both tranquility and expansion.

Great music can bring many kinds of solutions. It can help you to repair broken relationships and inspire you to build new ones.

HAL A. LINGERMAN

We need to find God, and He cannot be found in noise and restlessness.

MOTHER TERESA

If one is master of one thing and understands one thing well, one has at the same time insight into and understanding of many things.

VINCENT VAN GOGH

The more we cultivate great music in our lives, the greater will be our attunement to unlimited sources of the Creator's power and direction.

HAL A. LINGERMAN

The trance or transcendent state of awareness becomes a learned state of awareness through repeated journeys of the spirit into their mythical planes of reality.

MICHAEL DRAKE

Rhythm is our universal mother tongue. It's the language of the soul.

GABRIELLE ROTH

Task: Playing It Safe.

Listen to your Safety Music and allow yourself to write for twenty minutes about risks you long to take. I often do find that the trick of keeping my hand *moving* keeps my thoughts moving as well.

Another simple way to do this task is to play your Safety Music and write for twenty minutes, finishing the sentence "I wish" over and over. The very monotony of this technique will drive you both crazy and into new territory.

Task: Expanding Your Light Through Sound.

It is sometimes helpful to think of the Imagic-Nation as being a place we can get to by crossing a bridge or dropping down a well or tunnel. Some people find it by climbing a ladder or a staircase. However you choose to envision the crossover, music can help you to do it.

My friend Paul Pascarella, a wonderful painter, tells of using a particular and repetitive Laurie Anderson song when he was looking for the "window," as he calls the crossover, into a series of buffalo he was painting. Every night, he would cue up the song and dance until he felt his consciousness shift. (With dance, you can move across the bridge even faster.)

As is probably clear by now, these are essentially shamanic techniques that many artists discover intuitively but also can be consciously employed. A friend of mine recently asked me what, exactly, a shaman was. I defined it this way: a shaman is someone who journeys to other realms of consciousness to bring back healing for the tribe. This, I believe, is also a good working definition of an artist. We are healers who journey on behalf of society to realms of the Imagic-Nation where we discover images and truths which we then share through our art. As with all shamans, one of our primary methods of journeying is with sound.

For example, in addition to Wheater's music like *Whale Song, Green Dream, Timeless*—or my own—I have also used Mickey Hart's *Music To Be Born By* as a bridge. (Hart made the composition to aid in the delivery of his son, and I have used it to birth some of my own creative thinking.) I have loved the Native American

flute tapes *Ritual Mesa, Journeys,* and *Migration.* I have also used
Gabrielle Roth's *Trance,* the percussion tape from Sound True's
Global Meditation series, and straight drumming tapes such as
Drums of Passion, by Babatunde Olatunji or Michael Harner and Ed
Gross's shamanic journey tapes.

For me, all of these pieces take me quickly across—although not
perhaps as quickly and ecstatically as would some African drum
rhythms. For me, the point is not always "quickly" and "ecstatically."
The point is *surely, gently, safely.*

Experiment this week with finding musical rhythms that
move you across into the Imagic-Nation. First, think of a topic or project you would like to work with. Plan on spending twenty minutes exploring and expanding the topic or creative project of your
choice.

*You can journey on sound using a rhythm as simple as a metro-
nome's. A rapid, even ticking or drumbeat is all that is required. (The
shamanic state is associated with the alpha brain frequency of seven to
thirteen cycles per second. If you repeat, "One, two, three, four, one, two,
three, four" or "tick, tick, tick, tick" as quickly as you can, you will be
in the right range.)*

*If a friend is drumming for you, prearrange a call-back signal. For
safety's sake, don't listen to shamanic tapes while driving, and if you are
using a metronome or drum, set a soft alarm to bring you "back."*

One last word about what it is, *exactly,* you will be doing. The following brief excerpt is from Michael Drake's excellent book *The
Shamanic Drum:*

> The drum's pulse synchronizes the left and right hemispheres
> of the brain. When these hemispheres begin to pulsate in har-
> mony, there is a change in the actual physiology of the brain
> waves that produces a heightened state of awareness. The
> awareness is expanded into the ecstatic state—the divine octave
> of resonance. With the divine frequency attuned, access to mul-
> tidimensional increments of knowledge and wisdom is gained.
> These realities are utilized as tools in this dimension. In this
> way the shaman creates a bridge, linking the Earth and sky—
> the spiritual realm above and the physical realm below.

*In the beginning was noise.
And noise begat rhythm.
And rhythm begat every-
thing else.*

MICKEY HART

*Though the mythical par-
adise is lost in our physical
mode of perceptual aware-
ness, it still remains accessi-
ble along the intuitive and
imaginative frequencies.*

MICHAEL DRAKE

*The drum is sacred. Its
round form represents the
whole universe, and its
steady beat is the pulse, the
heart, throbbing at the center
of the universe.*

NICK BLACK ELK

The ethereal rainbow, arching high into the heavens, symbolizes this harmonious union of body and soul. . . . Drumming rebuilds the Rainbow Bridge.

In working with this tool, you may wish to keep a journal and log your impressions of the subtle voyages you undertake.

Breaking Camp

In leaving the Kingdom of Sound, you may notice something mysterious and delightful—even more so than with the other kingdoms,
you will carry the tools of sound with you as *companions*. Sound is at
once the most portable and the most potently pervasive of the creative tools. Even blinded by the dark night of the soul, you can still
muster a Spirit Song or croon yourself a snatch of a lullaby. Remember, as composer Steven Halpern says, "Sound is the carrier wave of
consciousness." Let's look at some of the tools you have practiced:

You have learned to ventilate and elevate emotions through the
use of Spirit Songs. You have written yourself a lullaby—the first of
many songs, I would hope—specifically to comfort yourself. You've
learned how to wash your environment with sound; how to form a
Sound Round and raise energy as a group. You've practiced Silence,
established a Sound Shield, chosen Safety Music and Expansion Music. (Be sure to glance through the discography in the resource section
at the back of the book.) You have become aware of how to "travel"
shamanically using sound as your gateway to the Imagic-Nation. In
short, you have learned to make sound a central part of your life, the
"beat" in "heartbeat."

As you go forward into the Kingdom of Attitude, all of these
tools will serve you. Be sure to continue their use on your Daily Walks
and remember they are there to serve you as processing skills.

The
Kingdom of
Attitude

Although this kingdom is called "Attitude," it might equally well be called "the Kingdom of Altitude." We are at the point in our pilgrimage where our consciousness must be lifted if we are to be able to complete our spiritual trek. Attitudes are what determine our spiritual altitude. If we are mired in resentment, fear, and animosity, we will interpret events and people through that negative filter. Once we have done that, we will act—actually, re-act—accordingly. The burden of bad attitudes weighs us down. On a creative pilgrimage we cannot afford them.

It is our attitude that allows us to view difficulties as lessons or opportunities, challenges instead of setbacks. It is our attitude that allows us to embrace self-compassion or flagellate ourselves with perfectionism. It is worth noting that often an artist's early work is fueled by anger and resentment while the later work takes on subtlety and *lightness*.

In the Kingdom of Attitude, we will undertake a series of "attitude adjustments" that will enable us pursue our creative endeavors with lighter hearts. The tasks of this kingdom are challenging in a far different way than those we have previously encountered. They are more playful, less labor oriented. Your Skeptic will protest! Picasso remarked that as children we are all born artists and that the trick is remaining one. That is the trick we will seek to master through these playful tasks.

The Paydirt in Pay-tience

. . . I was taught that the way of progress is neither swift nor easy.
MARIE CURIE

She who loves roses must be patient and not cry out when she is pierced by thorns.
OLGA BROUMAS

It may try your patience to begin with an essay on patience. "Haven't we been patient long enough? Let's get on with it!" you may think. Learning patience *is* getting on with it.

You may have heard the story of the prospector who worked for years sifting through low-grade ore, hoping to hit the jackpot. Isolated and alone, discouraged by his meager gains, he finally resolved to give up his search—when he finished that day's work. All afternoon, the thought plagued him, "Quit now, you're quitting anyway," but his years of work had trained him to finish what he began—and so he plowed slowly and methodically ahead, sifting, sifting. Scooping up the final handful of his day's labor, he found the enormous nugget that was the reward for his years of faith.

This story has come to me in several versions, and as an artist, I have had my own experience with it: the book that fought for years and then abruptly revealed the jewel within.

We live in a results-oriented society. We are trained to confuse process and product. We want "cup-of-soup" creative careers. Presto! You're an artist! The big sale or show or deal proves it.

Rather than create (or recreate) for the sheer love of it, we focus on what's-it-going-to-get-me. In our business-minded culture, if you tell someone you wrote a novel—the writer's equivalent of the

190

Boston Marathon—the reply is likely to be, "Have you got a pub-lisher?" (Imagine asking a weary marathoner, "Did you *win*?")

So obsessed are we with the stamp of approval that sale of our work implies, we don't even want to read a novel until someone (someone *else*) has decided it's worth publishing. We write for publi-cation, we paint for sales, not the pleasure of stretching our souls. This is toxic thinking, if it can be said to be thinking at all.

You may want to remind yourself that "art" is a form of the verb "to be." Many of us have the idea that there's such a thing as a real artist, and "one day we may be one." My feeling is that if you are making art, you are already a real artist. Over time, you may become a better one, more skilled in your craft, but what do real artists do? They make art. If you're making art, even beginning art, you are a real artist—at least today. And the day, the process of days adding up and experience adding up, is all we have for sure. So give yourself credit.

Being a real artist has nothing to do with getting published, gal-leried, or hired for a feature film. I wish it did. Then we could settle the question for good. The truth is, much of my best work has never been bought, and a lot of my lesser work has been. Continuing to do the work—good, bad, mixed—is what makes me a writer. Writers write. Occasionally, but not always, we do it very well.

(This is not to say artists do not aim for excellence or hope to at-tain it; merely that we cannot let the "aim" keep us from firing the arrow.) It is not the consistency of quality which makes me a writer. It is the consistency, period, that makes me one.

Somehow, this fact often can get lost in the shuffle. My Perfec-tionist can hold my artist at gunpoint and try to replace process with perfection. Perfection in art is not only impossible, it is undesirable. "Perfect" art rapidly becomes airless, arid, and dead. And so we need patience with ourselves, patience with our imperfections.

I have an observation, born from watching the creative process in me and in many others. No matter what our art form, we work along on a certain level and then the creative syntax breaks down and falls in a heap (*&%#*!), and it's really hard working for a while. We paint, act, or write "badly." Then something shifts, and the work

Commitment is a matter of pleasure.

NATALIE GOLDBERG

*Art is neither a profession
nor a hobby. Art is a Way
of being.*
FREDERICK FRANCK

*He only can enrich me who
can recommend to me the
space between sun and sun.*
RALPH WALDO EMERSON

*The best way out is
always through.*
ROBERT FROST

comes back together at a different level. Hopefully better, but certainly different. I think that anyone who works long enough and regularly enough goes through these spasmodic seizures and learns to just work through them, perhaps weeping and gnashing teeth, remembering the wheel will turn.

These periodic seizures of difficulty sort some people out and they quit, maybe mistakenly but maybe not, since being an artist is more about making art than about doing it well. Again, to survive as an artist you must be willing, at least periodically, to be a "bad" artist.

As a writer, I am rather like a word processor. Give me something to write and I will probably write it better than a non-writer. Sometimes, however, I will write really well and other times not so well. I'll have my good writing and my bad writing. Over time, the good and bad writing even out. In any case, I don't know how to get to the good writing without going through the bad. (This takes not only patience but also humility!)

Recently, the project I've been rewriting has not felt good at all. So what? My job is just to do it. That's a Survival Rule: Don't confuse the end result with the process. Process is what gives us credibility. Just process. (And, yes, process takes patience.) As creative beings we must learn, and therefore practice, patience. Patience . . . patience . . . patience . . .

I do not mean passivity, which is frequently mistaken for patience. It is passivity that tells us not to fight for our work. It is passivity that takes "no" for a final answer. Passivity is exactly that: pass-ive. We take a pass on growth on our own behalf. Patience is very different. Patience is not the acceptance of weakness. It is the quiet, slow, deep funding of strength. Let me add, building patience feels terrible.

Ironweed was rejected forty-nine times, William Kennedy's agent told me. Did the buy make it a great book? Did the buy make Kennedy a writer? No. Writing made Kennedy a writer. Patience did.

John Nichols is a hero of mine—not just because he is a fine writer, although he is one. Nichols is fifty-five. He sold *Sterile Cuckoo* at twenty-three, *The Wizard of Loneliness* at twenty-four. He was a bright hot literary star, and when the hoopla died down and when no one bought *nada* for the next decade, he kept writing.

Eventually, that writing brought us *The Milagro Beanfield War*, then more silence as more books weren't published, more books, more silence as other new books weren't published, then more books again. Through it all, Nichols kept writing. His recent book, *Conjugal Bliss*, is one of the funniest I have ever read.

I am sure the years of not seeing print were not funny for Nichols, but he soldiered through. That is what makes him a hero to me. He shows up. He does the work. He made a recent speech explaining how. Although he was talking to an audience of writers, his point applies to all artists:

> One thing I learned real early in my career is that if you wait for the perfect mood, or the perfect place, or the perfect situation for writing, you'll never write a word. If you're gonna be a writer, you have to learn to write no matter what. On the backs of napkins in restaurants. In bars and cafes. In your car while traveling sixty-five miles per hour down the highway, if need be.
>
> And you have to write if you're miserable. If you're uninspired. If you're sick. If you're totally depressed. If you're in the middle of a divorce. It doesn't matter what, 'cause there's never a perfect time for writing. Even the concept is absurd . . .

This brings up a Survival Rule: "Do it; don't judge it."

The longer you do creative work, the more you realize mood has nothing to do with it. Artists are life processors. Life processors cursed with opinions. One day, we'll like what we create. One day (more days), we will hate it. Keep on making things long enough and you will learn, to your embarrassment, that the good work and the bad are often not so far apart. In fact, some of your bad work looks pretty good. And some of your good work, well . . .

So you might as well just do it, and do it stubbornly, and do it all the time. Because mood is a slippery thing and what it tells you cannot be trusted—but process can. And process is the reward of patience.

One of our myths about artists is that we lack the capacity for intimate relationships. This is not true. We have a very intimate, long-term relationship, and it is with our work. Over time, through the use

The Meaning of Life is to see.   HUI NENG

I do the very best I know how, the very best I can.
ABRAHAM LINCOLN

Self-creation is an art of fire.
M. C. RICHARDS

*"I have done my best." That
is about all the philosophy of
living that one needs.*

LIN YUTANG

*... Perform every act in life
as though it were your last.*

MARCUS AURELIUS

of judicious listening, cycles of activity, and cycles of quiet, we learn the rhythm of our creative nature. Learning this rhythm not only requires patience, it rewards it.

It is useful here to talk about creative ideas in gardening terms. Morning Pages and Artist Dates can be thought of as a gently disciplined routine of watering and weeding. Walking—and the meditative thought or prayer that ensues from it—can be thought of as a nutrient.

While all of us might wish for fast and sustained growth, hothouse creativity, that is not the ideal. Forced creative growth, like vegetables that are artificially rushed, tends to have a flat, cardboard taste to it. There is something hollow, mechanistic, even flavorless in work that lacks the succulence of full germination.

In order to succeed creatively, we must learn to be discerning gardeners. We speak of having the "seed" of an idea, and we need to take that image literally. For a seed to sprout and mature into a healthy adult plant, it requires both care and nourishment. Plants must be placed a proper distance from one another. The patient gardener both watches over them and leaves them well enough alone.

The seeds of our creativity likewise require enough solitude and space to grow unhindered. Gardens that are overcrowded choke to death on their own growth. So, too, creative lives that are too rushed and jam-packed stifle or even kill the deeper creative dreams.

Conversely, an overzealous gardener can overprune a plant. We, with our where's-it-gonna-get-me thinking, can overweed our creative ideas. Creative thought is messy—a tendril here, a tendril there. Until we learn patience, we may uproot our best ideas as weedlike, or try to create product rather than produce. This misplaced emphasis yields us work with all the flat flavor of gas-ripened tomatoes with thick, unbruisable skins. By insisting on premature conformity, we lose the mutant beauties that are the seedbed of real art. It takes patience to allow our work to be self-perfecting over time. To be blunt, it also takes faith.

It is patient faith, not instant inspiration, that shows up at the easel, the page, the piano. It is patience that doodles with the same-old-same-old, while keeping one ear cocked for the new. Patience is tolerant of creative missteps, expects rough drafts, learns from failures. "Do not fear mistakes, there are none," Miles Davis advised us.

Even the fiery Davis had learned patience: play it again, Sam, and maybe this time it will lift off. Scales take patience, and patience takes the scales from our eyes. It is patience that allows us to see, and be encouraged by, tiny increments of growth. It is patience that washes out the brushes thoroughly, patience that runs spell-check over the day's work.

Without patience, short stories are aborted because we can't see where they're going and we don't hang around to find out. Without patience, the poem is abandoned when the rhyme scheme hits a sticking spot. Without patience, the play becomes all work, and we chop off its head before it finds its legs.

Creative growth is not a straight line steadily ascending to the heavens. Graphs like that one belong to real estate fraud. When I teach creative writing, I tell my students they will write along on a certain plateau and feel pleased with themselves until they hit a period of chop. In that chop, a set of creative rapids, their syntax will fall apart, their sentences will mutiny and collapse in heaps, grammar will be something where they went to school. Lots of writers quit when they hit the chop.

"Chop is necessary," I tell my students. "Chop means you're growing. Just you watch. You'll come out of the chop up a level, if you just keep writing."

And they do.

Patience teaches us to bear with chop. Patience teaches us the rewards on the other side of failure. Chop is a period of creative vulnerability in which your style shifts, becomes malleable and porous—in other words, open to inspiration. Without chop, our work becomes canned, repetitive—*product* instead of process.

"Mr. Edwards," I once heard a young, arrogant critic ask Blake Edwards, "did you set out to make a bad film?"

Clearly, the critic knew nothing of chop, less of sustained creativity. Blake Edwards has made some great movies. In order to make the occasional great movie, a director must be willing to make the occasional bad one. It's all part of the learning curve, all part of the

Patience is the companion of wisdom.

ST. AUGUSTINE

If the Angel deigns to come it will be because you have convinced her, not by tears but by your humble resolve to be always beginning: to be a beginner.

RAINER MARIA RILKE

I expect the gift of good and industrious hours....
RAINER MARIA RILKE

A job is what we do for money; work is what we do for love.
MARYSARAH QUINN

process. Filmmakers have a very public learning curve; theirs is, to my eye, a heroic art. Whether as filmmakers or as homemakers, however, it is patience that teaches us to bear with the pressure of creative chop.

Patience!

A stubborn, unwilling, spiteful student, I slowly learned that patience is the one requirement of sustained creative survival. If the wheel has turned, it will also turn again.

You, of course, may know this. Choose your "rag" and read all about it. In the pages of the *National Enquirer* or *People,* in *Vanity Fair* or the *New York Times,* you can follow the soap-opera spills and chills of celebrity artists. Movies, albums, novels, breakdowns, and breakthroughs—what you learn, reading, is that for those patient enough to persevere, the wheel turns again.

Most of us, if we focus on it, can think of times when our patience has yielded rewards. Ellen committed four years to night school, finishing a B.A. and then a master's degree. Now she is a wizardly financial planner—a creative career she was patient enough to *slowly* pursue.

For twenty years, clothing designer Jo Dean Tipton worked with hand-dyeing and hand-painting silks and cottons. For many years her design business was jammed into her home, taking up every stitch of space. This year, thanks to her patience, she has both a new home and a new studio. Based out of Taos, New Mexico, her gleeful, comfortable, superbly designed "creativity dresses" are in demand from coast to coast. Jo Dean laughs at her "overnight" success.

Houseplants may be the best teachers when it comes to patience. I am thinking now of two beauties that belong to my friend, a writer. The plants came to him as sprouts when he was working on Morning Pages and dreaming of being a writer of books. "The girls," he called his plants, as if they were the tree-trapped nymphs of Grecian folklore.

"The girls" are now six feet tall, sproutlings no longer, and the writer is at work on his third book. It is patience that allowed the plants to slowly flourish. It is patience that built the books, draft by draft.

∽ Task: Patience. ∽

Look back over your Narrative Time Line. Name five times in your life when your patience has served you. Write a few sentences about what was gleaned from each experience, how the depth and strength you gained helped to fund your future life.

- The Sundays I took Domenica to the pony rides and led her around at a snail's pace over and over. At nineteen, she still loves horses and is an expert rider. Horses are something we have always shared.

- The hours I put in learning rudimentary music notation. I no longer feel like an idiot when someone says 4/4 time or dotted half note or adagio.

1. _____

2. _____

3. _____

4. _____

5. _____

Keep the faculty of effort alive in you by a little gratuitous exercise every day.

WILLIAM JAMES

It takes a long time to bring excellence to maturity.

PUBLILIUS SYRUS

Take three-by-five cards and symbolically record these occasions. Hunt for images that bring them back to you instantly. Whenever you are engaged in a task that requires the practice of patience, post these cards where you can see them. Remind yourself through their use: Yes, I can have creative stamina!

∽ Task: Use "Just a Little" Patience. ∽

Look over your household and select one item that would look a whole lot better if it were freshly painted. This can be anything from the classic leftover-from-college bookshelf to a chair or the trim on your kitchen windows. Do *not* choose anything that is a major project. We are after (almost) instant results.

Go to a paint store, select a swatch of every color you enjoy, not just the "probable" or "suitable" color for the item you are going to transform. Bring those colors home and select one of them for the chosen item. (Store the others for later use.) Now, get your paint and paint your chosen item.

Voilà! The reward of "just a little" patience.

Courage

Courage is necessary to creativity, but not as necessary as most of us think. Too often, we confuse courage with comfort. We want to wait until something *feels* comfortable before we try it. There is a certain touching childishness about this notion. It has lingering overtones of Jack and the Beanstalk, Aladdin, and even Merlin.

It goes like this.

"One day, *magically*, we will feel safe and protected and powerful. When we do, *then* we will let ourselves begin the novel, the piano lessons, the acting class . . ."

But what if we never feel that safe? Then we will end our lives sorry—sorry we didn't muster the courage to write that novel, good, bad, or indifferent. Sorry, too, we skipped the risks of an improv comedy class, the joy of watercolors, however botched, the rite of playing "Chopsticks" (and maybe even Chopin) on the piano.

When we look for the courage to come into our creativity, we typically look for more than it takes. Signing up for a beginner's video class, we demand to feel the strength to withstand our panning by Siskel and Ebert. Rather than let ourselves play with clay, we visualize our grossly misshapen bronzes and tell ourselves sculpting is an outmoded art form, so why should we risk not getting into juried shows? When an idea for a movie script scuttles across our conscious-

Big-heartedness is the most essential virtue on the spiritual journey.

MATTHEW FOX

Jump.

JOSEPH CAMPBELL

*To know oneself, one should
assert oneself.*

ALBERT CAMUS

ness, we tell ourselves, "I could never learn screenplay format" or "What are the odds of selling an original screenplay?"

Whenever we raise the question of reviews, whenever we ask ourselves to consider the odds, we are indulging in emotional terrorism. Be certain of one thing: the odds of selling an original screenplay are a lot higher if you've written one. The odds of being a good sculptor (actor, comic, painter) are a lot higher if you let yourself be one at all. In other words, the only courage you really need is the courage to begin.

Creativity is a step-by-step process, and so is courage. You don't need the courage to live through your rotten page-one review to begin a novel. You do need some paper and something with which to write on it. That something doesn't need to be the laptop that will take six more months for you to afford. Writers have written long-hand for centuries. Some of us still do.

Whenever we demand we have perfect tools for our work, we are indulging in childish thought: "I didn't write the book, my Power-book did!" Artists are notoriously superstitious. We have lucky pens, pencils, pajamas, notebooks, cafés, waitresses, cameras, calligraphy nibs, brushes, and shoes. Remember Bette Midler's remark, "Give me the right shoes and I can play anything."

Most of us feel the same way, although our totems may differ. "I was dating Sheila," we say, as if Sheila wrote our novel. Ever eager to deny our creative powers, we attribute our creativity—and our courage—to any source or condition that is currently elusive. City living or country living is what we need, depending on whether we live in the country or the city. The girl who got away or the boy who's leaving—how can we be creative without them? A private place to write, a decent studio, two months off from work, a year's sabbatical, a move to the Southwest (or St. Thomas), a simple million dollars in the bank . . .

The list goes on and the price goes up as we speculate on what could make us feel safely, comfortably creative. Like the Cowardly Lion, we fantasize a life without fear and, childlike, we tell ourselves real artists have those lives instead of those fears.

Nonsense.

What "real artists" have is courage. Not enormous gobs of it. Just enough for today. Creativity, like breathing, always comes down to the question, "Are you doing it now?" The awful truth is that there is always some small creative act for which we can find the courage. If you can't mail your manuscript today, you can Xerox it and address the envelope. Perhaps tomorrow the envelope can be dropped in the mail. Just for today, even if you can't start a new canvas, you can stretch one, gesso one, and clean your brushes. As with housework, there is always something, and all the little somethings add up, over time, to a flow. Courage, after all, is a matter of heart, and hearts do their work one beat at a time.

When we beat ourselves up for lacking courage, we should actually commend ourselves for having imagination. It takes considerable imaginative power to conjure up the goblins that we do. Although many of us profess to being woefully short on ideas, we actually have scads of very specific ideas—all related to catastrophe. For years before I directed my first feature, I *knew* my reviews would read, "Director's Ex-Wife Makes Vanity Art Film." With headlines like that, who wants to race headlong into filming? Not *moi*. (I made the film anyway.)

Many of us apply the same scenarios to our creativity that we do to our love lives. The specter of a first dinner date has us married, divorced, or defending ourselves against hostile accusations against our character. We read our romantic obits before we get through the hors d'oeuvres offerings.

"Oh, come on. Just show up," our friends advise us. "Maybe it won't be so bad."

The same advice applies to creative risk. "Just show up . . . maybe it won't be so bad."

I'd like to say here that creative energy and sexual energy *are* alike. In both cases I've had the experience of thinking, "Oh, my God, this will never work . . ." only to change my mind as momentum develops and carries me forward. The sexual analogy is not a capricious one. Artistic anorexia and sexual avoidance have the same root fears—fear of intimacy, fear of exposure, fear of failure. When people ask me how it feels to be a "creativity expert," I tell them it's a lot like being Masters or Johnson. I help people do what tickles their fancy. I urge them to proceed slowly, by titillating, manageable

Granted that I must die, how shall I live?

MICHAEL NOVAK

*I always entertain
great hopes.*
ROBERT FROST

*Dance is one of the most
powerful forms of magical
ritual.... It is an outer expression of the inner spirit.*
TED ANDREWS

steps, instead of scaring themselves to death with a demand for vir-
tuosity and stunts.

"Have fun? How can I have fun doing something that terrifies
me?" people ask.

I recommend bribes. Our creative self is more easily seduced by
treats than persuaded by browbeating or entreaties. "Buy the stamps,
address the envelopes, put them in the hall, ready to go . . . and you
can go roller skating," I tell myself. Or, "Sketch from five-thirty to six
thirty, and I'll take you to a seven o'clock show. . . ."

Courage, it seems, has more to do with encouragement than with
bludgeoning ourselves into bravery. I think of my creative self as a
balky toddler—hardly as godlike a self-image as one might wish, but
a godsend in terms of effectiveness. "Julie, come on. You can take a
train ride to the Grand Canyon if you finish that book."

As I write this, I am aboard the Southwest Chief, shuttered away
from telephones and distractions. I have bribed myself successfully:
"Write from sundown to bedtime. Then you can read your new book,
ride through the desert all morning, and you don't have to write more
than one hour tomorrow."

If bribery strikes you as a cheap trick—like froufrou lingerie,
feathers, potions, and candlelight for sex—please remember that
cheap tricks usually work, and that we are after tools that work, not
tools that look good, sound good, and fail you. In the final analysis,
courage has nothing to do with emotion and everything to do with
action.

Do we care whether the firefighter who entered the burning
house and rescued the child was scared to do it? Not really. The
fear adds poignancy to the heroism, but the action is what interests
us: the child was rescued. In creative recovery, it is our brainchildren
we are rescuing. All creative ideas are children who deserve our protection.

In seeking to do this, it is helpful to remember that courage
stems from the French root *coeur,* for "heart." *We must love our Creative Children and ourselves.* When we act with gentleness and affection toward our creative selves, we are able almost always to act
bravely. Like that fireman, we sometimes think we're rescuing somebody else.

I am thinking now of my friend Michele, a born comedienne, phobically frightened of her own talents.

"You should take an improv class," friends would urge.

"I can't," Michele would wail. "It would kill me."

What was really killing Michele was her artistic anorexia. How to allow herself to get near the water?

"Go watch some comedy. Take a friend," I urged her.

"Oh! I know who to take," Michele picked up her cue. "I know someone really funny. . . ."

So did all of Michele's friends, but we didn't point that out. Let her think a few good laughs would help her suffering girlfriend, the closet comic.

"She *loved* it," Michele reported. "We're going back. I might even help her write some material. . . ."

Really?

"We're pretty funny together," Michele reported later. "We're thinking of doing a live radio show. . . . Of course, that's about as appealing to me as doing tightrope without a net."

Really?

"They said we were pretty great. Of course, she—my friend—is."

Really?

"You won't believe this. My friend doesn't want to do the show anymore, but this radio station is after me to do one, solo. Of course, it would kill me, but . . ."

But Michele now has her own radio show. Her talented friend has gone back to teaching, and Michele is almost too busy to notice she's on that high wire alone.

Only when you truly inhabit your body can you begin the healing journey.

GABRIELLE ROTH

~~ Task: Dance a Power Dance. ~~

Very often, contemplating a hero, we say, "He embodies courage." This is a literal term. Courage—and any other trait—can be invited into our lives through our bodies. In this task, you are going to use your body to empower your spirit.

Name five things you would let yourself do if they weren't so "risky."

- Go to Hawaii alone for vacation.

- Pursue a class in performance poetry.

- Ask my sister not to call me up every night to complain about her boyfriend.

1. _____

2. _____

3. _____

4. _____

The most basic, fundamental tool of magic is the body.
VICKI NOBLE

Dance has always been a way of accessing the other worlds, especially whirling or spinning.
CAITLIN MATTHEWS

Choose one of the risks from the list above. Get into some comfortable clothes—pajamas are ideal. Cue up a piece of music that moves you to dance. For some of us that's a Strauss waltz. For others, it's a salsa. For still others, it's African or Native American drum music with a strong, propulsive beat. Now, dance the risk. Imagine yourself in Hawaii on vacation, winning at a bout of performance poetry, telling your hostile friend just where to get off.

Dance, dance, and dance until you have really placed the power of your body and your mind behind the risk you are contemplating. We so often think we have to "force" our way through blocks; we can dance our way through them as well. Remember that change begins in the Imagic-Nation. When you can successfully picture yourself doing something there, you can far more easily manifest it in ordinary life.

Baby Steps

Drummer Mickey Hart tells us, "Adventures don't begin until you get into the forest. That first step is an act of faith."

Hart is right about that, but I'd take it further. *All* steps are an act of faith; we just become more practiced. A toddler steps away from the couch and strikes out for the middle of the room. A business writer sets sail from the solid comfort of facts and makes a first venture into fiction. What's the difference? Exactly this: a toddler has no judgmental expectations and is thrilled by any success. An adult, seeking to annex new creative territory, has a world of ego judgment and expectation.

"I better be good at this," we think. "I don't want to make a fool of myself." Picture a baby attempting step one to such feedback.

"No way! I'll just stay right here, doing what I'm doing, clinging to this couch . . . I mean, *job.*"

As a culture, we focus on results, not on the rewards of risk. Anything worth doing is worth doing badly, but we don't tell ourselves that. Instead, we indulge in a litany of self-abusive mantras, all designed to keep us squarely at step one, or before it.

"You'll never pull this off," we mutter to ourselves. "What a fool to sign up for this class. Who do you think you are, trying to write a novel?"

Real genius is nothing but the supernatural virtue of humility in the domain of thought.

SIMONE WEIL

Forgiveness multiplies and melts rigid postures. Try again and again with self-forgiveness. Be the kind parent to yourself you may not have had.
SARK

What we need is more people who specialize in the impossible.
THEODORE ROETHKE

Most of us approach creative risk with the same assurance and self-confidence a shy teenager brings to walking in front of the jeering bleachers at a basketball game. We know we'll make fools of ourselves. In a cultural climate where movies are judged thumbs-up or -down like at the Colosseum, a learning curve is not permitted. Having never seen the beginner's films of Spielberg, Lucas, Scorsese, or Coppola, a budding filmmaker compares his student work to their masterpieces. Is it any surprise discouragement sets in?

A decade ago, I was working at a prestigious film school that numbered some accomplished filmmakers among its faculty. It was my thought that we should show the students some of our early, sometimes dreadful, work. My colleagues were appalled.

"But, Julia," many wailed, "they'll never respect us!"

"Sure they will. They'll know we've been through what they're going through—and we lived to tell the tale."

"Well . . ."

Unable to muster enough faculty support for a full festival, it was decided to ask famous directors for their early work. Most gleefully complied. Screened cheek to jowl with the faculty work, it was a toss-up over whose work looked bumpier. True, there was the occasional flash of pure gold, but I will never forget the electrified air in the auditorium as students realized *all* artists have a learning curve. For the first time, many of them felt the freedom to try and to fail. Without the freedom to fail, real creative success is impossible. The work that avoids failure avoids risk, and safe work is dull by definition.

Ask yourself: if I gave myself permission to take baby steps, what would it be fun to try?

When I first taught Pamela, she was a seasoned journalist interested in writing a movie script. The black-and-white newsprint of her conservative metropolitan daily did little to reflect the shades and nuances she found in her life as a black American writer. A lady to her delicately arched eyebrows, and a brilliant one at that, Pamela found racial stereotyping an excruciating daily experience. A gifted writer, she was widely assumed by her colleagues to have been hired for her color, not her colorful prose. She needed an outlet for her creativity and her frustration. She thought screenwriting might just be it.

Meeting around some trestle tables at Chicago Filmmakers, a venerable filmmakers' co-op, Pamela and two dozen other skeptical adults were there to transform themselves from screenwriting wanna-bes into the real animal.

"What we will do in this class is write movies," I warned the class. "We're not going to talk about writing movies, we are going to do it. Now, here's how . . ."

"But, Julia!" came the predictable wails as I assigned a regime of Morning Pages, Artist Dates, and other unblocking tools prior to the screenplay launch.

" 'But, Julia' what?" I asked back.

"Do you really believe . . . ?"

"Yes."

"But I've wanted to do this for years and I never have. What's the secret?"

Goaded, I leaned forward and told them The Secret:

"Baby steps."

"Baby steps?"

"Yes. In order to write a *good* screenplay, you have to be willing to write a *bad* screenplay. The minute you become willing to write badly, you'll be able to write," I promised. "And you will do it just like you do your Morning Pages—one day at a time."

Pamela's head snapped up. An excited glint flashed in her eyes. She all but winked: got it.

"There's a reason we call them *rough* drafts," I continued.

By now Pamela's head was bobbing an excited yes: got it, got it, got it.

The rough draft of Pamela's first screenplay, *Natchez*, was exactly that—a *rough* draft. It was a huge, toddling baby step forward. The second and third drafts improved it—more baby steps. In its final draft, *Natchez* won third in a national screenwriting contest. By then, Pamela was trying her baby legs at playwriting. Within a year, she had mounted a highly acclaimed one-woman show.

Whether you are contemplating a screenplay, piano lessons, a move to another job, or a novel, play, or sculpting career, baby steps are the way to proceed. They allow us to travel far further than we may at first imagine.

. . . just a tender sense of my own inner process, that holds something of my connection with the divine.

PERCY BYSSHE SHELLEY

The first prerequisite for education is a willingness to sacrifice your prejudice on the altar of your spiritual growth.   LUISAH TEISH

A real artist is nothing if not a working man and a damn hard one.

EDWARD WESTON

Remember, ours is an art- and artist-toxic culture. Creative beings are often straitjacketed into expressing their creativity along a very narrow gauge. In a sense, we are all learning impaired when it comes to realizing our creative potential.

When someone is discovered to be dyslexic, the work undertaken to help the condition involves crawling and creeping—literally reprogramming the toddler part of the brain. This is what we will be doing toward our creativity. Without declaring ourselves as any specific type of artist, we will be taking baby steps in all forms. You may find your creativity expanding, hydra-headed, in multiple directions.

As I write this, Pamela is now not only an accomplished journalist, but also a seasoned screenwriter and playwright. Her willingness to fail—to take baby steps and fall—gave her the freedom to succeed. Her baby steps took her into the forest, where the adventures began.

... One little step at a time, lest I be presumptuous, lest I hurt myself, lest I hurt others.

JOAN HALIFAX,
quoting her teacher, Ogobara,
a Dogon

~ Task: Playing House. ~

One of the things we often do as children is "play house." I am asking you to do it again, on paper, so that you can create a blueprint that will enable you to begin building a more creative life, one baby step at a time. Here's how this game is played: Go to a five-and-dime. Buy cheap versions of the following supplies:

Crayolas

Magic Markers

Children's modeling clay

Watercolors

Acrylics

Set aside one half hour and use any or all of the five to make a small representation of a house. This is your emotional house you are drawing, a primary symbol of your life as it is currently constituted. Don't try to make this drawing "art." Think of it more as a child's drawing. You remember: a couple of lopsided windows, a door, maybe smoke curling out a chimney.

Next, list five qualities you would like to see more of in that house. They might be musicality, humor, plant life, friendship, intellectual pursuits. Finally, list five baby steps you can take toward bringing those qualities in.

For example, I wanted more whimsy and magic and adventure. I decided to consciously invite those archetypes into play. Because the creative mind responds to symbols more than to language, I used symbols to get the message across. Right on the table where I work I now have three toys, one for each quality: George, a whimsical green lizard who doubles as a paperweight on all my manuscripts; a magical statue of Merlin with a baby dragon so that I remember to create what I want and not just what I "should"; and a small adventurous-looking sterling silver sailboat that reminds me my horizons are as vast as the ocean if I will just allow myself to set sail.

Go to a five-and-dime or a toy store. Seek out small toys and trinkets that capture the qualities you seek to expand in your life. Place these tiny totems where their presence can serve you: a kitchen windowsill, desk-side, next to the phone—anywhere where you can use the friendship of these creative companions to shape your life more holistically.

. . . the art of creation is not entirely a rational and conscious one.

SALMAN RUSHDIE

A sheltered life can be a daring life as well. For all serious daring starts from within. EUDORA WELTY

~ Task: List Every Place You Have Ever Lived. ~

You may find yourself surprised by the emotional potency of this simple task. It may, additionally, be a valuable help to you in filling in your work with your Narrative Time Line. All you need do is start at the beginning and name every single place where you have ever lived. As you do so, you may find yourself flooded with very specific memories of the "you" you were at that time and place in your life. These "remembered yous" are very important to your creativity. They have things to tell you as well as things that they wish you to tell *for them.*

Scan your list of places and use it to write a Cup.

Boredom

Be patient toward all that is
unsolved in your heart and
learn to love the questions
themselves, like locked rooms
and like books that are written in a very foreign tongue.
Do not seek the answer,
which cannot be given you
because you would not be
able to live them.
RAINER MARIA RILKE

A little boredom is good for creativity. The trick is to maintain momentum through it. Used properly, boredom builds stamina, and stamina is always needed. We need to learn to work through boredom and despite boredom. We also need to start talking about what lies beneath boredom, and that is a queasy-making combination of fear and petulance.

Art is about making something, not about making ourselves something special. When we are bored by a project, we have very often lifted one eye from the work at hand and glanced down that dark and scary tunnel toward its reception. "Boring" is a mini-review that flattens our ego and our will to work when we have temporarily allowed our ego instead of our heart to be doing the creating. Boring is a defense we use and an exit we look for when we feel low on stamina or inspiration.

Boredom is the symptom; excessive ego is the underlying malady. When we are bored, we are usually sulking: "Why hasn't anybody noticed how special I am yet? Why isn't my work being singled out more? Why is all this such drudgery? I hate cleaning out my damn brushes, retyping my damn story, taking out the crooked hem. . . . Ahem! I am important!"

"It just doesn't seem very interesting to me anymore." (So I might as well stop.)

"I think it's gone flat." (So I might as well stop.)

"I keep feeling it's been done, and why should I do it again?" (So I might as well stop.)

"My characters feel stale." (So I might as well quit.)

"Do we really need another still life?" (So I might as well abandon this one.)

When the heart creates, it lovingly explores both the familiar and the unfamiliar. When the ego creates, it does so with one eye on the competition. The familiar, the known, must be bettered and improved upon. We must be interesting at all costs.

"Interesting" is a heartless word.

One of my favorite books about music is W. A. Mathieu's *The Listening Book*. In the final essay, "Big Ears," Mathieu describes a turning point in his own music, which heretofore had been reviewed as "interesting":

> I saw that my mission had been to compress the world's music into a personal style, to squeeze the wisdom and beauty of cultures into a many-colored ball which I threw into the air to win esteem from my listeners. . . . Naturally, people found that interesting.

When Mathieu was ready to deepen his music and his life, his awakening occurred. First, he realized something was wrong; he thought to himself, "If one more person tells me my music is interesting, I'm going to kill myself." Instead, after one more "interesting" concert, a friend asked a provocative question: "What is the purpose of your life?"

The question stopped Mathieu cold. He realized his life had two separate threads—his teaching life and his performing life. He further realized, "In teaching, the act of showing off or parading my abilities would be obscene."

And in performing?

"I realized that my music had gotten stuck because I was trying to prove something. Too much ego in it. I hadn't stepped out of the way."

When we demand to be entertained and interested by all we cre-

Learn to wish that everything should come to pass exactly as it does.

EPICTETUS

Alas, I have done nothing this day! What? Have you not lived? It is not only the fundamental but the noblest of your occupations.

MICHEL EYQUEM DE MONTAIGNE

We are all apprentices in a
craft where no one ever
becomes a master.
ERNEST HEMINGWAY

ate, when we demand never to be bored or boring, we have too much ego in the creating. We want too much to be special (which is different from being valued).

But of course we want to be special! We live in a society drenched with images of the importance of being important. We travel first class, business class, or merely coach. We get VIP treatment, the red carpet, or tourist. Our credit cards come in gold or platinum. It is all about pecking order, and the pecking order is pecking us to death.

Nowhere is this more evident than in the business of the arts. If art is always about being important, then we'd better be making important art instead of those delicious little cartoon doodles we love. Our music had better carry a Big Message. Our writing had better be Right On.

All this importance gets exhausting. It also channels our creativity along known and approved-of lines. Being important is a function of the ego. Being creative is a function of the heart and soul. Art created by the mind alone may be brilliant, dazzling, and important, but it stops short of connecting us to one another. Instead of communicating to the listener, reader, or viewer, it asks to be admired. In a hundred little ways, it draws attention to the kind of pecking order that says, "Admire me. See how deep, how rigorous, how special I am?"

There is a vast difference between being unique, as we all are, and being special, which smacks of self-importance. The ego loves special, but special puts us in a precarious position.

This is where it is useful to make a small distinction.

Very often students worry about their work not being special enough, not being original. At this point I usually point out, as I have before in this book, that the root "origin" is in the word "original." I urge students to remember that their work passes through them as through a prism, and that in passing through it acquires their coloration; hence, it is original.

"But it's been done before!" they wail, reluctant to acknowledge that everything we do in life has been done before—birth, loss, love, the works.

Yes, and with any luck, it will be done again.

～ Task: Do Something That ～ Has Been Done Before.

Some of you may remember the work that artist Jim Dine did with simple, multicolored hearts. Using hearts of uniform size and shape, he made us see them and understand them afresh by using their similarity to make us appreciate their differences as he drenched them in saturated rainbow hues. Many a sophisticated collector fell for the resultant work. Taking a cue from him, we will try our hand at something of the same notion.

I recommend using watercolors and cookie cutters for this exercise and making a row of something very simple—hearts, daisies, stars. Let yourself play with making these any colors you like. Do several sheets of this very simple exercise.

Then ask yourself, "Isn't this fun, even though it's been done before?"

We can do anything we want to do if we stick to it long enough. HELEN KELLER

It is only with the heart that one can see rightly; what is essential is invisible to the eye.

ANTOINE DE
SAINT-EXUPÉRY

～ Task: Oh, All Right! Make Something Unique. ～

We often remark that each and every snowflake is unique. This is a chance to prove it to yourself. Perhaps because she felt her seven children might need some reinforcement in this area, this task is one that my mother had the Cameron children perform every Christmas season. Some of my happiest childhood memories center on this task and the individual magic that I could create with a simple sheet of paper and a pair of scissors. Here goes:

Take a square sheet of paper. Fold it in half horizontally. Now pinch that horizon line in the middle and, using the "pinch" as an anchor, fold the two wings in diagonally so that they form a cone. Turn the cone over and cut straight across the top back, getting rid of the extra peaks. (You'll see them; don't worry.)

Now you've got a triangle. Fold it in half lengthwise. (You are making a snowflake.) Using a sharp pair of scissors, cut notches, slashes, points, and circles. Carefully unfold your flake.

Make six of these. They're great on kitchen windows and bathroom mirrors.

Time

There's plenty of time.

"What do you mean there's plenty of time? There's never enough time. There's no time."

When we believe there is "no time," that is what we experience. As all of us know, time is a marvelously malleable commodity. A day can go by in a flash or stretch out endlessly. We like to pretend that the tempo of our time is not our own; however, to a large extent, it can be.

Composers, as many of you may know, tend to live longer than the rest of man. It is my contention that this is true because they are always, continuously, playing with time. Music is the mathematics of time. A composer looks at a musical measure and says, "Shall I fill it with tiny little notes or make it feel elongated, like a cat taking a big stretch? A composer knows that the same amount of time can be experienced in any number of ways—as something rushed and pressured, as something languid, as something expansive, or something crowded with tension.

Our lives are our music. The movements within our lives are determined by our use of time—*and by our perception of time.* Just as a composer builds a variety of tempos into a piece of music, so, too, we can build a variety of tempos into our days. Rests (a musical term) do not need to be long to give us a sense of luxury and space. Pausing to

We're afraid of feelings. We rush through our lives searching yet not living. For those who have the interest to look closely, life becomes art.
DIANE MARIECHILD

214

note (another musical term) how we feel and what we might best do next can keep the tempo of our day from running away from us pell-mell, prestissimo at all times.

As mystics have told us for centuries and as Einstein and modern physicists now tell us in the scientific terms we can hear with our modern ears, time is relative. In the precise "now" we always have plenty of time. By focusing on each moment of the now—like playing each note of the music—we can move through our days, however rapidly paced, with a sense of timeliness. That is what we are really after: the feeling that we are "on time."

Too often we feel we are falling behind. We want to race ahead. We want to do more when we are already exhausted. There is, we say, "not enough time." The reason there is never enough time is because our time is not our own. We do not make it that way. Therefore, we do not experience it that way.

"Well, how could we?" you may want to quarrel, citing family, commitments, responsibilities. And justifiably. My point is that there is always some excellent, justifiable reason why our time is not our own. There is always something we should be doing—and usually, it is something for somebody else.

"I'd love to," we say, turning aside an invitation. "But I have to . . ."

"That would be lovely," we say. "But I really should . . ."

What we really should do is make ourselves a priority, and our time our own.

This is easier *done* than *said*. Making our time our own sounds like a grandiose and dramatic venture: we picture quitting the job, leaving the pregnant wife, never again helping out with the homework, the overtime, the yard work. Sure, we could make our time our own. All we'd need to do is move to the bush.

Moving to the bush is one way to do it, but those who have often report that while conventional time drops away, the experience is a little like living inside a radio set: they sense the consciousness of the outside world—its thought forms tug at their consciousness even more acutely.

Very often, this "tug" is what we are talking about when we say we have "no" time. What we want is time when we have no looming

Time is the stuff of which life is made.
BENJAMIN FRANKLIN

Without discipline, there's no life at all.
KATHARINE HEPBURN

The important thing is to create. Nothing else matters; creation is all.
PABLO PICASSO

*You must learn to be still in
the midst of activity and to
be vibrantly alive in repose.*

INDIRA GANDHI

commitments or concerns. Such time exists very seldom for most of us, and so we must learn to use the time that we do have as efficiently and effectively as we can.

No. Do not move to the bush unless you like being a radio very much. Instead, clear the underbrush out of your life. Weed it a little, just around the edges. Prune back your commitments slightly. Start with twenty minutes a day.

"But, Julia," I had a painter friend exclaim to me, "maybe a writer can do something in twenty minutes, but it can take a painter twenty minutes just to squeeze out paints, oil, and spirits."

"True," I acknowledged, "but even a painter can find something to do in twenty minutes that would further his art."

"No! . . . Well, maybe I could get a drawing . . . a drawing or two."

That is my point. By learning to use our small windows of time with velocity, we are able to use our big windows of time much more effectively when they are upon us. In other words, in order to practice your art, you need to practice your art, and "practice" is the key— regular, daily practice.

Often, when we are procrastinating with starting a project—gobbling our time as we do so—we are really trying to "rev" ourselves up so that we can create a masterpiece—or something pretty damn good, even inspired. We are waiting for the right mood to fill our sails and send us sailing toward the horizon of high art.

That wind, like a vast stretch of "free" time, may or may not come no matter how long we wait for it—and if we are willing to work from a more modest attitude, all we need is a little puff of energy. The amount it takes to make a drawing or two. The amount it takes to write a single paragraph. The amount it takes to start right where we are instead of waiting for a large amount of time or a larger, more heroic version of ourselves.

So much of a creative life has to do with finding ways to quickly and smoothly cross the bridge into our creative consciousness and so much of "quickly and smoothly" has to do with humility.

I do not mean to minimize here the amount of frustration we can feel when we don't have clear spaces of time for our creativity. I know that frustration very, very well. For many years, I was a full-time single mother, a full-time writer, and a full-time teacher. It was during those years that I was forced to find ways to use time more and more effectively.

Morning Pages, which appear to take time, actually prioritize the day and tend to help keep time my own. Artist Dates, which appear to take time, actually keep my image well filled so that when I go fishing, there is something there to catch. Walking, another time-burner, generates an image flow and allows me to override my talking, worried, rational brain and listen to the shortcuts and suggestions my artist brain has to offer. Every single one of these techniques has to do with getting the most out of my time.

One of my close friends, a fellow writer, is always saying to me, "Julia, you are the most prolific writer I know." This is because I have learned simply to write. I am willing to write badly. I am willing to fix it later. I am willing to just show up on the page, obedient to my posted sign: "Okay, Higher Power, you take care of the quality; I'll take care of the quantity."

Ordinarily, when I am doing a first draft, I write three pages a day. That's ninety pages a month. That *is* prolific, but it is prolific not by virtue of long binges of work or vast savannahs of time. It is prolific because I simply start where I am—mood-wise, mess-wise—and go from there. Kabir advises, "Wherever you are is the entry point." I have found this to be true, and an enormous time-saver.

So very often, it is using time for ourselves that is the tricky part, not finding time. In order to have enough time, you do not need to own everything to the horizon. What you need is a parcel—that and a hoe and the will to use it. Creativity is more like a vegetable garden than it is like ranching or homesteading in Africa.

One of the tricks we use to be anorectic about our art is the persistent, culturally supported notion that we must have vast savannahs of time if time is to be of any use to us. In my own writing experience, which is considerable, vast savannahs of time, like vast savannahs of anything, can be daunting. If you look from your back porch to a mountain a hundred miles off, as I do, you may get a sense of the sweep of things, but you may not feel like walking the fence line. It seems overwhelming. Well, you think, I could and I could and I could and I could . . . What you could do is what you are doing, wasting

I must govern the clock, not be governed by it.

GOLDA MEIR

*. . . To get where you want
to go, you must keep on
keeping on.*
NORMAN VINCENT PEALE

Make haste slowly.
AUGUSTUS CAESAR

your time surveying the horizon, like a hunter in old-time Africa, when the plains were teeming with game and deciding what to shoot was like playing eenie-meeny-miney-moe.

Instead of trying to pick something you could do, try picking something you *would* do. Some small, manageable something that looks do-able and is. For example, on a daily basis, you would be able to find twenty minutes. Oh yes, you would.

Stop looking for the sabbatical—or even the weekend when everyone is out of the house. Solitude is wonderful, but vast swaths of it can be like bolts of vintage silk—so lovely, so hard to come by that we're reluctant to cut into them, and so they sit unused while we say we "could . . ."

Yes, we could. But we don't. It's too much of a big deal. So shrink it. Stop thinking about years, days, and hours. Start thinking of minutes. That's right: all you need is a minute amount of time. Make your time piecemeal. Start thinking of a patchwork quilt instead of time by the yard. I've been writing an extra ten minutes now. That's no big deal—keeping our creativity no big deal is what lets us do it in the first place.

Big deals are always time-consuming. Remember wanting to call someone and making a big deal out of it? Think of all the time you spent: Should I? Shouldn't I? If I do, will he . . . ? If I don't, will she . . . ?

Making something a big deal creates obsession, and obsession gobbles time. Even when we are here, we are really there.

We are all familiar with the glazed-over look first on a friend's face and then on our own as we listen to the ninetieth rendition of "does he/she love me?" Unused creativity becomes obsessional in the same way as unrequited love. We become so fixated on longing for real creative fulfillment that we skip getting any creative fulfillment at all.

Creativity is an awful lot like sex. If it always has to be great, that creates a certain amount of performance anxiety. If, instead, you experiment a little, even when you're not in the mood and don't have time for a long candlelight dinner with your muse, interesting things may start to develop. You are married to your creativity, not just out on a first date. There has to be some comfort here. There has to be some room for compassion and "bad artist days." Let yourself write badly. You can rewrite later. Paint rotten canvases. You can paint over them. Just do ten minutes at the piano. It's better than none. Think of yourself as a skittish horse. Keep the jumps small.

Dash off twenty minutes of creative noodling. Call it a kiss on the cheek. A little daily affection can be more tender than a high-voltage night on the town. Treat your creative self to a nosegay instead of a dozen roses. Perfection is a little hard to live with. Improvisation, on the other hand, can be a sweet romance.

~ Task: I Never Have Time To . . . ~

Carry a sketchbook every day for a week and sketch places where you are kept waiting. Remember that these sketches are not high art and that you do not need to be a visual artist to do them. I carried such a notebook for a year once and I still love looking back over the entries and seeing how powerfully they draw me back to memories of a time and place far behind me when I had wasted time that wasn't wasted at all because I used it so creatively.

~ Task: I Never Take Time To . . . ~

Purchase five cards or postcards. Be sure you have stamps as well. Put on your Expansion Music and note the time. This task will take you less than fifteen minutes. First, list five people you love and "never" write to because you "never" have the time. Next, work down your list and give each person a single card with a sentence or two: "I so often think about you and wish we lived closer! How are you? All's, well, well with me. Love . . ."

At the end of fifteen minutes—probably sooner—you will have freed yourself from a burden of guilt and proven to yourself that you do in fact have time for something you didn't before. All you needed to do was be willing not to make a major production when a skit would do.

Motion is the significance of life, and the law of motion is rhythm.

HAZRAT INAYAT KHAN

Economy is the art of making the most of life.

GEORGE BERNARD SHAW

Time for a little something.

A. A. MILNE

~ Task: Stay Up Late and Read a Book. ~

One of the things we often claim is, "I don't have the energy I used to have." Very often we don't have the energy because we are depressed, and we are depressed because we do not "have" the time—or make the time—to do the things we used to love doing. Any of us can survive sleep deprivation one night. Pick a book you would love to read, not one you "should" read. Let yourself wallow in the naughtiness of staying up. You may even want to treat yourself to college-style snacks—cocoa, popcorn, cookies. Make this your own party and enjoy using *your* time *your* way.

~ Task: A Stitch in Time. ~

This is another exercise in doing something we claim we never have time for—mending our clothes and our ways. To begin with, gather up a stack of things that need mending. Hand mending is best: the slightly open seam, the missing button, the lapsed hem. Get out needle, thread, and a problem you have not been able to solve.

Put on your Safety Music, set the clock for twenty minutes, and set to work on your sewing. "That so-and-so," you may find yourself thinking at the beginning. Sew on. Sew for the entire twenty minutes. At the end of this time, you will have made progress on another undo-able task—in fact, two of them. Very often, we are able to mend not only the hole in the sock but the hole in the heart as well. So often it takes only time to find compassion for ourselves and solutions for our problems.

If, when you do this task, you find yourself more than ever resolved that the rift between you and your friend or that your problem at work really is unresolvable, that's fine, too. Sometimes we need to take enough time to see where our self-esteem has been torn and mend it up a little. You've done that, too.

Containment

The first rule of magic is containment. Because we don't realize that we *are* magical, we seldom practice containment. We don't even realize we should practice it. Actually, practice *them:* our magic and our containment.

In the section on self-disclosure, we worked with the idea that as we became intimate with ourselves we could practice discretion in the personal disclosures that we *chose* to make. This essay carries that thought a step further: we are now focusing upon the kind of containment we must practice in order to give our creative projects a safe vessel in which to develop.

It is an oft-repeated bromide of twelve-step recovery that "we are only as sick as our secrets." This may be true with negative secrets, but not with positive ones—not with secret dreams. This phrase, intended to help people break through their isolation, may actually serve to isolate them further if they tell their positive secrets (a.k.a. dreams) to the wrong people.

Creative success may occur in clusters, but so does creative frustration. We tend to hang out with other people who share an invisible but perceived creative ceiling. In other words, there is a consensus about what is and isn't possible.

Most of the time, though not always, our intimates are the wrong people to tell our secret dreams to. They love us, they wish to protect

For a fortress to be secret, it must be invisible. It must have no boundaries of exclusiveness—it must be an Internal Fortress of Practice.
NGAKPA CHOGYAM

The alchemists knew the necessity of creating the inviolate vessel and giving the elixir all the time it needed to transform into gold. Our writings—that is, our innermost selves—require the same attention, patience, and seclusion.

DEENA METZGER

... The whole purpose of entering a sanctuary or participating in a festival is that one should be overtaken by the state known in India as "the other mind."

STEPHEN LARSEN

us—and not coincidentally, they wish to protect themselves. Our secret dream, to study pottery, learn Chinese, to write a novel, or stage a play, may threaten them. They may worry about our being hurt by critics—or their being left behind. Share a secret dream with a person like this and you will receive your own doubts and fears back at you.

Carl sent his first writing to his longtime friend Brigitte, a blocked writer herself. "You're not Hemingway," she shot back. (And "shot" is the operative word there.) Brigitte loves Carl, but she is a creative sniper. Blocked in her own creative expression, she fires volleys of censure at Carl for expressing his.

The practice of containment is a very healthy form of self-protection. You are excavating your own archaeological site, searching for creative gold. You do not want other people trampling the site! This is why archaeological finds are roped off and casual visitors are not welcome. Our creativity deserves the same sacred enclosure.

Yes, we need to share our secrets, but we need to share them with safe people. For this reason, creative toddler steps should be kept absolutely secret until safety is assured. When in doubt, don't.

Repeat: When in doubt, don't.

One of the most damaging ideas our culture perpetrates is the idea that we cannot trust ourselves or our perceptions. We are raised to doubt ourselves, to seek outside validation for our perceptions, to assume that someone other than ourselves can tell us our truth more clearly than we can tell ourselves.

"What do *you* think?" we are taught to ask.

Even our criminal justice system reflects an increasing dependence on expert advice. A jury of peers is no longer sufficient. It is as if we believe we are no longer equal to the task of living our own lives. Instead, our lives are led by consensus. Is it any wonder we feel dissatisfied?

The right job.

The right man.

The right car.

The right house.

The right retirement plan.

Right to whose eyes? In whose terms?

Rather than learning from our mistakes, we try not to have any! We fall into the habit of listening to others more closely than we listen to ourselves. It follows that when we begin to reverse this, listening closely to our own perceptions, we will feel some anxiety about this new behavior. Feeling that anxiety, we will need to be self-protective, which means we will need to practice containment.

Although we may not have acknowledged it previously, all of us pass through periods in life where our perceptions are not in sync with the perceptions of those around us. Anytime we are moving up to or through a major psychic change, we do so best by drawing our energy into our own core and beginning to keep our own counsel.

In other words, we must stop being guided by consensus and begin to listen more closely to that inner voice that says, "I know they all say it's [safer to live in the suburbs, impossible to sell a movie script, dumb to quit my high-paying job, necessary that I dump Ralph, whatever], but *my* instinct, which I am going to trust, is that I should not do what they say because it feels wrong to *me*."

When we are in such a self-validating passage, we often feel at odds with those around us. We must remember, in these times, that they mean well, and that the advice and mirroring they offer us is intended to support us as well as the status quo. They aren't really out to sabotage our change. They just don't want to see us get hurt.

What they don't understand—and they don't, because we don't, either—is that something in the status quo has become so painful that we are compelled to change. Even if it frightens us, the change offers us relief from a known pain. That pain may be a sense of suffocation in a high-paying job that doesn't interest us, a sense of self-loathing when we sell out our dreams because we are afraid of the odds, a feeling of claustrophobia in the homogeneity of the suburbs, or a terrible nagging sense that Ralph and I might be keeping each other from True Love rather than embodying it. The fact is, our friends worry that the unknown pain we are choosing might hurt us even more.

Of course they worry about that! So do we! That is why, as we contemplate change, we often pull back a little and stop rehearsing our lives with our loved ones.

Is this secrecy? Not really.

The quieter you become, the more you can hear.

BABA RAM DASS

*Thou shalt decree a thing,
and it shall be established
unto thee:
and the light shall shine
upon thy ways.*
JOB 22:28

*The beginnings of all things
are weak and tender. We
must therefore be clear-
sighted in beginnings....*
MICHEL EYQUEM DE
MONTAIGNE

The first rule of magic is containment, remember? Whenever we want our life to be more magical, we put this principle into action by beginning to build a sacred space in which our dream is alive and well and doubt is not allowed. In other words, we draw a circle of safety, and we rehearse not the reasons to stay stuck, but the possible reasons to take the risk we are drawn to.

Friends, for all their friendship, often find it hard to offer room enough for dreams. Whenever we move into trusting our dreams, we move into territory that both thrills and threatens those who watch us with interested eyes. "I believe I can" we say—can sell a novel, find another job, live without Ralph.

"Maybe that's just your ego," a well-meaning friend will often respond.

The idea that something is "just our ego" suggests a nasty duality. If we want something and that desire is just our ego, then we and the Universe are truly at odds. The "something" is smart and wonderful, while we are just a bunch of shallow, shortsighted dummies.

Ours is a thoroughly Calvinist culture. We are taught that our desires for fun, pleasure, and delight are somehow ungodly. We are taught that renunciation and martyrdom are spiritually superior. Even if we renounce our Western religious training, we often espouse an Eastern spirituality that asserts that all matter is illusion, *maya*, something other than and removed from God.

Frankly, I don't believe any of this anymore.

We are the Universe. We are made of it and it is made of us. If it is intelligent, we are intelligent. If it is wise and all-knowing, so are we. If it knows what is best for us, we too know what is best. There is no separation between God and us, God and matter. It is all consciousness. We are all consciousness. We are God dreaming God. We are God making God. We are creators co-creating the Universe. If we can trust the Universe, then we can trust ourselves.

Even better, if we can trust ourselves, then we can trust the Universe. Although many creative people have suffered excessively at the hands of envious and destructive friends, we seldom jump to the conclusion that criticism may spring from envy or insecurity. "Why would anyone be jealous of me?" we wonder, feeling the tremulous nature of our own creative unfolding. The joy of creativity is so innocent, it has so little to do with others and their perceptions, that we do not realize that from the outside it looks like power, and that power can be threatening.

When I have worked in academic environments, I have often found the faculty to be apprehensive and hostile when faced with the exuberance of raw creative talent.

Creativity is alive and breathing. It is, in fact, the breath of life. Brainchildren must be treated like children. They are not to be hurled onto the operating table and dissected. Time enough to shape (not dissect) a piece of work after it has found form. Trying to find form prematurely, trying to force form, is unnatural and inappropriate and inhuman.

Just remain in the center, watching. And then forget that you are there.

LAO-TZU

As experienced artists know, sometimes a piece of work needs a little time to find its legs. Its early steps, toddling but in the right direction, may be promising but unsteady. They are, after all, baby steps. Do not let someone break the baby's knees in order to straighten out its gait! In other words, practice containment. Put differently, do not give away the gold.

"But what gold? How will I know the gold?"

You will know the gold. Not immediately, perhaps, but eventually. It takes time to trust that your creative bliss may be enjoyable to others. It takes time, and it takes locating the right others. Most creative people are far too afraid of being grandiose and far too unaware of the possibility of being crippled. In the glow and exhilaration of a creative breakthrough—a first song, painting, poem—we want to show it to the world. We are like little kids. We want to crow, "I did it! I did it!"

Don't do it. Crows are considered noisy birds and are often told to shut up!

Don't show. Don't tell. A first song played to the wrong person may be the last song. A first painting criticized by a critical eye may be the last painting in what was to have been a series.

But shouldn't we toughen up?

No. In order to be creative we must be vulnerable. We block our creativity when we toughen up. The same hard shell that protects us keeps us from being open to our own experience. Shutting down to protect ourselves from creative pain, we shut out creative joy. And so you must draw a sacred circle, a protective ring, around yourself and your fledgling work. Think of yourself as a creative child and your work as brainchildren. Remember that not all of your adult friends are friendly.

At the risk of being repetitive, I will say it again: some of your friends, maybe even most of them, may be blocked in their own creativity. Blocked people are typically very critical. François Truffaut maintained that film critics were blocked directors. As a critic, he himself was, and his criticism was earmarked by a deadly stinginess, just as his films were marked by luminosity, generosity, and light.

What your friends may comfortably call discernment actually may be a perverse perfectionism that sets standards so high they can never be successfully met—not by you, and certainly not by them! It's easy to see what the payoff is, really. If no work of art is ever good enough, we don't need to make the nasty stuff, do we? Leave it to a few certified creative geniuses. The rest of us can just sit on the sidelines and cavil.

Blocked creatives are like village gossips. They delight in bad fortune, and good fortune makes them very, very nasty. Before you show, tell, mention any fledgling creative endeavor to someone, ask yourself: is it even possible that this person might be blocked, envious, threatened? Be compassionate to your blocked creative friends. (And remember, they may not look blocked to the casual eye.) But be far more compassionate to yourself. Practice containment. The results will be magic.

> *Some people will never learn anything ... because they understand everything too soon.*
> ALEXANDER POPE

～ Task: Creative Snipers. ～

List ten friends you consider to be creative snipers, those who take potshots at your efforts.

You know who they are. They're the people who mirror you back to yourself as smaller and more helpless than you are. These are the people who say, when you tell them you are writing a screenplay, "Do you know the odds of selling an original script?" (Higher than the odds of selling one that isn't written.) Some people, doing this exercise, find that no names come to mind at all. Claire, a publicist, put it this way, "I had a childhood full of them. Now I've got them weeded out!" If that's true, that's excellent, but it's seldom true.

Look in both your childhood and your adulthood for your snipers. You may have weeded them out, or you may be practicing denial about having them.

~ Task: Believing Mirrors. ~

List ten friends you consider to be believing mirrors—those who mirror back your dreams in a possible, positive, affirming way. Every artist needs a few good friends. Not sycophants, but positive thinkers. As creative beings we *need* believing mirrors. These are people who mirror back to you the possibility in you and your work.

Find yours and cultivate them.

All Higher Self communication begins in the heart.
SANAYA ROMAN

Getting Current

"I'm sorry I didn't get back to you sooner," we gasp to a beloved friend. "I haven't had a chance to get current!"

We all know what we mean by that. We mean that our lives have been rolling over us, pell-mell, and we have been caught in the thresher of speed and events. Our personal priorities—friendship, family, creative projects—have gotten mishandled or misplaced. Our lives have not been our own doing.

"I know I should have called you sooner. I wanted to, but . . ." (But I was swept along, pummeled, overworked, underappreciated, stressed out, strung out . . . miserable.)

"Let me get back to you when I get back to me."

What we are really talking about here is the act of getting current and staying current with ourselves. We are talking about the act of checking in, honoring ourselves, our intentions, perceptions, and intuitions. We are talking about something very simple that is often difficult to do amid hurly-burly. We are talking about paying attention to what we love.

Many spiritual teachers call such conscious, moment-to-moment focus being "mindful." I like to call it "getting current" because it has less to do, for me, with mind than spirit. I am checking in less to see what I think with my mind than what I know with all of me: body, mind, and spirit.

The poet Mary Oliver writes beautifully on this:

You do not have to be good.
You do not have to walk on your knees
For a hundred miles through the desert, repenting.
You only have to let the soft animal of your body
Love what it loves.

But what do we love? For that matter, what do we hate, resent, envy, or dream? We must ask to know the answers.

"How do *I* feel about that?" is an exceedingly valuable question, one posed daily by Morning Pages, by walking with ourself whenever we sense we are in the rapids or snagged by a submerged log. "What do *I* think?" "What would *I* like to do?" our line of questioning might continue.

We are checking our circuits, looking for where our circuits are blown or shut down. This is delicate work, work that requires care and consciousness. All dealings with electricity require focus. Dealing with creative current is no exception. "Getting current" requires attention to detail in both the inner and outer realm.

When we take the time to ask and answer questions like these, we move from watching the inner movie of our own unresolved preoccupations to a clear-eyed and authentic encounter with the world. As artists, that is our job. Ours is the front line, not the ivory tower. Too often we hang back, afraid that our creative urges are "just our ego." It is my belief that they are a sacred imperative, a spiritual job. We are meant not only to get current but to use that current.

"You must give birth to your images. They are the future waiting to be born," poet Rainer Maria Rilke urged us. But in order to give birth to our images, we must contact them and know what they are.

When we are not current with ourselves, we tune out on our lives and our environments. The world around us becomes lackluster, even invisible. Far from filling our creative wells with an inflow of fresh images and their resultant insights and art, our vision is blurred by the veil of self-absorption. Our world worsens for our lack of attention.

Existence is sustained by the on-off pulse, the alternating current of the two forces in perfect balance. Unchecked, the life force is cancer; unbridled, the death force is war and genocide.

STARHAWK

*Genius is mainly an affair of
energy....*
MATTHEW ARNOLD

*Know the true value of time;
snatch, seize, and enjoy
every moment of it. No idleness, no laziness, no procrastination; never put off till
tomorrow what you
can do today.*
LORD CHESTERFIELD

To get current, we must deliberately and decisively focus on our-selves and our concerns. When we avoid such focusing on ourselves, we avoid focusing at all.

There is a reason we call it "getting current." We are quite liter-ally talking about dowsing for the flow of juice or electricity in our lives. The energy of the body can be thought of as rivers. When we seek our enthusiasms and honor our true loves, we are working like spiritual geomancers to find the underground stream that flows with force and majesty. It is always there when we stop and seek it. When we do so, we find the nurturing sap, the vital flow of our lives.

Getting current works wonders for the flow of creative energy. Current, we move *with* the current. We move at our pace, find our thoughts less snagged and troubled by the whirlpools of others' emotions and agendas. *We* have the "juice" to act—and act we have to!

Writer and mystic Mechtild of Magdeburg speaks of every artist's dilemma, every artist's war between self-effacement and the necessity of fulfilling his or her creative role: "I am forced to write these words regarding which I should have gladly kept silent out of fear of vainglory. But I have learned to fear more the judgment of God should I, God's little creature, keep silent."

In other words, we must not only "get current," we must use that current to act. Some of us, additionally, will use our creativity to help us get current. Often when I feel stymied in a relationship, I will write a poem or a song "at" the sticking point. It could be said that pointing my pen is pointing a finger, but I prefer to think of it more like the pointer on a compass. Writing points me toward True North.

When we get current with ourselves as individuals, we tap more forcefully into the flow of universal energy. One way to think of this is to imagine "us" (humankind) as a sort of giant pipe organ. We are all one huge creative consciousness and yet each of us, individually, is a pipe. Each pipe both partakes of the whole and informs it. When we are current, our personal energy channel is clear. This allows us to both draw from and pump into the universal creative consciousness a greater volume—voltage, to continue our metaphor—of creative power.

Task: Getting Current. ~~~

One of the best ways to get current is to write very quickly, so quickly that we do not allow our hand to stop moving as we free-associate on certain "loaded" phrases. The trick is to go very quickly and to repeat the phrase often enough to work down through our layers of denial. Here are some phrases that I complete twenty times each whenever I want to get current. Take pen in hand and try them twenty times each yourself:

1. If I let myself admit it, I feel . . .

2. If I let myself admit it, I think . . .

3. If I let myself know it, I suspect . . .

4. If I let myself enjoy it, I am . . .

5. If I let myself have permission, I could . . .

The crisis of yesterday is the joke of tomorrow.

H. G. WELLS

Well begun is half done.

HORACE

~~~ Task: Get Current in Your Household. ~~~

This is another task that, like the painting task, will give you an immediate, visible result. It is also very cathartic. Begin by finding one or two large cardboard cartons. Now, go through your house and into one of the cartons toss all of the extraneous papers you have accumulated—except for ten old magazines with pictures that you will be using later.

This means that into the box go newspapers, old letters you really won't reread, scraps of wrapping paper that you don't really like, broken-down smaller boxes, at least some of the nine hundred folded paper bags you have been saving for the day you will need them to take groceries back to the store. You get the idea. Work until you can see some clean surfaces, until you have some empty drawers again. Dispose of this paper carton as seems environmentally best to you.

Carton number two is for closets and clothing drawers. Into it goes all your "low-self-worth clothing" to be quickly followed by those things that are lovely *but you just don't wear*. Be a little ruthless.

Look at that wardrobe and pare it down, toss it out, send it back into the Universe. How can anything new come into a life that is over-stuffed with everything old? On with the show!

～ Task: Get Current in Your Spiritual House. ～

For this task, you will need a shoe box or small carton and a good dose of honesty. Set aside an hour of uninterrupted time. Cue up your Safety Music and write out the attitudes and toxic habits you wish to clear from your life. Do you waste time gossiping? Do you have a habit of junk food, reading, or TV? What about envy? Do you indulge in resenting others instead of taking steps toward what they have which you covet?

(Those of you who worked with the Artist's Way may remember the "Jealousy Map," which asked you to name those you were jealous of, exactly why, and what action step you could take toward whatever they embodied that you yearned for.)

This is a good time to take a look at the Deadlies. Have you sabo-taged yourself through alcohol, drugs, food, overwork, draining rela-tionships, needy friends, toxic sex, over- or underexercise? Write out your negative inventory.

When you have finished writing out what you want to be rid of, toss that paper into the shoe box. Now you have a chance to be cre-atively, constructively destructive: burn the box or bury it!

Breaking Camp

Congratulations on having completed a difficult and necessary kingdom. The housecleaning you have accomplished will stand you in good stead as you move forward. Before we do, let's take a look at what it is you have just done for yourself. Taking the time to acknowledge the difficult work you have undertaken can help you to a greater confidence in your capacity to undertake and bring to fruition creative projects. A backward glance then:

You have inventoried the times when patience has served you. You've used this muscle to paint a brighter present. You've focused on what risks you would like the courage to undertake. You've begun dancing into those risks one baby step at a time. You've surveyed your environment for the qualities you value and want more of. You have symbolically opened yourself to more of these traits. You've revisited your past, place by place, reconnecting to the parts of you that each embodied. You've faced down boredom by trying your hand at the worth of simple pleasures and you have turned your hand to the snowflake intricacies of your unique creativity. You have found time to get current with yourself and you have found the resultant energy to build a protective circle of creative containment.

Good work and lots of it! With these attitude adjustments as part of your creative repertoire, you now move into the challenging Kingdom of Relationship.

The
Kingdom of
Relationship

We have been traveling for some time now in our inner landscape, encountering our own internal resistance, developing our stamina and spiritual dexterity. We have altered our attitudes and we have gained in altitude. We have reached a higher and clearer perspective on the terrain of our lives. At this point in the our pilgrimage, we are about to begin the thrust to reach the summit. This means we must now evaluate our relationships with absolute clarity and choose as our continued companions only those whom we can really trust.

Now is the time to scrutinize, sort, and discard those patterns of relationship that no longer serve you and will jeopardize you as you push for the heights. My friend Julianna McCarthy, a consummate actress with the beauty and ruthless discernment of a Celtic queen, calls this point in the journey, "Who would you take to the war?"

What an interesting, terrible, *useful* question! Ask it and we may discover many who cannot be brought forward with us. We suddenly see, "Oh, Phyllippa would sleep with the enemy. Terry would compete, arguing about strategy instead of helping get the troops across the mountains. Andrew would never be able to execute what we planned. Joyce would want me to carry her pack as well as my own. . . ."

The challenge of the Kingdom of Relationships is to become self-serving in the very highest sense.

Equality

Many very creative people feel guilty about claiming the gold in their own lives and personalities. This kingdom's work is aimed at sifting through our lives and reclaiming our power. Sourced in the Universe, we are each of us, esoteric Egyptian teachings tell us, the direct recipient of "the Golden Ray." Gilt, after all, can be spelled two ways!

One of the most difficult, pivotal, and threatening principles of creative recovery is very simple: we are all equal. There are no stepchildren in the Universe. We all know the right Someone, or if you prefer, the right Something. In order to contact sufficient force to alter our destiny, we need only go within—which is what all of the tools in this book are designed to help you do. Going within, none of us needs an agent, or even an operator. We all have a direct dial.

"Ah, yes, equal . . . mm . . . Yes, I suppose we are in the absolute sense," a friend of mine chuckles nervously.

We *all* chuckle a little nervously at this concept of true equality. We may like to believe that the idea of *inequality* is what threatens us, but it's not so. We're used to that idea. We all know all about "insiders" and "outsiders" and "favorites." We've grown up with these concepts . . . or should I say excuses? (Don't sugarcoat it!)

If we are all equal, then we don't need to hide our light under a bushel to save the feelings of others—be they parents, spouses, blocked friends. If we are all equal, then we have a right to use our talents and a right to expect those talents to be appreciated and supported. If we are all equal, then the support for those gifts may come from anywhere—we have an equal draw on the Universe, although the form it takes may surprise us.

In other words, if we are all equal, the "odds" don't matter. There's no such thing as odds.

Of course there are odds, we want to say. And the odds are against me. (Or, alternatively, the odds are against other people, so I shouldn't be greedy or take my share because then they'll feel bad.)

Forget about it.

That's right. People who believe in odds already feel bad. They've joined a club of their own devising. They are the also-rans, the "outsiders," even the losers. It's actually a comfy little club because you don't have to do much in it. You can just complain about how "they"—the insiders, the winners, the lucky ones—won't let you do much.

Among our culture's many toxic myths about artists is yet another one, the idea that there is a magic insiders' club that determines who makes it and who doesn't. "It's all politics," you'll hear disgruntled artists say. "It's all who you know, not what you do." This is a seductive block. If the game is really rigged, why even bother to try? If you have to know the "right people," why try to do the real work? "They" are against you anyway.

But who are "they"?

They are our own ideas, our fears or misapprehensions, our predetermined ceilings for our worth. They are not other people. If we are all equals, no human being has the power to block our good. Think of a pipe organ. If our good can come to us from any of the pipes, why focus on the fact that a few appear to be blocked to us?

So who are "they" again? They are our perceptions that some people have more power than we do. To be precise, we believe that some people have the power to say yes or no to our dreams.

Even at the remove of the written page, I can hear you thinking, "Oh, come on, Julia! This is too much . . . too New Age . . . too metaphysical . . . too . . ." Threatening?

Life is *sacred. Life* is *art.*
Life is *sacred art.*
GABRIELLE ROTH

The sage is one who has first discovered what is common in our hearts. MENCIUS

If we are all equal, we are all equally sourced. We all have access to support that can empower us if we will just encounter it.

"That's a big if," you might say.

Yes and no. Accessing this power is really a decision. All too often when we want something, we choose a source for it to come to us. This source is typically a specific person or company. If they do what we want, then . . .

But "if they do what we want" gives away our power. It gives the other party power over us. Of course, that power is an illusion, but it doesn't matter. As long as we believe someone has power over us, they do. As long as accessing power for us is someone else's job, we don't have to do it ourselves. Further, we can continue to believe that we can't.

"If only my agent were more aggressive," we whine, turning aside our friend's offer to send the manuscript to his friend in publishing.

"If only Hiram would send me those tapes of our great songs from ten years ago," we grumble, and we don't call the composer who said he needed a lyricist, *now!*

No wonder we are steeped in our resentments. In a world where we are not equal, where we must hold on to every advantage, every toehold on the hill, we must also hold other people to our agendas—whether the agendas continue to serve us or not.

"If only Robert would help me with this video. I know it would be good if we did it together. We've always collaborated well. So why quit now? It's hard to find someone else. . . ."

"If only Adrienne hadn't quit as my assistant," we grumble at the office, too surly to interview someone new, happier wallowing in the mess of our affairs—a good excuse to function poorly for a little while and get some sympathy for it, too! How delicious it is to wallow in the injustice of the "system" rather than ask: "Is there *anything* more for me to do myself?"

So much energy is wasted knocking on doors that won't open and refusing to walk through others that open to the touch. We pound on the door to certain establishments, wanting someone, the *right* someone, to open the door, invite us in, and certify us as "real" artists. We crave a stamp of approval we are meant to give to ourselves. Ironically, when we all give ourselves, by our own hand, the dignity we crave and the right to support and validate our own work, so many locked doors mysteriously open.

"I am living in the expectancy that every good thing in my life is multiplied," wrote Dr. Ernest Holmes. It is our job to maintain that expectancy in ourselves.

"The timing isn't ours," says my friend Dusty, but it is ours to remember that "not yet" does not mean "No."

"Build it and they will come," the hero of Phil Alden Robinson's movie *Field of Dreams* is advised by a mysterious voice. Trusting that voice, he builds a ball field in the middle of an Iowa cornfield. To his surprise, "they" do come—not only the mythic ballplayers of his dreams, but also fellow dreamers who believed in them as well.

When I left home to be a writer, I left with fifty dollars and dreams. Six months later I was writing on the arts for the *Washington Post*. How did that happen? I had no contacts. I had no letter of introduction. What I had was an old high school friend who called me to say there was a job opening, sorting mail, did I want it?

When I went for an interview, the editor, Tom Kendricks, said, "I hope you don't think you're a writer."

"I am a writer," I told him. "I hope you don't think I'm a journalist." (I kept on writing.)

Kendricks saw something in my bravado, because I got the job. Six weeks later on his way out to dinner, Kendricks stopped by my desk. "What's the matter? You look depressed," he said.

"I just typed a story for tomorrow's section and it stinks," I told him.

"If you think you can do better . . . ," he said.

And so, I wrote my first story while he was at dinner. The following Sunday, it ran Style front, as the arts section was called. In the next six months, I had lots of stories Style front, and lots of book reviews and magazine pieces, too, thanks to the believing faith of Bill McPherson and Shelby Coffey.

When it came time to hire a reporter full-time, however, their support was little aid: this was back when hiring young women

One of the reasons our society has become such a mess is that we're isolated from each other.

MAGGIE KUHN

Fair play is primarily not blaming others for anything that is wrong with us.

ERIC HOFFER

wasn't considered a necessary thing to do. And so, I thanked them, quit my letter-opening job, and went back to writing short stories. Six weeks into that, *Rolling Stone* called me up—they'd read me in the *Post*—and my career in journalism took off again. *Against all odds...*

The point is, the "odds" were against my getting breaks like these. The point is, the odds don't matter. The point is, there's no such thing as odds. Consider this prayer from Ernest Holmes.

> As I desire to do only that which is good and constructive, life-giving and life-expressing, the Divine Abundance forever manifests in my endeavors. Therefore I know that I shall prosper in everything I do. I know that I exist in limitless possibility and that the infinite Good is right where I am and active in my experience.

⌇ Task: Write a Positive Prayer. ⌇

Using your own words, write a prayer that states firmly and powerfully that you are, in fact, not a victim but a fully endowed creative being whose possibilities for growth and accomplishment are unlimited:

> Beloved Source,
>
> I gratefully claim my birthright as a fully endowed child of the Universe. I accept that for every need of mine, there is a universal flow waiting to fill it. I thank you for that flow. I thank you for the divine plan of goodness for me and my work. I accept and embrace the idea that there is no dream too large for the two of us to accomplish together. I open my limited thinking to your unlimited creativity. I invite you to move through me as a channel, pushing my creative ideas into the world as an extension of the divine nature that I share with you....

In the act of writing this prayer, you may meet with inner resistance in the form of historical situations and beliefs that you blame for blocking you. Write the prayer anyway and then move on to the next task.

～ Task: Illuminate Your Prayer. ～

Many of the most beautiful documents of the Middle Ages are scriptures that were painstakingly "illuminated" by monks as part of their spiritual practice. A sacred document like your prayer deserves such treatment.

Go to the five-and-dime or an art-supply shop. Get yourself a small bottle of gilt paint and a brush. Gold gilt pens and markers also are often available. Working with either a calligraphy pen or a printed copy if you prefer, write out your prayer, decorate it, and post it. You may wish to use the trick I learned in grammar school: burn the edges of your paper with a match to make it look like a "real" antique.

That is why art as meditation is so democratizing a movement: It returns responsibility to each of us for the images we believe in. And with the responsibility goes the fun. MATTHEW FOX

～ Task: The Blame Game, Round One—Events. ～

Please list ten historical situations that you perceive as blocking your good. Next, list ways in which you can remedy this in your current life.

- If I'd gone to a better college, I'd have better intellectual self-worth. (Take a night course or a correspondence course in an area where you feel weak.)

- If I'd had more supportive parents, I'd have been able to talk out my options and get some guidance. (Seek out older friends or relatives, a minister, or social worker and ask to talk through your current options.)

- If I hadn't poured all of my energy into Harry's career, I'd have my own master's degree by now. (Send off for information about master's degrees in your field. List all of the great things you did for Harry and do at least one of them for yourself.)

*A man cannot be comfort-
able without his own
approval.*
MARK TWAIN

1. _____.

2. _____.

3. _____.

4. _____.

5. _____.

6. _____.

7. _____.

8. _____.

9. _____.

10. _____.

*Remember that you are listing not only the problem but also the so-
lution!*

The Voluntary Victim

One of the most potent lies we tell ourselves is that our life is someone else's fault. If only they . . . then we . . .

Almost always, if we are stewing up a nice big resentment, we're stalling. We know what it is we'd like to do and what it is we need to do, and we're not quite ready to do it yet, so we blame someone else for our feelings of discomfort. Our sense that we need to move on and take an action is duking it out with our desire to remain safe and sorry. The punching bag in this internal dialogue becomes our friend, our boss—almost anyone who can stand in for our quavering self, poised on the diving board but not ready to jump yet.

Rage and blame are often symptoms of impending change. Change is frightening for many of us much of the time. We resist it, and the way we do it is by blaming someone else for the state we're in (angry and frustrated) so that we don't have to do anything that might make us less angry and less frustrated. Blame and resentment keep us stuck in the victim slot. They create blinders that make it difficult to see our options. If we "have to wait for a phone call" from a thoughtless friend who left us hanging, then we don't need to change clothes and habit patterns and get out the door to see the new play we have two free tickets for, do we?

Anger creates adrenaline. Adrenaline makes us feel strong. Strong is what we want to feel—not vulnerable, not frightened, not

> *Some people actively retain illness and energy blockages, usually because it is more convenient or familiar to live this way.*
>
> CAITLIN MATTHEWS

open to new events, people, places, and experiences. Strong but stuck: there's a nice, secure position!

Doing it wrong is what we are trying to avoid, and so we often avoid doing it at all. We avoid by blaming someone else and getting good and mad at them. We pump up our systems with adrenaline and anger or fear until we are drugged by our body's own chemicals.

"If he weren't such a jerk, not calling, leaving me that weird message with the secretary, then I'd be feeling calm and centered enough to try writing out this phrase of music. . . ."

Who says (besides our Inner Perfectionist, who is always doing sit-ups) that we have to feel calm and centered to write out a piece of music? Maybe we can feel and be a wreck and do it anyway. Maybe we can do it and do it wrong and fix it later. Maybe we do not have to be or perform perfectly. Maybe we are allowed to have a learning curve. Maybe part of what we need to learn is a little compassion. Of course we're afraid to try something new: writing out a piece of music, making a monoprint, sewing a set of curtains! We may have never done it before!

The fact that we have never done something before inspires no compassion in our Inner Perfectionist. No, to the contrary, that is exactly when he sharpens his little claws. The needling begins when we even think about doing something at which we have no demonstrable track record of success—and it doesn't really matter whether that something is love or music or riding a horse saddle seat. What matters to our Inner Perfectionist (*all* that matters to our Inner Perfectionist) is that we are about to pry loose its hold on our life and actually live a little.

The Inner Perfectionist is a gatekeeper. It is helpful to think of it (it/him/her—whatever form it is currently taking, and the form does change, at least for me) as a well-programmed, not particularly imaginative troll. This troll is just carrying out its orders to keep you from straying off a certain path. It has strict instructions not to allow any exploration, any wandering into the woods of invention or imagination. Why, you could be hurt in there!

So if you can't get your Inner Perfectionist to muster up any compassion for you—and I'd say the odds are slim—then try mastering

Loneliness is the way by which destiny endeavors to lead man to himself.
HERMANN HESSE

Too much agreement kills a chat.
ELDRIDGE CLEAVER

some compassion for the poor little troll your Inner Perfectionist really is. *Its* Inner Perfectionist won't let it do anything differently. Maybe it, too, wonders about the woods of invention. Maybe your expedition into the unknown world of music or drawing or an improv class sounds pretty intriguing to it. No wonder it's setting up such a racket! You're . . . *changing the rules*. And the rules cannot be changed.

If this sounds like the world of Alice in Wonderland, it is. Some things do make you bigger, and taking risks is one of them. Not taking risks is the way we insist on staying small. I want to give you two very painful case histories to drive this point home. If you find yourself thinking, "Enough! Enough! Enough!" the stories are probably hitting a nerve. Many of us have wasted considerable time and energy blaming others for "trapping us" in our own lives.

Clarisse, a wanna-be writer, was a hardworking single mother— too hardworking, too single, as she'd be the first to tell you, but that was her daughter's fault. "My daughter needs a real mother," she would volunteer.

"If I had time, I'd write," Clarisse said.

Of course, Clarisse had time, but she used it reading other people's books. She used it watching television and videos about other people's lives. Clarisse got her adventure vicariously. Although officially she bore up nobly and bravely, Clarisse was really a bitter and timorous woman, unwilling to commit herself to change, to growth, to risk, or vulnerability. At root, she was jealous and not a little judgmental.

"Maybe a man could find the stamina to write," Clarisse would tell herself, echoing her mother's dictum that men could have real dreams while women could have daydreams. And so, dutifully, Clarisse had married a man who could do what she herself had dreamed of doing: write a book. Typing his pages, editing his awkward phrases, Clarisse made herself a live-in Florence Nightingale, nursing his book to health.

"How could he leave me after all I did for him?" she wondered, reviewing her fate to her long-suffering friends. "'Write your own book,' he finally told me. Where would I find the time?"

I'm not going to limit myself because people won't accept the fact that I can do something else.

DOLLY PARTON

You've got to find the force inside you.

JOSEPH CAMPBELL

It would be good to find some quiet inlet where the waters were still enough for reflection, where one might sense the joy of the moment, rather than plan breathlessly for a dozen mingled treats in the future.

KATHLEEN NORRIS

One of the oddest things in life, I think, is the things one remembers.

AGATHA CHRISTIE

Lest this sound too sexist, let me be clear that men are equally adroit at binding their lives to the wheel of obligation, blaming family and responsibility for their irresponsibility to themselves.

Justin is a very fine painter—when he finds time to do it. His real claim to fame, the one he is known for, is being a perfect father. Not for him any absentee fathering! Every single night, he is there with his three sons. He eats with them, watches TV with them, tucks them into bed. What little painting he manages is an hour or two on the weekend—unless the boys have another agenda that takes precedence.

"What can I do? They're only young once," he says virtuously. Although no one has the nerve to point it out, Justin is working on being young twice; he uses his kids to avoid responsibility to his own adult dreams. This is very different from using your creativity to model its use for your children.

My father had a basement workroom where he made furniture—a wonderful bench out of an old headboard, a trunk that opened from its seat. He also made picture frames and used many of them to frame our work. I remember my excitement when one of my paintings made it into the living room, but I also remember that there was a framed crayon drawing of my sister's palomino horse, "Miss Caroline," that hung amid the photos in the basement game room.

As a young man, my father had played the banjo. He gave that up but set up a music room for his kids, even building a washtub bass and teaching my sister to play it. At our house we had two pianos, one good one and one old honky-tonk that I was allowed to paint with gold leaf. One was upstairs and one was downstairs. Both of them were almost always occupied.

As a young woman, my mother worked with my dad as a writer-editor combo, but later, when she was a "full-time" mother of seven, she still wrote regularly—poems for all manner of family occasions and many, many letters—often filled with a leaf pressed between waxed paper or some other bit of beauty she had found. Both my parents modeled creativity in their own lives.

One project I remember with particular affection is the time that my mother and I made gilded pinecones for Christmas baskets. I still keep a huge basket of pinecones here where I write. They are a touchstone for me of creative joy.

In her fifties, my mother suddenly took a belly-dancing class. We were all astounded and a little mortified. ("Never marry a man who can't dance," she told me once. This was probably her solution to the fact that she had.)

In his sixties, my father took his first acting job since college, playing a priest in my movie *God's Will.*

My parents worked very hard and they did not do everything perfectly—but they did remember to play. Because of their example, all seven Cameron siblings are active creatively. (Truth be told, I find my siblings a little bit dazzling in the multiplicity of their gifts.) And so, whether you are parenting flesh-and-blood children or your Creative Child, I say, play a little; it will change your life a lot.

People are always good company when they are doing what they really enjoy.

SAMUEL BUTLER

~ Task: The Blame Game, Round Two—People. ~

Please list ten people whom you blame for curtailing your endeavors. What do they "keep" you from doing? How can you get around this?

- My children: no time to paint. (Move an easel into the TV room with them.)

- My sister: always on the phone with me at night during my writing time. (Let the machine pick up after six.)

- My jealous friend: never encourages me to take risks. (Stop telling her the risks I am planning.)

1. _____.

2. _____.

3. _____.

4. _____.

5. _____.

6. _____.

7. _____.

8. _____.

9. _____.

10. _____.

Now that you have listed what you could do to get out of the victim slot in each of these situations, choose one of the above and actually do it. When you have, cross it off your list and move on to a second item. This list, like your Morning Pages and your Narrative Time Line, should be kept for your eyes only, but it would be best if you kept it where you could refer to it often. As you move on to some of the more threatening shifts, you might wish to engage the help of one of your cluster list people to support you in making the shift. I call this making a creative sandwich. Here's the recipe.

You: I'm going to do it. I'm going to _____.

Ally: Okay. Call me back right after.

You: I did it! I _____!

∼ Task: Play a Little. ∼

Very often when I teach I am asked, "Julia, what can we do to help our kids stay creative?"

"Stay creative yourself," I answer. "If you are practicing your own creativity you will know exactly how to foster it in your kids. Besides, kids learn from what we do, not from what we say."

I think back for a moment to my own childhood, the long winter afternoons making paper ornaments with my mother, multi-pointed stars covered in paraffin and glitter. Our house, made by an old Swedish woodworker, had a winding spiral staircase. My mother used the staircase as a rotating gallery: Matisse, Van Gogh, Gauguin, Monet, one by one, a month at a time, just to give us a taste. My guitar-playing siblings were excused from dish duty. If they would serenade, my music-loving mother happily scrubbed. The following five things are difficult to do without feeling just a little bit playful, just a little bit non-martyred. Please do all of them!

1. Buy yourself a bell. Very often import stores such as Pier One Imports have bells or chains of bells that cost very little. Five-and-dimes and fabric stores have small silver bells that can be sewn on your socks or threaded through the laces on your sneakers. It is almost impossible to be depressed when you make a merry, tinkling sound with every step.

No one can make you feel inferior without your consent.
ELEANOR ROOSEVELT

2. Buy or make yourself a rattle. Get dried beans from the health food store. Fill and decorate a tin can or container. The kind that foreign teas come in make excellent little rattles. Use your rattle every time your energy gets "stuck."

3. Buy or make your favorite, very favorite childhood food. There is something about chocolate pudding or Jell-O with marshmallows that does cheer us up.

4. Make Christmas cookies no matter what time of year it is. You can invite one of your clustermates to do this with you or you can bake some and send them as a madcap gift—as well as remembering to eat some yourself.

5. Make homemade fudge or homemade vegetable soup. Make enough that you can freeze some. Make enough that you can give some away.

Where Does It Hurt?

When our feelings are stung, and those stung feelings affect our artist's capacity to function, we can usually find ourselves repeating some telltale phrase that is the clue to what it is that's ailing us.

My unlisted phone number rang during my writing time. Thinking it was my teaching partner, I picked up the phone.

Anger is an integrity-producing response to the invasion of your personal boundaries.
GABRIELLE ROTH

"Hi," I said. A strange woman was on the other end. I explained that it was my writing time, not a good time for me to talk. No matter. She couldn't hear the boundary.

"But I *want* to talk to you," the caller went on. She explained that she was having trouble with her creative life but didn't want to do any work that involved "inner child."

"I've never found creativity that didn't involve it," I said. "My experience is that unfaced inner-child wounds tend to sabotage our creative projects. I think of it like the Loch Ness monster. You're drawing this calm lake and suddenly a weird neck and head come poking up from nowhere. . . . That's your inner child's Creative Monster saying, 'You can't!'"

"Maybe," the woman said doubtfully. "But your work isn't what I want to do."

"Then don't do it," I told her. "It's up to you. I can't make that decision for you."

"I wasn't asking you to make it . . . ma'am," she snapped, sarcasm dripping through the phone.

Ouch! I got off the phone and went for my rattles—toys I keep to remind me to lighten up. I shook a few rattles. Stomped my feet. Shook my hands like a rag doll. Did "bug-a-bug-a-bug-a!" And I was bugged. *It wasn't fair* that she'd called and interrupted my work and been mean. *It wasn't fair. . . .*

I asked myself, Now, where did that come from? Did I have a painful pattern of "it isn't fair"? Was it being retriggered?

Yes! My telltale phrase was the iceberg's tip.

As an artist, I must remain vulnerable to pain or I will not have the sensitivity necessary to do my work. Ideally, we want our adult self and our artist child in constant communication. In this way, the adult can function not as a tyrant, but as a defender of the vulnerable artist self, while the artist self can function as a guide, playmate, and companion to the world-weary adult. I must listen to both of me.

As an artist, my worst angers and depressions center around the feelings of my artist self who, like a child, is very vulnerable to being frightened, bullied, hurt, and discouraged. I am not alone in this. I often feel that the greatest healing that comes out of creative clusters is the simple opportunity to tell each other "where it hurts," because hurt it does!

Danieli, a gifted set designer, mysteriously fell afoul of his director on a large project. Nothing was said, but suddenly Danieli was no longer included or welcome at key meetings. Because of the ambiguity, Danieli began to feel paranoid and defensive. At all times on the set, he felt he was walking on eggshells. Even now, at a decade's remove, the memory is very painful for him, and he suffers from artistic scar tissue.

The crazymaking director that Danieli worked for knew very well that he could engender paranoia by cloaking his thoughts in secrecy. His movies were known for their conspiracies full of Machiavellian intrigue, and so was his daily life. Hapless Danieli, who was a sunny man with a preference for bright, clear communication, found the joy in his work being overshadowed by the director's foggy be-

Remembering the past gives power to the present.

FAE MYENNE NG

But the artist persists because he has the will to create, and this is the magic power which can transform and transfigure and transpose and which will ultimately be transmitted to others. ANAÏS NIN

haviors. On the director's part, such behaviors were inbred, if not actually intentional.

"Where exactly did it hurt?" I asked Danieli. "How exactly does it make you feel?"

"It makes me feel invisible," Danieli replied instantly, and with considerable emotion.

I asked Danieli the same question I had asked myself: Was this phrase he had just used a clue around his creative scar tissue? Did he have a pattern of being treated as though he were invisible?

Did he ever!

The artistic child of artistic but narcissistic parents (and the two *do not* need to coincide!), Danieli had had his youthful creativity overlooked and undernurtured. Early on in his professional career, he had generously offered his services to a young director who gladly took Danieli's help—but then took all the glory for Danieli's work, *never acknowledging, even long after he was very famous, exactly how pivotal Danieli had been on his early masterpiece.*

From there, Danieli traced a pattern of invisibility: the stint as acting coach that went uncredited while another director claimed the gold, the "help" given as set designer when others claimed the results as totally their own. . . .

Two decades of a destructive pattern suddenly became clear. Danieli saw that he had frequently functioned as a creative booster rocket to someone else's rising star. Such "invisible" help on his part had created a bitter residue that left Danieli in the dark as to his own considerable powers. Being invisible is no fun!

Talking about it, Danieli was taking a step into visibility. Whether or not the famous director *ever* acknowledges Danieli's work, at least now Danieli himself has, and that is a very large step in the right direction.

When we are angry or depressed in our creativity, we have misplaced our power. We have allowed someone else to determine our worth, and then we are angry at being undervalued. In short, we have fallen for the fool's gold of worldly approval instead of continuing to pan our own rich resources, valuing the nuggets of inspiration we find there.

The realm of the psyche seems to respond to us much as we approach it.
STEPHEN LARSEN

Nobody can give you wiser advice than yourself.
CICERO

In point of fact, no other human, no institution, no critic can either bestow or destroy our creativity without our consent. *However,* sometimes it is appropriate that we fight for recognition—credit on a script we wrote, timely payment for a painting that a gallery has sold and collected on. Very often, though, the action that we need to take is internal: acknowledging where it hurts, how it hurts, and what we can do to heal it. Since the largest thing we can do to heal an artistic wound is to value ourselves *ourselves,* the tasks that follow are steps in that direction.

~ Task: Taking Back Your Power. ~

List five times you have allowed your creative worth to be determined by others. In doing this task, take a look for the times that it has happened as a positive as well as a negative. ("She said I was brilliant, therefore, I'm brilliant.") Setting too much store by an outside opinion, negative or positive, can deflect us from determining our own creative course.

~ Task: Relationship Collage. ~

Collage one of your toxic creative relationships. This is a very powerful tool and one that may give you unexpected clarity and relief. I used this task to clear a relationship that had grieved me because a promising collaboration was aborted. In the process of doing the collage, I finally passed through my grief and gained a renewed sense of self-worth that I had pursued the work alone and completed it. That accomplishment had been lost to me in my sorrow over the "could have been."

~ Task: Abundance Collage. ~

Put on your Expansion Music. Find a recent picture of yourself. Using a large sheet of poster board, collage yourself dead center in a field of valuable images. Let them point to you and your worth. This

It is life itself that must be our practice. It is not enough to hear spiritual truth or even to have our own spiritual insights. Every aspect of what happens to us must become part of a learning experience.

DIANE MARIECHILD

As you grow spiritually your words gain more power to affect people.

SANAYA ROMAN

is an Abundance Collage, one in which we work with returning ourselves to a well-sourced position, abundantly fed by the Universe.

~ Task: Counting Coup. ~

In Native American tradition, a warrior returning from battle would "count coup," adding up all the wins he had acquired. Going back through your Narrative Time Line, list one hundred of your favorite wins, things you are proud of. This list can range from "writing a play" to "standing up to my sister about what she said about me to my *other* sister!" The wins can be very small—and even things no one else might be proud of. I, for example, am proud of the fact that in grade school I socked a boy who was beating up on all the girls!

~ Task: Who's Got The Gold? ~

Sit down with a legal pad and a pen. Begin at the beginning and list every single creative thing that you have ever done that you can remember. Developed in Arts Anonymous, this is called taking a creative inventory. It is a very powerful tool and one that helps to put your power in a very different perspective!

For double the vision my eyes do see And a couple vision is always with me.
WILLIAM BLAKE

Batteries

Now that we have looked at the many small ways in which we are discounted, let us pause to double-check—yes, one more time—to see if we have any large leaks in our lives, places where we are hemorrhaging time and energy. Very often creative people are unaware of how creative they are because they are not using their creative powers in their own behalf.

When some of us try to carve out for ourselves time away from our intimates, they act as if we have committed a crime—perhaps assault and battery. Our requests for a little space fall on them like blows. That's the assault part. The battery is something else: it's the role we often play for them. Many very creative people can be found sublimating their own creativity into the service of the creativity of others.

This is the weekend you have set aside to write your proposal about the big rehab job you would love to snare. This is also the weekend that your partner is staging a fund-raiser. The deadline for your proposal is Tuesday. The fund-raiser is one day only. Of course, you've already put in several weekends of good-sport time organizing the event for which your partner will take full and glorious credit. (When you even think about credit, you feel guilty, don't you?) Since it's only one more day, what will pitching in again hurt . . . ?

Well, let's see. Pitching in will cost you your time, your energy, and quite possibly your shot at the job. The proposal is due Tuesday;

I think knowing what you cannot do is more important than knowing what you can do. LUCILLE BALL

I need to take an emotional breath, step back, and remind myself who's actually in charge of my life.
JUDITH M. KNOWLTON

Monday will find you exhausted—not to mention the fact that you will have a full day's work at your job. Of course, you could always pull an all-nighter, but that would leave you in no shape to go to work on Tuesday, and you do work for a living.

Let me say that again: you do work for a living.

Many very creative people work for a living when the "living" involved is living together, not working at a job. We are the ones who stay up until two A.M. brainstorming with our partners or calming their nerves before and after their big events. We are the ones who wait to be thanked, wonder why we weren't, or if we were, wonder if a thank-you really suffices for the damage we have sustained to our own life plans.

"Don't be selfish," we tell ourselves. It's what many of us have been told our entire lives, especially when our plans conflict with someone else's plans to use us as their creative battery.

It's time we got selfish. Let me define my terms here: in a healthy sense, to be selfish means to act in the interests of the self. This means, at the very least, we should ask that self how, what, and *if* it feels something about every request made on us for our energy.

"Could you?" we are asked.

"Of course," is often off our lips before the question's ramifications have time to register.

"Could you help me with my book?" means "Could you give me your time, expertise, opinion? Could you give me your weekends, evenings, vacation time?"

"Could you type my book for me?" means, "Would you help me do mine in the time when you could be writing your own or taking that painting class that meets two nights a week?"

Many creative people have been taught that their gifts make other people feel rotten—like our less musical siblings, for example. We have been told either to hide our light under a bushel or, at the very least, to share the wealth and use our creativity for the betterment of others. Is it any wonder we grow up to be batteries?

Mimi, a talented writer, was told by her mother that her real job, as a good wife, was helping her husband to advance his career. Robert, a gifted musician, was told, "Your brothers are special, too, and they don't have to traipse off to the ends of the earth to prove it."

For Mimi, the message was loud and clear: "Serve, serve, serve."
For Robert, the message was: "Don't grow, and whatever you do, don't abandon people to pursue your dream."

Although we seldom look at this squarely, many of us who have gone through life as other people's batteries were programmed early on to do exactly that. Perhaps "programmed" will strike you as a sinister word: "You don't mean they did it on purpose!"

Yes. They did do it on purpose. No. They didn't do it on purpose. What difference does it make? The point is, do it they did, and it falls to us to undo this programming in ourselves and lay claim to the power, energy, and time that is rightfully our own.

~ Task: Assault on Being a Battery. ~

In this exercise, you are asked to name ten people for whom you have served as a battery. Begin with historical situations—writing your big brother's term paper, designing your sister's science project—and move forward. Designing the project your boss took all the credit for, writing your husband's or wife's business proposals, doing all the grunt work for the PTA dinner, the sales conference, etc., etc.

Don't make promises until you thoroughly understand what you have to do, what impact the promise will have on your other commitments, and the importance of the promise to your own goals.

PAULA PEISNER

1. _____.

2. _____.

3. _____.

4. _____.

5. _____.

6. _____.

7. _____.

8. _____.

9. _____.

10. _____.

WARNING! Don't simmer here in the stew of reactivated resentments! Go directly to the next task, where resentments are alchemized into the golden ore of self-worth.

∼ Task: Write Your "Shadow Résumé". ∼

One of the ways in which creative people are manipulated is by never having their contributions acknowledged. Those who use them as batteries often act as if the creative fuel they receive from us is theirs instead—as is, needless to say, the resultant accomplishment.

One woman I know "co-wrote" books with her Ph.D. husband. The truth is, she wrote those books. She was the writer of the two of them but he never acknowledged that, and neither did she. When I saw her recently, she asked me to read her first solo book, which I did—it was excellent. I called to tell her.

"You really think it's good?" she asked anxiously. "You really think I can write?"

"Of course you can," I told her. "Who wrote all those books with your husband?"

"Well, actually, *I* did," she said, a little surprised by this information.

Very often we have done far more work in far more fields than we have ever claimed credit for. Claim credit now. Get out your Narrative Time Line and go back through it, looking for places and people that used you as a battery. What did you do that you have never acknowledged?

Take the time to add to your Narrative Time Line any accomplishments that you now realize you had overlooked or undervalued.

Giving another person too much power or taking too much power yourself are both sides of the same coin: misunderstanding personal power.
MARION WEINSTEIN

It is important to know when to assist people and when not to.
SANAYA ROMAN

Here lies the great gift of the Spirit; though we may have lost our way, when we come to that realization, we discover the path once again.
DR. LAUREN ARTRESS

Obsession

Before we move off the topic of drains on our time and energy, I want to look at one more way in which highly creative people frequently sabotage themselves—"unrequited love," a.k.a. obsession.

For blocked creatives, unrequited love has a purpose: it keeps us from loving ourselves. If we don't love ourselves, then we don't deserve any of the adventures, achievements, and accomplishments we might deserve if we were lovable. So pick someone unresponsive, and the payoff is terrific in terms of inertia and the increased capacity to stay stuck.

If only so-and-so would love me, then I could ... and then I would ... go to Europe, take riding lessons, get a new car, take a correspondence course, join a spa, get a new stove, submit my short stories, raise capital for a theater troupe. Why, with a little support (so-and-so's support, of course) I could do almost anything I wanted ... Oh, dear, I wonder if he/she loves me?

Wondering takes a lot of time and even more energy. An ambiguous love affair, the kind that leaves you craving more, is by definition addictive. Scientists have long known that sporadic reinforcement will habituate a rat to a desired behavior far more effectively than steady reinforcement will. Ambiguity is always addictive. Put cheese at the end of a maze every time and the rat loses interest in

Develop interest in life as you see it; in people, things, literature, music—the world is so rich, simply throbbing with rich treasures, beautiful souls and interesting people. Forget yourself.

HENRY MILLER

*There has to be some balance
of things that move on
the earth.*
JAMES WRIGHT

*All nature is at the disposal
of mankind. We are to work
with it. Without it we
cannot survive.*
HILDEGARD OF BINGEN

the cheese. Put it there only so often and the poor rat will race to see what's there.

Ironically, sporadic reinforcement is exactly how the rats we love condition *us*. We make them the focus of all of our love. They pay us back for all this attention every so often and . . . Oh, rats! We get hooked.

We get hooked by the stop/go. By the off again/on again. By the chimera, the shadow dance of a now-you-see-it/now-you-don't affair. This business of red light/green light love is a very distracting addiction. Many of us use it to avoid our own creative lives. It goes like this:

"I could rewrite the top of that story and send it in by the deadline. . . . I wonder if he loves me. . . ."

"I could clip the dog, and get myself a nice new haircut, too. . . . I wonder if she loves me. . . ."

"I ought to at least read the job opportunities and get myself out of this dead-end situation. . . . I wonder if she loves me. . . ."

Is it any wonder that when we are seeking to avoid our creativity, we locate a red-hot/ice-cold unrequited love? Of course we do! If we can just keep the drama in the middle of our lives, we don't have to put it on the page, the canvas, the clay, the stage, or the screen.

Instead, watching our inner movie ("He left a sweet message when he canceled our plans. Was that a hopeful sign? . . ." "She turned her head and looked at me twice when she was really out with him. . . ."), we can avoid the plot turns of real life. Turning a blind eye to the cost of our obsession, our vision dulls creatively as well. Is this any wonder? How can we marvel at this year's abundant lilacs and play Miss Lonely Hearts at the same time?

In its most basic form, unrequited love is a glorified tantrum. We've stamped our foot and made a demand of the Universe: "I don't care what your plans are for me and my time. I want this person to love me now!"

Of course, we've made a demand of our love object as well: "I will be miserable unless you love me and fix my life!"

Forget free will. Forget respecting the needs of others—their right to choose companions, their sense of timing. Forget, too, the ebb and flow, the essentially tidal nature of human affairs. A heart opens and closes to circulate both love and blood. We want a flood instead.

We want something and someone that will sweep us away. We want love, and we want it from X.

Is it any wonder we're resented? The person on the receiving end of our demand can feel the coercive nature of this interest. No wonder they feel like a food source. They *are* being eyed as a food source: the empty calories we want to use to medicate our dissatisfaction with a life we are refusing to create.

"You love me!" we demand, instead of asking, "How can I love myself?" If our love has to come from one person, and that person is not me, myself, or I, then that certainly lets us off the hook about doing anything to love ourselves. It works like this:

"A nice dinner out?"

"No, thanks. I'm too depressed. He/she hasn't called, and . . ."

"What about coffee and a film?"

"No, thanks. I'm waiting for a phone call."

"What about phoning them?"

"Oh, I couldn't do that. . . ."

The reason that we can't phone them is that clarity is non-addicting. Clarity and real communication leave time and space and energy for creativity, friendship, and risk. That's scary, isn't it? We might do something, notice something, even change something.

Obsession is almost invariably linked with procrastination. In fact, the most surefire way to break obsession is to move into the creative act that you are avoiding.

∼ Task: Obsessions (Past Tense). ∼

Look back over your Narrative Time Line to see if you have ever used a grand obsession to avoid creative work. Write a Cup about this period in your life.

∼ Task: Obsessions (Present Tense). ∼

Look at your current life. Do you have a lingering obsession blocking you at the moment . . . even a little bit? Make a collage of your (actual) relationship with this person.

If the world is to be healed through human efforts, I am convinced it will be by ordinary people, people whose love for this life is even greater than their fear. People who can open to the web of life that called us into being, and who can rest in the vitality of that larger body.

JOANNA MACY

Seeing is never from memory. It has no memory. It is looking now. The total organism is involved in seeing. Not thinking about what is said from memory, but listening and looking openly now. TONI PACKER

We are nature. We are nature seeing nature. The red-winged blackbird flies in us.
SUSAN GRIFFIN

When I am alone the flowers are really seen.
MAY SARTON

The act of painting is a spiritual covenant between the maker and the higher powers.
AUDREY FLACK

~ Task: Snap Out of It. ~

Do these actions to snap out of your obsession:

1. Carry a loaded camera every day for a week.
2. Take pictures of all of your friends' hands and feet.
3. Make a pillow in the shape of an animal.
4. Call one "lost" friend whom you can still track down.
5. Send yourself a rave review of your lovemaking.
6. Write your ideal epithet.
7. Write your Oscar speech.
8. Paint one kitchen chair with folk-art patterns.
9. Go to a fabric store and look at bolts of silk to determine which colors really cheer you up.
10. Go to Chinatown and buy one great plate and saucer.

~ Task: Get On with It. ~

Okay, begin what you have been avoiding.

Breaking Camp

"When an inner situation is not made conscious, it appears outside as fate," Dr. Carl Jung told us. It is for this reason that we have done the work of bringing to consciousness our difficulties in the Kingdom of Relationship.

We have reaffirmed our essential equality and our birthright to creative fulfillment. We have dismantled patterns of voluntary victimhood. We have revisited and reshaped creative woundings that left us blind to our own accomplishments. We have reclaimed our right to our own use of our creative energies. Finally, we have confronted any patterns of obsession that have blocked our access to our own creative powers.

In setting off again, we find our hearts and our burdens lighter. Freed from the deflective pull of others' agendas, we are able now to set our course with greater accuracy and attain our goals with greater celerity. Moving into the Kingdom of Spirituality, we find that we have indeed left false gods behind us.

The
Kingdom of
Spirituality

It could be argued, correctly, that *everything* is spiritual and that we have been traveling in the realm of the spirit from the very beginning. True enough, but now we are going to focus on spirit directly, examining and strengthening our conscious contact with higher realms.

For many of us, such spiritual venturing is an exercise in semantic flexibility. We find that the language of spirituality can be too nebulous, too ethereal, or too impractical sounding for us to feel fully grounded. Perhaps we have even had run-ins with "officially" spiritual people who didn't feel that way to us.

The essays and tools of this kingdom are designed to focus on actual experience rather than theory. You will no longer be dealing in "God as told to you." Instead, read with a tablet in hand and note down any actual memories that are jogged. You may discover you have, in fact, had a good many spiritual experiences. Once you are open to recognizing them, you will discover yourself having many more. In time, the sense of a working partnership with an unsuspected inner resource may emerge. The tools of Morning Pages, Artist Dates, Daily Walks and entering the Imagic-Nation all serve to nurture that relationship. The tools of this kingdom serve to both ignite and enliven it.

Name That God

"God is voluptuous and delicious," declared the mystic Meister Eck-hart. I believe he was right. I believe in a festive God. I believe the Creator loves creativity. After all, Somebody had an awfully good time making hibiscus blossoms, red clay cliffs, rivers, starfish, pine-cones, coral snakes, and stars.

Somebody—or, if you prefer, Something—didn't know when to stop. Beetles exist in myriad varieties. Butterflies, a little loftier, make it into high digits. In our culture, God is so often thought of in terms of Calvinist austerity and renunciation that we forget there was clearly a godly glee in creative excess, an artist in love with the materials themselves.

"We are related to God as a painting is related to a painter, as a clay pot to a potter, as a book to its author," declares Matthew Fox.

"Let all the rivers clap their hands and the mountains shout for joy," exclaimed David (Psalms 98:8).

"My beloved is the mountains, And lonely wooded valleys, strange islands, And resounding rivers . . . ," wrote John of the Cross.

"We all get the God we believe in," my friend Julianna Mc-Carthy tells me. (After thirty-plus years on her spiritual path, I sus-pect she knows.) Another way to look at the wisdom of her words is to realize that many spiritual traditions advise us to address specific deities or aspects of the deity. (Jungians might say we are activating the archetype of a particular god/goddess within us.)

Soundhealer Ted Andrews explains it this way:

> The ancient god names are specific signals, signals that can be used to call upon aspects of the one divine force throughout the universe. . . . The use of god names in rituals, prayers, affirmations and mantras has been practiced probably as long as humanity has been on the earth. They can be used to attune to the specific force represented by the name. . . . We use the ancient divine names and words to invoke and awaken energies that are normally associated with them, yet that live within us.

In Christian tradition, we might pray to God the Father, God the Son, or God the Holy Ghost, according to which aspect of the Godhead resonated with our situation. Traditionally, the Christ child is associated with creativity while the Holy Ghost is the aspect we address for grace in a given situation. God the Father might be prayed to for protection.

In each of these cases, we would be invoking a force aligned with our needs. The Kabbalah contains ten call-names in the Tree of Life—each name addresses a different divine aspect, again, according to need. Eheieh ("eh-hah-yeh") is the call used to invoke creativity. Shaddai el Chai (shah-dy ehl hy) is the call to sharpen psychic abilities. Each call-name invoked a different power of the divine—and of the divinity within.

One way to think of this is in terms of bloodlines. Thoughts, concepts, names—all carry a flow of history and, more important, *energy* with them. In much the same way that if you follow a family over several generations you may see grandpa's nose reappear on grandson's face or Aunt Dorothy's eyes blinking back at you from little Dorothea, so, too, when we call to mind a god concept, we are calling into our experience the cumulative weight of that thought, the influences of that energy family of thought through time. It is like tapping into a computer using the code words that give us access to certain banks of information. For this reason, it behooves us to be very conscious of which god we believe in and invoke.

All creation is a manifestation of the delight of God—God seeing Himself in form, experiencing Himself in His own actions, and knowing Himself in us as us.

ERNEST HOLMES

*This we know: All things are connected
like the blood which unites one family.
All things are connected.
Whatever befalls the earth
befalls the sons of the earth
Man did not weave the web of life.
He is merely a strand on it.
Whatever he does to the web
He does to himself.*

CHIEF SEATTLE

Troubled in our relationship with a demanding child, we might, for example, invoke the compassionate heart of the Christ who said, "Suffer little children to come to me." We might enlist the aid of Sarasvati, goddess of music, if we were having trouble with our piano lessons. The goddess Athena might be invoked if we wanted to be judicious in managing our employees. We might invoke the god Mercury if we wanted our communications to be quick-witted and direct.

By clearly focusing on what sort of god we believe in, by addressing it by name or by naming it as feels right to us—Great Goddess, World Mother, Mother/Father God, Higher Power, Force, etc.—we are able to act with a sense of support and protection, even levity, all dependent on the "type" of god we invoke.

Like most of us, I have had the experience of being a sort of "cosmic straw"—the poem that sprang out fully formed, the painting that painted itself, the melody that just arrived. And yet, for me, I have come to feel that not only is this the flow of God's energy, it is *therefore* the flow of mine. "I" am far larger than myself. As Walt Whitman exclaimed, "I contain multitudes."

Very often when we contemplate creative endeavor, we are daunted by a lingering belief in an anti-creativity god. You know the type: one who wouldn't laugh at our jokes; one that would find them uppity. Many of us have been raised with a humorless god. Not that it was done with malice aforethought, merely that it may have been misguided. In the words of mystic Mechtild of Magdeburg:

> Those who would storm the heavenly heights by fierceness and ascetic practices deceive themselves badly. Such people carry grim hearts within themselves; they lack true humility which alone leads the soul to God.

A number of saints agree with her assessment. Julian of Norwich, another mystic, put it this way: "The fullness of joy is to behold God in everything."

Creativity requires a certain amount of *joie de vivre*, at least a *soupçon* of chaos. One of our most pernicious myths about creativity is that we need solitude and silence in which to practice it.

Not always.

Silence and solitude are fine, but often both expensive and luxurious—and creativity does not require them. For that matter, neither does God: birds make a tumult; waves and winds twist and shout; plants and stones speak a sibilant, vibratory language. The language of life is a sibilant, seductive tongue: raucous, tender, reverent by turns.

And yet ours remains a predominantly Judeo-Christian culture in which our central creativity myth goes like this: Everyone is having a very nice day in Paradise until someone gets uppity and wants to try something new, like picking an apple (or writing a novel). This is too uppity for a jealous, territorial, competitive God. Adam and Eve may want that apple—God wants their heads! And so it's out of Paradise for the two of them. "Bear your children in pain and suffering!"

What if the story had had a different ending? What if we'd been raised with a creation myth that involved God's delight in our exploration and expansion? What if God were encouraging, loved to share creative collaborations with us, loved our steps into risk? What if God had said, "I'm so glad you finally noticed that apple! I made it bright red for a reason! What did you think of seeds? Aren't they a great idea? I really think they're fun. But if you have anything you two would like to try . . ."

It might have been very different for us emotionally.

Balking at a creative jump, it's well worth playing Name That God. You may be ducking the jump in order to duck the wrath of a God you no longer (officially) believe in.

Remember that most of our God concepts were instilled in us as youngsters. (They may differ significantly from our God experiences.) Remember that the part of you that creates remains a creative youngster. Your rational, adult mind may be an agnostic, a Zen Buddhist, a practicing Neo-Pagan, or Presbyterian. No matter. Odds are excellent that your creative child still believes in God-the-bogeyman. In other words, your Creative Child still believes, "Reach for that (golden) apple and off with your head!"

You may argue, correctly, that this essay has a disturbingly flippant tone, that my reading of Genesis has a certain levity, that I seem to be taking God too lightly. As I said at the beginning, my God has a

God as an entity separate from ourselves is simply another idea that we can either accept or dismiss.

DIANE MARIECHILD

To me the concept of the "Beloved" conveys not just a nice, cozy, warm relationship with God, but one that is joyous, uplifting, and exhilarating because it is a recognition of who I am.

NANA VEARY

*God, I can push the grass apart
And lay my finger on Thy heart.*

EDNA ST. VINCENT MILLAY

sense of humor. As a theologian, and as an artist, I am allowed to make mistakes.

~ Task: Recall Your Childhood God. ~

When working with this exercise many people can rapidly fire off a list that goes something like, "Distant, forbidding, male, judgmental, all-powerful, jealous, non-supportive, all-knowing, stern, all-seeing, withholding, stingy, unreachable . . ." Would the God of your childhood support your creativity? Often not. And, all too often, the God of our childhood was an invented God, not an experiential one. We were taught who and what God was rather than being allowed to discover God for ourselves. Even benevolent loving gods were none too interested in our creative endeavors.

After writing about the God you were taught about as a child, scan back through your Narrative Time Line to see if you have any examples of benign divine guidance—a "funny" feeling, a "miraculous" coincidence—especially as regards your creativity. Does this benevolent God match with what you were taught? If yes, wonderful! If no, learn from your experience and revamp your rote understanding of God.

List five examples of what could be divine guidance in your life:

1. _____

2. _____

3. _____

4. _____

5. _____

~ Task: Invent a Creativity God. ~

When I teach, I ask my classes to collectively brainstorm a "Creativity God." Instantly, working with this tool, the adjectives take on a festive tone. Very often, words such as "good-natured, nurturing, fun-

To me the sole hope of human salvation lies in teaching Man to regard himself as an experiment in the realization of God, to regard his hands as God's hands, his brain as God's brain, his purpose as God's purpose. He must regard God as a helpless Longing, which longed him into existence by its desperate need for an executive organ.

GEORGE BERNARD SHAW

I know not what you believe in God, but I believe He gave yearnings and longings to be filled, and that He did not mean all our time should be devoted to feeding and clothing the body.

LUCY STONE

loving, non-competitive, supportive, musical, humorous, sensual, abundant" come to mind. Suddenly jokes appear: "Loves to cha-cha, a good kisser." The whole room lightens up as people begin *playing* with the idea of God.

List ten traits of a Creativity God—for *you*.

1. _____.

2. _____.

3. _____.

4. _____.

5. _____.

6. _____.

7. _____.

8. _____.

9. _____.

10. _____.

⤳ Task: Create a Creativity Totem. ⤳

You may wish to clip images and collage a Creativity God. You may wish to draw, paint, or sew one. Think about doing a mural on the wall of the room where you work. What about a smiling God on your bedroom ceiling? You may want to create more than one Creativity Totem. You might want a green goddess reflecting your ecological concerns, a loving mother-father god for your parenting concerns, and a festive, many-armed dancer for the ebullient creativity that you seek to evoke in your dance work.

As I mentioned in *The Artist's Way*, for many people, the creation of an Artist's Altar is a very potent exercise. On this altar, you might place images of the benevolent god that supports you, also objects that awaken in you a sense of wonder. Wonder is a spiritual touchstone.

The rhythm of my heart is the birth and death of all that are alive.

THICH NHAT HANH

God is really only another artist. He invented the giraffe, the elephant, and the cat. He has no real style. He just keeps on trying other things.

PABLO PICASSO

Any creative endeavor is channeled, whether it be music or art or theoretical science. We have the capacity to tune into energies and to convert them into reality for ourselves.

FRANK ALPER

Remember that you can draw on gods from cultures other than your own. You may resonate to Sarasvati, Hindu goddess of music, to a recumbent Buddha, or a prancing Pan. You may want to collect objects associated with the god you are invoking. I associate Pan with the greenwood, and all creativity. On my altar, I have a large collection of pinecones gathered from wherever I find them in my travels.

If you have not created for yourself an Artist's Altar, do so now. Bedeck it with the god images that speak to you of abundant creativity. (If you remain an atheist or agnostic, choose images from the natural world that speak to you of the qualities you wish to invoke.)

Guidance

Guidance comes to us most clearly in solitude. It is called "the still, small voice" because we must quiet our minds and our lives enough to hear it. The poet Rumi importuned us, "No more words. Hear only the voice within."

Guidance comes to us in many forms, some of them so fleeting that we merely catch the thought like a wisp of movement out of the corner of our eye. It's a little like bird-watching.

"Was that just a yellow finch over there in the fall foliage or was it the foliage itself?" As neophytes, we need to pause and double-check. Yes, that was a finch. Yes, that thought *was* guidance.

"True intuition is subtle and graceful and will leave you secure if you listen," assures Sonia Choquette in her book *The Psychic Pathway*.

But listen we must.

Increasing and regularizing our times of solitude and quiet increases our ability to receive guidance. One way to think of it is that we are creating a sort of spiritual clearing. I have a centering song which goes:

> *In the center of your heart*
> *Is a still small part,*
> *Like a meadow in a forest made of green.*

To whatever degree you listen and follow your intuition, you become a creative channel for the higher power of the universe.

SHAKTI GAWAIN

In the center of your heart,
Is a still small part,
And that is where your soul must go to dream.

In other words, we clear space in our lives in order to center and clear space in our hearts. The soul's voice, the voice of guidance, then ventures into the clearing we have created for it. We do not so much tame it as coax it like a wild deer by acknowledging its wildness and creating an environment where it feels safe enough to speak to us and offer its higher perspective.

There are many times when the guidance we will receive will shock us. It sometimes suggests a subtle adjustment in our life as it is currently constructed, but it may also suggest a major realignment in a totally unexpected direction.

I am thinking back to 1980, when I was happily living in Los Angeles, writing a popular newspaper column and writing for the movies. As was my wont, I took long, solo walks in the Hollywood Hills, asking for and listening to guidance.

Most of the time, the guidance came in small, digestible bites: "Write a column about _____." One sunny day, high in the Hills, I put out my antennae and got, "Move to New York."

I was flabbergasted and quickly double-checked. "Move to New York," I got again.

This directive took a bit of processing! For several weeks more, I walked, listened, and resisted while the inner directive became more and more insistent. "All right!" I finally capitulated.

I did move to New York. In fact, I spent the next five years in Manhattan. There I began teaching the Artist's Way and returned to working in the theater. Perhaps more important, my coast-to-coast move allowed my daughter Domenica easy access to her father and to her grandparents. It allowed us regular Monday and Friday expeditions out to galleries and shops as we parsed through the good, the bad, and the spectacular.

In innumerable ways, New York was good for me both spiritually and artistically. I found a small shop, Enchantments, on a side street in the East Village. I ventured into the shop because its sign and window displayed symbols I had begun to spontaneously and compulsively draw: crescent moons, hands with spirals in the palm, pentacles. All were emblematic of ancient goddess worship, although I didn't know that until I made my way down the steep steps into the small grotto-like shop, where I encountered Starhawk's groundbreaking work *The Spiral Dance.* Stepping into Enchantments, I stepped through time into a world of knowledge that beckoned to me like a misplaced dream.

Fifteen years later, I can look back in awe at the tracery of my guidance. In California, I had encountered and admired the work of Susan Griffin speaking on behalf of our increasingly denatured planet. Oddly, it took me a move to lower Manhattan, where I could literally count the remaining trees and bushes, to move me emotionally and spiritually into a deepening commitment to global consciousness, a consciousness that spoke to me through women like sculptor/healer Nancy Azara and author Marion Zimmer Bradley, who gave us *The Mists of Avalon,* a spellbinding reworking of the Arthurian legends from the perspective of the goddess-based religion that Christianity had all but snuffed out.

"God is efficient," Julianna McCarthy always reminds me, "He brings us along like fighters."

I have to laugh, finally seeing the guidance fretting through my life like a golden thread, setting up plans and designs of which I was barely conscious, laying the foundation for future creative work—my musical *Avalon*—long before I could sense the outline of that work before me.

I took those steps that led me into Enchantments, and from there unfolded a world of teaching and healing all based on convening sacred circles, rather than conventional lecturing. Nancy Azara held a regular Friday-night circle. I began teaching every Thursday. With every circle I learned more about the power of sacred energy called into focus by the group, more about the healing that comes to us in clusters when we unite and commit to each other's growth.

Unseen by me and parallel to my teaching work, my explorations into earth religions, goddess study, and druidism were forming a root system from which *Avalon* would later emerge and blossom. *I didn't*

There is reason to believe that behind spurious notions and false concepts of God there lies a reality that is God.

M. SCOTT PECK, M.D.

Anything we fully do is an alone journey.

NATALIE GOLDBERG

*There are unknown forces
within nature; when we give
ourselves wholly to her, without reserve, she leads them to
us; she shows us those forms
which our watching eyes
do not see, which our
intelligence does not
understand or suspect.*
AUGUSTE RODIN

*When you really listen
to yourself, you can
heal yourself.*
CEANNE DEROHAN

know this, and I didn't need to know this. All I needed to do—all any of us need to do—is to listen and follow guidance a step at a time.

All of us receive clear and specific guidance. All of us can depend on the guidance that we receive. Learning to hear it is a little tricky, and so is the part where we expect the guidance to pay off in a linear fashion. This is the point where we can often feel that God or the powers that be have somehow duped us or set us up.

My friend Julianna has an explanation for this as well: "God knows exactly the right carrot to get us exactly where we're supposed to go."

Maybe so. In July of last year, I attended and spoke at the annual conference of the National Institute of American Doll Artists. I was lured there by my own love of dolls—or so I thought. As it turned out, I wasn't really there for me at all.

First of all, let me say that the artistry of the assembled creations was enormous. The dolls were less dolls than sculptures. While at the conference, I struck up a conversation with a non-NIADA doll artist, Alice Lester Leverett. On impulse, or so I thought, I asked her if she had happened to bring along any of her own dolls. She had. Could I see them? I could.

Her dolls were magnificent. I saw a doll based on a southwestern beauty. I saw a doll based on a southern belle. Last, but not least, I saw a doll named "Laura"—based, or so it seemed to me, on my friend Laura.

"Oh, my God!" I burst out. "She's exquisite. She's perfect. . . . She's Laura."

For twenty-one years a teacher of gifted kindergarteners and first-graders, Laura loves children, although she has none of her own. This doll—flaxen-haired with twin braids, clad in a pink balle-rina costume—resembled Laura herself as a young child. She looked at the world through my friend Laura's beautiful, wide-open eyes. I had to buy her for Laura.

My frugal Scottish side swung into action. "Julia! Be sensible! She's porcelain! Porcelain dolls break!"

"But she has her own little steamer trunk full of costumes, and Laura would *love* her," my guidance insisted. "Laura has to have this doll!"

"But, Julia! You could buy an old clunker car for the price of this doll. Be sensible!" my rational self protested.

Meanwhile, my artist self was completely enchanted by Laura, by her steamer trunk, by her change of costumes (black ballerina with fairy wings, queen, witch, bride), and above all by her serene, all-knowing gaze. She was "my" Laura's Laura, all right.

"She will be priceless to Laura," I thought, and I wrote out the check.

Six weeks elapsed before the limited-edition doll reached its destination. I came home one day to Laura's breathless voice on my answering machine.

"Oh, Julia! She got here! I haven't loved an *object* like this since I was a little child. I have to talk to you."

I phoned to hear the scoop. Laura talked of her favorite costume (the black fairy-winged ballerina); she talked of her plans to make Lilliputian beaded jewelry for her toy. Then she said, "Of course, you couldn't know this, but my favorite toy as a little girl was a flaxen, braided-haired doll—and she had a steamer trunk!"

No wonder my guidance had been so insistent! I was so glad that I had listened instead of brushing it off.

Events like this, surprises like this, are for me the silver lining to following guidance. They are the reward for resisting our "rational" mind's skepticism and venturing—perhaps cautiously—into the territory of the spiritual unknown.

As for myself, I enjoy hearing the adventures of previous explorers. One of my favorite books about listening to guidance is *To Hear the Angels Sing* by Dorothy Maclean. She tells of how the guidance first came to her:

> At that time, when alone in my apartment, a recurring thought kept coming: stop, listen, write. I ignored that thought until it became so insistent that I was forced to listen (if only tentatively, because my critical mind allowed me to write only trite safe truths). I kept these sketchy writings to myself, until Sheena [her spiritual mentor] found out about them. After reading them carefully, she told me they were truly inspired and asked why I didn't put their suggestions into action. With her encouragement, some inner floodgate opened to the most

... To learn to see, to learn to hear, you must do this— go into the wilderness alone.

DON JOSÉ
quoted by Joan Halifax

joyous thoughts and feelings. To me their source was God, because the inspiration derived from the same sort of place, or non-place, as that first experience of God within; but in their joyousness, they were unlike anything I had ever encountered as being attributed to God. My initial inner experience had come unsought, but now I could return consciously to that wonderful inner Presence, which was always different yet always the same.

Maclean began setting regular times to "check in": stop, listen, and write.

> There was no actual voice; there was a delicate, inner prompting which I tried to convey in my own words, as my art form. I wrote the words in shorthand while experiencing them, never losing awareness of my external environment ... Of course I doubted these writings. My mind said that it was nonsense that God would talk, for example, about "quick-silver- thoughts passing from his lips." But Sheena was delighted and gave me a schedule of sitting three times a day. Without that schedule, I would not have bothered with the times of quiet ...

How encouraging to hear that even Maclean needed to consciously schedule her spirituality! How often it is easy to believe that other people are spiritual giants by nature while my own balky willfulness is mine alone!

～ Task: Clearing a Clearing. ～

Working with this book, you are already doing Morning Pages, through which you may be receiving a great deal of guidance. This week, take a leaf from Dorothy Maclean and set aside two short additional times daily. They needn't be more than five minutes each. Take a pen in hand and simply *listen*.

If you find yourself getting "nothing," start finishing this sen-

I value my time. I choose to use it wisely and do not let others steal it from me.
PAULA PEISNER

Prayer is an opening of the heart, an alignment with the beauty of the universe.
DIANE MARIECHILD

The most beautiful emotion we can experience is the mystical. It is the power of all true art and science.
ALBERT EINSTEIN

tence, "I could _____." Finish it over and over. At each of your sitting times, listen first to see if any guidance is forthcoming. If not, use "I could" or "I'd like to" or "If I had faith" or "It's possible that," and finish the sentence until the five minutes are up.

Eventually, your guidance will come up spontaneously without needing such prompts. Remember, too, that guidance may simply bubble up as unexpected insights: "Jeffrey really likes you."

~ Task: Spend One Evening ~ in Silence—of All Kinds.

Because the written word is still "words," and words "speak" to us, this will be an evening of reading deprivation as well. This is not a night to watch TV or go to the movies. It is not a night to enjoy music. It is a Silent Night.

In order to do this, you may need to enlist the prearranged agreement of your family or spouse. Simply tell them that you are conducting a scientific experiment. Explain that you are going to be observing the effect of silence and that you will *tell* them about it later.

For many of us, silence amplifies the voice of the soul, of inspiration, and of creativity.

No more words. Hear only the voice within. RUMI

Why do you weep? The source is within you. . . . RUMI

Many people pray and receive the answer to their prayers, but ignore them— or deny them, because the answers didn't come in the expected form.

SOPHY BURNHAM

~ Task: Write a Spirituality Cup. ~

Scan your Narrative Time Line for something that you can identify as a spiritual experience. Write the experience out fully.

~ Task: Create a Deck of Spirituality Cards. ~

Buy a packet of three-by-five lined cards. You will need fifty-two. Take ten of them and on each one record a spiritual experience or answered prayer. You may wish to decorate these cards, paint them, make them with a calligraphy pen, or edge them in gold-gilt paint.

Next, take another ten cards and write out ten spiritual quotes that "speak" to you. Illustrate or illuminate these quotes as well.

Now take another ten cards and write on each card the name of one thing you love: frosted windowpanes, raspberries, scallop shells, acorns, blown glass. . . . Decorate these cards as well.

Take a fourth set of ten cards and name ten people whom you love. You may wish to use photographs on these cards.

Take a fifth set of cards and name ten artists or pieces of art that ignite in you a transcendent feeling.

Take the final two cards and design one to symbolize you and one to symbolize what you conceive of as God source.

Place all fifty-two cards in a special box, fabric square, or bag. (Small velvet bags are available in many metaphysical stores.) Use these cards at least once a week whenever you feel your consciousness needs a spiritual lift. As those of you familiar with tarot, medicine, or druid cards would know, there are a number of ways you might want to use them:

1. Draw a card at random and experience any synchronicity in your selection.

2. Shuffle all of the cards slowly, allowing multiple associations to accumulate.

3. Formulate a question and then lay out three cards, one for the past, one for the present, and one for the future. What guidance does each card give you regarding the situation at hand?

4. Shuffle the cards and select those which offer you support and inspiration in your current endeavor. Post the selected cards where they are very prominent. Use them as archetypes to invoke energies you wish to work with.

5. If you find the above exercises particularly rewarding, you may wish to explore the use of tarot art and jewelry. Gino and Judith Schiavone of The Cornmaiden Shop, Taos, New Mexico (505-751-3739),

make exquisite and relatively inexpensive tarot and goddess earrings and pendants in brass and sterling silver.

An artist might choose to wear the Magician for help in manifesting a desired dream or the Empress in order to invoke universal supply. A flute player I know has a Schiavone Pan pendant, a Hermit, *and* a Magician.

Spiritual Experience

What does mysticism really mean? It means the way to attain knowledge. It's close to philosophy, except in philosophy you go horizontally while in mysticism you go vertically.
ELIE WIESEL

I love reading about other people's spiritual experiences, but I hate to write about my own. I say I am afraid of sounding pretentious or "off the deep end." What I don't say is that not writing is a way of not owning my spiritual experiences.

Like many of us, I have been known to practice a deliberate ignorance of rewarded faith, synchronicity, and its benign implications. The most blatant synchronicity is dismissed as coincidence, turned aside as too good to be true. I ask for guidance, for some sign, and then refuse to read the billboards as they come into view. I ask for a path and ignore the freeway that opens before me—or perversely lay rubber in the opposite direction, a creative U-turn.

Although I do believe, I am afraid of believing. We say we crave the security of faith, but I for one find a great deal of security in my lack of faith. Lack of faith keeps me cautious and complaining. It has a real payoff. Risks can be postponed, insights discounted, beneficial synchronicities ignored. In short, I can dally in "stuck" just a little longer.

Sonia Choquette calls this the "Yeah, But Syndrome." Hearing that, I want to say, "Yeah, but, Sonia! It's scary to believe in the invisible realities."

And it is. It's scary to see the invisible hand of God or other help-

ing forces. On the other hand, over time, what is even scarier is the re-
fusal to see. At this point in my life, I have seen enough to believe. I
have also seen enough to recognize my own disbelief as hedging. I often discount, downsize, trivialize, discredit, minimize, miniaturize,
and, if possible, ignore spiritual surprise packages. I forget or out-
right deny them. I do this because the alternative is threatening.

A life where spiritual dimensions are as real to me as our concrete, agreed-upon "actual" life is as scary as it is thrilling. (You mean
I can count on spiritual support . . . ? Uh-oh . . .)

Spiritual hedging, like any fence straddling, becomes uncomfort-
able the longer you try to sit with it. Discomfort more than faith can
be the goad to moving forward, but moving forward has its own discomfort. The velocity can be frightening. Is it any wonder many of us
teeter-totter between belief and disbelief, straddling the fence as
long as we can bear it?

Seeing that spiritual life is a reality carries some consequences.
Eventually, you have to come creeping out of the spiritual closet and
admit that, yes, you are some kind of believer in . . . well . . . in
Something. In other words, you have faith. Worse than that, you have
some degree of spiritual experience. Experience moves faith out of
the theoretical and into the personal. Once you admit you have it,
even a little of it, faith becomes a tool for taking risks, and these risks
generate further faith, which generates the possibility of further risk.
No wonder we balk!

As long as we can continue to deny the possibility of spiritual
support for our endeavors, we can comfortably set a low ceiling on our
dreams and goals. The phrase "I'd love to, but" can often be found
smooching with the Yeah, But Syndrome. Spiritual experiences are,
well, *spirit*ual experiences. They may feel weird. Some of us may feel
self-conscious or frightened by them. If we can deny them, we can
back off both from our spiritual support and our creative possibilities.
Remember that the phrase "it would take a miracle" is often used to
refuse to invite one.

When we look at adventurous lives, we often see the large and
small leaps their owners' faith impelled them to take. When Carl
Jung broke with his friend and mentor Sigmund Freud, he risked

*I did comprehend the whole
world . . . and the abyss and
ocean and all things. In these
things I beheld naught but
divine power.*

ANGELA OF FOLIGNO

*Yet it is in our idleness, in
our dreams, that the sub-
merged truth sometimes
comes to the top.*

VIRGINIA WOOLF

*Our culture's entire value
system is firmly based on
this belief that the rational
principle is superior and,
in fact, constitutes the
highest truth.*
SHAKTI GAWAIN

*Spiritual experience is a
transhistorical transcultural
phenomenon and can break
through in individuals
at any time.*
HOLGER KALWEIT

professional ruin. Freud's ideas—namely that our action and thought and image patterns originate in a personal unconscious—were very potent, popular, and in vogue.

Jung begged to differ. His own leadings led to him to the notion that we each partake of a collective consciousness or race memory as well. This ocean of consciousness (a staple of mysticism everywhere) was dismissed as primitive by his colleagues. They were done with all that "magic thinking." They were beyond it. They were modern. Rational. (And, need I say, somewhat smug?) Jung's colleagues viewed him as a gullible unfortunate, a man who had derailed a brilliant career to chase an errant star, or even his own tail.

This dismissal of Jung was especially true when he began exploring the more occult systems of knowledge—Egyptology, astrology, and the ancient Chinese oracular system, the I Ching. Such systems hinged on significant coincidence, an uncanny intermeshing of microcosm and macrocosm, the inner world and the outer world. Jung called this intermeshing "synchronicity." His explorations and experiences led him to a belief that an invisible spiritual realm interlocked, influenced, and responded to actions and thoughts taken in our own mundane realm.

As modern Freudian thinkers saw it, we had outgrown such childlike ideas as Jung's concept of synchronicity. Ancient systems of knowledge were outmoded and faintly ridiculous. Although he faced ridicule and a degree of professional isolation, Jung stuck to his personal path. From his private spiritual explorations, he forged work of great dignity and originality—work that is catching fire in people's imaginations now, decades after his death. As the new physics and the new mathematics unfold "new" theories such as morphic resonance and the observer's Universe, we see that Jung's theories were really neither before his time nor behind his time, but timeless.

Late in his life, when questioned about whether he had faith, Jung responded, "I don't believe . . . I know." To say that we *know* requires great courage. What, exactly, do we know?

For myself, I have a bias toward regarding spiritual gifts as spiritual gifts—that is, blessings to be unwrapped rather than marks of spiritual attainment, and yet, we can invite spiritual gifts to "happen" to us, and that, in large part, is what this book is about.

I will tell you a little of what I know, and what I have been try-ing not to know. In other words, I will own up to some of my spiritual experiences, past and present, in the hope that by my tracing this thread through my Narrative Time Line you will be able to detect it and trace it in your own.

Before turning to some of my spiritual adventures, I would like to quote briefly from Machaelle Wright Smith, the remarkable ecol-ogist whose farm Perelandra has been called an American Findhorn. (Findhorn is the famous devic Scottish garden where all manner of flora flourishes on barren soil.) In the introduction to her spiritual odyssey, *Behaving as if the God in All Life Mattered*, she writes:

> I offer this search for the spiritual thread in my life as an ex-ample for you to use when looking back into your own life. I can't adequately express how wholeheartedly I recommend this exercise for anyone. . . . By seeking the spiritual thread I saw the purpose contained within the individual events and how each event was built on top of the previous ones, creating a pat-tern of oneness, wholeness. I saw the light of synthesis. The re-sult has been that more and more I don't look back in anger and disappointment—instead, I look back in gratitude, even cele-bration.

And now to my story, but with this proviso: it is my belief that we *all* share a common spiritual dowry, that we *all* have a grab bag of spiritual gifts that we can uncover, and that *all* of us have the same gifts as an inherent part of our humanity. Like Jung, I believe that we partake of an archetypal ocean of shared consciousness, and that per-sonal spiritual experiences are really universal in nature and far more commonplace than we ordinarily allow. I also believe that if we be-gin working to open ourselves to our creativity, spiritual gifts will manifest as a matter of course. They simply come with the territory, so it is time we learned to be less spooked and more accepting of them. I know that can seem easier said than done, so I will share a lit-tle of my own journey into this acceptance in the hopes that it will make you more comfortable in your own.

Because this is a good story, and a spooky one at first, let me be-gin as those stories do: "It was a dark, stormy night."

To bring forth the soul of our being, we must be in our bodies, rooted to the Earth, able to draw from the uni-versal source of energy.
DIANE MARIECHILD

My body has certainly wan-dered a good deal, but I have an uneasy suspicion that my mind has not wandered enough. NOEL COWARD

It *was* a dark, stormy night. I was visiting, not yet living, in Taos and I had an appointment north of town, "just past the yellow blinking light," to visit a woman I had never met before. She was a spiritual reader, a.k.a. channeler, and because I did not understand some of the things that were happening to me, I decided to talk with her about them. They were, after all, her forte. "Lois West"—a normal-enough-sounding name. I had spotted her card at the local metaphysical bookstore, Merlin's Garden, and called her up.

"I can see you at nine tonight," she told me. "Is that too late?"

And so, at nine that night, I was driving north through a dramatic storm (and there are few things as dramatic as an electrical storm in New Mexico). Suddenly, I caught myself thinking, "I know how to do what this lady does." The thought startled me, I brushed it aside, and then I was at her house, an oddly shaped stone house—a veritable witch's cottage.

Lois West herself was a blond, sensible-looking woman with a friendly, no-nonsense manner. "I used to be a reporter, so they tend to work with me in a very succinct way," she told me. "I hope you don't find your reading too short. They usually get straight to the point."

The point "they" got to in my reading was that I had been "sent to teach about the relationship between creativity and spirituality."

"That's funny," I interjected. "I am writing a book about that." I reached in my bag and took out a snippet of what would later become *The Artist's Way*.

"Mm. It will be very successful," West went on. She flicked the tape back on. "You've done this many times before." The tape unspooled, flashing me forward into the life I now have. As promised, the reading was brief but fully packed—just like a good news story. I thanked West and went on my way.

Back in Chicago, I mentioned this adventure to my friend Eleanor, and the funny thing I had said about thinking I, too, might be able to do readings.

"Oh, do one for me!" she exclaimed.

I did, and Eleanor proclaimed it very accurate. A short time later I found myself working on a film with a very gifted woman producer. During the shoot, she discovered she was pregnant and soon after she miscarried. She was heartbroken and I, as her friend, was sympathetic and concerned.

"I don't know what caused it," she said tearfully. "We want a child so much. I seem healthy. I've been checked out as healthy. My husband's healthy . . ."

As I listened, I mentally scanned her as if searching for clues to answer her questions. That is when I "saw" several odd masses of tissue, like marbles and a golfball, in what I took to be her uterus. I blinked.

"What is it?" she asked. I must have looked startled.

This was my first experience of a gift you might call healing sight. To say the least, it surprised me. What I saw felt crazy to me, but not telling my friend what I saw seemed even more crazy. What if the masses really were there?

"I think . . ." I searched for words. "I think you should get checked to see if you have growths or something. I see . . . I see these round masses . . ."

Now my friend blinked.

"I think you should get checked," I concluded. "Checked again."

My friend went to the gynecologist and reported back that, yes, three such masses did exist, and she was scheduled for surgery. We both talked about how amazing my intuition had been. I am happy to tell you the surgery was successful as was a subsequent pregnancy, which yielded a beautiful baby girl. My friend, meanwhile, thanked me profusely for my "diagnosis." Predictably, for me, I wanted to pretend it hadn't happened. I certainly didn't want to think what, if anything, it might mean.

For six months after that, I seemed to have developed a new and disconcerting specialty. I sent three other women friends off to—or in some cases, back to—gynecologists for maladies that were clear to me in my mind's eye. In all three cases, the medical help was needed, and needed for the conditions that I had somehow intuited. I began to feel like a covert nurse practitioner, hardly my self-image. Furthermore, there was that part of me that was afraid of making an error, of missing something I should have seen or seeing something that simply wasn't there.

To be surprised, to wonder, is to begin to understand.

JOSÉ ORTEGA Y GASSET

Man can learn nothing except by going from the known to the unknown.

CLAUDE BERNARD

The world of reality has its limits; the world of imagination is boundless.
JEAN-JACQUES ROUSSEAU

As exciting as it was to catch these psychic glimpses, I also found them frightening and did not know what they meant or where they were leading me. Every time I saw something and the something that I saw checked out, I would put a tiny little jot on my mental blackboard: "Intuition right again." Then I would promptly erase the jot. As more and more friends would ask me for intuitive readings, I became more and more fearful. This whole thing was getting out of hand!

I remember one particularly disconcerting incident. An editor friend asked me for a reading and I sat down to do it, only to be confronted with a persistent image of pomegranates.

"She is really going to think I'm nuts," I thought, but I finally began the reading with the image of pomegranates. I did not feel it was my place to censor even if I clearly was stepping into the deep end. But pomegranates?

Imagine my shock when she exclaimed excitedly, "Pomegranates! I carried them in my pockets all the time as a little kid! I loved them. They were my favorite things!" Evidently, she was still carrying them in some mental pockets, because they were clearly enough still with her for me to see them.

Being psychic was scary. What if I were struck *really* psychic? Would I be doomed to a lifetime of wearing purple diaphanous robes and crystals? What about my daughter? Would she like having such a New Age witch for a mother? I preferred denial. In fact, I preferred it with a vengeance until I felt I was being split down the middle between the two worlds. On the one hand, it felt crazy to believe. On the other, it was crazy not to.

About this time, a wise therapist named Barry Cecconi suggested I find a role model, someone who was psychic and at ease in the real world. I thought instantly of Sonia Choquette, a graceful woman, happily married, the mother of two, who lived in a regular Chicago brownstone and was a lifelong, third-generation psychic and spiritual teacher with a thriving livelihood reading for spiritual seekers and the generally baffled.

About fifteen years earlier, my brother's girlfriend Beth had invited me to spend an evening with her. She had someone she wanted me to meet—Sonia Choquette. Sonia and her husband Patrick were teaching a short workshop on manifestation. It was called "Your Heart's Desire" (now a Random House book).

The workshop, then held in their second-floor Chicago apartment, was fascinating to me. Outside the window, a concrete playground was enclosed by a chain metal fence. The image reminded me of the way that life can sometimes seem—too small, too harsh, too determined by insurmountable boundaries, limits not of our own making.

Inside the apartment, Sonia was talking about the power that we had to create our own lives, choose our own boundaries, set our own limits. Life was to be lived from inside out, not vice versa, she said. Psychic gifts were gifts of the soul. We created our own fences, our own limits and boundaries. We did it with language.

What? Wait a minute, Sonia . . .

I was in complete agreement with all of the concepts she spoke of until she reached her eighth law: "Your words are the building blocks of your life."

Perhaps because I was a writer, I resisted this notion strenuously. Words were important enough to me! I didn't want them carrying anymore freight than they already did!

"Well," Sonia said, "you can resist the idea, but we do get exactly what we ask for psychically—so watch what you say. Some people say, 'I'm always getting colds'—and they do. Some people say, 'I've got terrible luck'—and they have. Our subconscious takes every word we say literally. It carries out what we command it to do. If we persist in using negative language, negative things happen."

I was not convinced. I left the workshop thinking that Sonia was onto some wonderful things about the quality of our lives being essentially self-initiated, but that with the business about words, she was carrying it a little bit too far.

I soon learned differently.

Helped by the generosity of my family and friends, using money I had earned writing for television, I shot a small feature film. Incredibly, we had it in the can in three weeks and it looked very good.

The real voyage of discovery consists not in seeking new landscapes, but in having new eyes.

MARCEL PROUST

If the doors of perception were cleansed, everything would appear to man as it is, infinite.

WILLIAM BLAKE

I took time off to recuperate before editing and in that rest period I came to an abrupt insight.

I realized that there were many times in my life when I listened to what people said instead of paying attention to what they were really doing. In other words, if the voice-over was soothing enough, I would ignore all manner of personal pain and indignity.

What would happen, I suddenly thought, *if I watched the picture without the sound?*

I felt as though I had stumbled across *the key*. The greedy colleague who was always telling me about how generous he was? He didn't look anything but stingy when I tuned out his words. The man who told me he was leaving his girlfriend so we could be together? He certainly wasn't doing anything of the kind if you watched just his actions.

"Watch the picture without the sound! Watch the picture without the sound!" I kept repeating, decoding some of the tangled messes my life currently entailed. I must have repeated the phrase a thousand, ten thousand times—right up until the moment when the sound man on my film called to tell me that the movie's sound had been stolen.

Stolen! Reels of quarter-inch tape of no use to anyone and invaluable to me! The Chicago cops had murders to solve and weren't too concerned about some missing quarter-inch tapes. ("Lady, go back to Hollywood," their attitude seemed to say.) It was the dead of winter. Icy fingered, frozen hearted, I dug through Dumpsters all over the north side of Chicago to no avail. The tapes were truly missing. The sound was truly gone.

"Watch the picture without the sound." I ruefully thought of my mantra. Had I brought on my own robbery? I wasn't happy about saying, "Yes," but I wasn't so sure I could really say, "No." Hadn't I been warned? Hadn't Sonia described the subconscious as a sort of silent army that stood ready to carry out our repeated commands? Didn't she say that our words shaped our reality?

Like it or not, now I *had* to watch the picture without the sound. I also had to cut the film silent, reading lips, dub the entire movie, and satisfy myself with a European release, since an English-speaking film dubbed in English could never be released in America. No matter how I looked at it, this was a very expensive lesson in the value of words.

Perhaps Sonia was right after all, I belatedly concluded. Perhaps psychic phenomena really were gifts of the psyche, the soul. I certainly hoped so!

I called Sonia and asked for an appointment.

That appointment began a friendship that continues to this day. From Sonia, I learned to see psychic gifts as normal human endowments. Under her careful tutelage, I saw that just as we are all creative, we are all also intuitive. In fact, I would have a very hard time parsing out intuition from a creative inkling.

If you have been working with your Morning Pages for the last weeks, if you have done some Artist Dates, you have probably experienced, noticed, and perhaps minimized your own episodes of spiritual synchronicity—those times and events where the gears between your inner reality and the outer world seem to intermesh. If so, you may already have become an adroit practitioner of Sonia's Yeah, But Syndrome.

Frankly, I think it's time we all gave up "Yeah, but . . ." just a little bit. The key to doing that is the cultivated practice of open-mindedness. Notice I did not say "empty-headedness." It is my belief that we need to be grounded and specific when we explore spiritual realms. This is why those Daily Walks are so important: they keep our head in the clouds and our feet on the ground.

Another extremely valuable tool in allowing your own spiritual unfolding is the sharing of others' spiritual adventures. I am lucky in that Taos, now my home, has not only Merlin's Garden but a second, used bookstore, Ten Directions, which is crammed with books on spiritual topics. It was there that I found one of my favorite books, *ESP: A Personal Memoir*, by Rosalind Heywood. Despite its rather lurid title, the book has a delicious skeptical and humorous tone:

> The aim of this book is to record certain experiences of my own which may have been due to the alleged capacity nowadays

Today I do affirm that I am Divinely guided. . . . There is That within which knows what to do and how to do it, and It compels me to act on what It knows.

ERNEST HOLMES

Is it possible that . . . the path of spiritual growth leads first out of superstition into agnosticism and then out of agnosticism toward accurate knowledge of God?

M. SCOTT PECK, M.D.

known as extra-sensory perception, or ESP for short. Only may: there is no cast-iron evidence that they were. It is safer to call them ESP-type experiences, and I do not know of any sure way to explain or interpret them. Nor am I trying to use them to prove or disprove ESP. Things are what they are, I am no missionary, and as Faraday said, the truth will always make itself known in the end. . . .

Now, I do have one quibble with Heywood: her modesty. She was, in fact, a missionary (her book was published in 1964) and she had traveled to unknown realms before me. I, for one, was grateful that she had and grateful, too, for her account of her travels.

It was Heywood who first spoke of a phenomenon I had encountered my whole life: an insistent inner voice that urged often improbable but retrospectively correct actions. "Guidance" Dorothy Maclean called this voice. "Marching Orders," I call mine. Heywood called hers "Orders," and hers seemed every bit as puckish as my own. So did her trepidation at explaining this voice.

Let me quote from *Memoirs* again:

> "Freeing my mind of all thoughts of the problem, I walked briskly down the street, when suddenly at a definite spot which I could locate today—as if from the clear sky above me—an idea popped into my head as emphatically *as if a voice had shouted it.*" That is a description by a scientist of how an intuitive idea came to him. He was wiser than I when a somewhat anti-ESP psychologist asked me to tell him how I received what I called Orders.
>
> "Well," I replied innocently, forgetting those precious words *as if,* "I hear a voice."
>
> "Ah, a voice," he broke in, and his own voice could not have said more clearly, "Obviously an unbalanced type . . ."

As we begin to hear more and more specific guidance and get more and more clear spiritual or intuitive information, we ourselves may begin to think, "Obviously an unbalanced type." It is also possible that we may be surrounded by people who say that very thing. For this reason, it is important that we find spiritual allies—if only on the written page.

Very often when I am teaching, I am approached by students who have had amazing and unsettling experiences of guidance and synchronicity.

"What's going on?" they want to know.

What is going on is, quite simply, that their spiritual gifts are unfolding. Very often I refer them to Sonia's excellent book *The Psychic Pathway*, which demystifies so many things and offers so many helpful techniques for staying grounded and open at the same time.

For right now, let me close with a few words that I hope are reassuring. Western culture is alone in acting as if spiritual realms are not a reality. As spiritual realms become more and more a part of your experience—which they will as you move further and further into your vein of gold—please bear in mind that you are not becoming unbalanced; rather, your cultural base has broadened.

It is interesting that visionary and mystical inspiration are behind many of the world's greatest inventions and scientific breakthroughs; even those of such giants of the mind as Albert Einstein and Nikola Tesla.

DAVID TAME

We are told that prayer brings angels down. But if prayer is thought, concentrated and distilled, the clear, pure yearning of the heart, is prayer itself also the manifestation of the divine? The desire itself being granted as a gift of God, in order that its satisfaction may be given us by God?

SOPHY BURNHAM

~ Task: Open the Door. ~

Cue up your favorite piece of Safety Music. Lie down or sit very comfortably. Close your eyes. Breathe gently and deeply until you are centered and ready to begin. When you are, visualize your mind as a room in which you keep a certain number of ideas you are comfortable living with. Picture the door to your mind as being open just a crack. Now see the gleam of a dazzling golden light shining in from just outside. That golden light is the gleam of spiritual possibility. While you allow your Safety Music to comfort you, begin to imagine what new ideas you would like to invite into your room:

A belief in accurate, internal guidance?

A belief in synchronicity?

A belief in angels or higher guiding forces?

What you choose is up to you. As your Safety Music plays, allow yourself to enjoy the expanded sense of possibility this new belief brings to your life. When your music ends, return to normal consciousness. Make a small note to yourself and post it where you will see it: "I now officially believe in _____."

~ Task: It's a Wide World After All. ~

I like to start this task by looking at a globe: yes, there it is, the place where *you* live. And, yes, there is all the rest of the world—so many cultures, so many beliefs. So many alternative ways of looking at things. . . .

Now, over a period of several days, execute the following short tasks. They are designed to help you enter into psychological spaces that allow you to entertain alternative belief systems:

1. Light a candle, douse the other lights, and ask yourself to imagine a world lived only by candlelight.

2. Go to an ethnic restaurant that is not part of your culinary repertoire. Imagine that this is your ordinary, everyday food.

3. Contemplate this thought:

Once every people in the world believed that trees were divine and could take a human or grotesque shape and dance among the shadows; and that deer and raven and foxes, and wolves and bears, and clouds and pools, almost all things under the sun and moon, and the sun and moon, were not less divine and changeable. . . . They dreamed of so great a mystery in little things that they believed the waving of a hand, or of a sacred bough, enough to trouble far-off hearts, or hood the moon with darkness.

W. B. YEATS

4. Pick a totem animal. Get a picture, statue, or image of it. You may wish to make an entire collection of images of this animal. What is it about it that speaks to you?_____

(You might also enjoy Bear and Company's Medicine Cards, which feature Native American animal

Artists are channels for cultural feelings and creators of images that the culture is hungry for and doesn't even know it.
VICKI NOBLE

The devas say that they are our source of inspiration in many fields, including science.
DOROTHY MACLEAN

mythology or, my personal favorite, the animal cards
from Druidic tradition by Philip Carr-Gomm.)

5. Dance that animal. Cue up music that you think
   "your" animal might really enjoy. Let yourself play
   at dancing as that animal might: smoothly like a
   snake or a fish; with great swoops like a hawk or an
   eagle; with the canter of a pony; the rollicking waltz
   of a bear. . . .

Saying "Thank You"

We like to believe we must make things happen. We also like to believe we can't. This means we can worry about our powerlessness and get steeped in our own bitterness. The truth is, we are meant to co-create. In other words, we both make things happen and let things happen; we imagine and then we release the imagined dream into the Universe for it to manifest it properly. Far from being powerless, we have all the power of the Universe available to us, if we will cooperate with it in its unfolding. In other words, we must accept the Universe's helping hand.

The late Unity minister Jack Boland called this cooperative process Master Minding. He believed in working with spiritual prayer partners so that they could see and speak each other's dreams aloud—and then release those dreams to the Master Mind for it to manifest them.

When I lived in Chicago, I did this process weekly with my beloved friend Laura. We would meet in a coffee shop, order our cappuccinos, and then, together, list what we wanted or needed help with. Our spiritual aims ranged from the large ("a new place to live," "help with the detective novel") to the very particular ("the right words when I talk to him").

One person would list a request and the other would mirror it back as actualized. "Julia, I see you finding a way to move to Taos. I see you finding a home there that suits you perfectly. . . ."

We kept a journal of our requests and every week began our session by checking in on what progress we had made—or, more accurately, what progress the Universe was making in our behalf.

Very rapidly, I realized I was blind to a spiritual helping hand when it was proffered. It wasn't that my prayers weren't being responded to, it was that I tended to have fixed notions about what quarter the help should come from. Even worse, I was always looking for abrupt, spectacular, and dramatic reversals of negative situations. I wanted blinding flashes of light, not little twinkles of improvement.

"We're still fighting," I would say if my relationship was in the rapids.

"I thought you said you did find a way to tell him what you meant, and that you had a good talk after going to the movies the other night."

"Oh, yeah . . . but we squabbled over breakfast!"

Working as a team, Laura and I were able to nudge each other into noticing the often unexpected ways in which prayers were answered. I began to feel a little bit like a shopper who wailed, "But I wanted it in blue!" when actually pink was very pretty.

When I was moving from Chicago to Taos (a large answered prayer) I needed to move three horses and despaired of finding the money to do it. Feeling that it was a pretty tall order, I put it on my request list and a week later, talking with my ex-husband about the move, he offered, "Why don't you let me move the horses for you and Domenica?"

"Oh, I couldn't let you do that!" I replied.

At my next Master Mind session with Laura, she found this behavior hilarious. "Oh, yes, you can!" she said. "You call him back and say thank you for his generosity! Besides, you're supposed to be asking the Universe for help, *not* telling it how you'd like it delivered!"

Oh, yes . . .

It is because of the "catcher's mitt" aspect of a partner that I have loved praying in tandem. Not everyone is comfortable with this

Joy is a landmark of the psychic pathway.
SONIA CHOQUETTE

Come, Love! Sing on! Let me hear you sing this song— sing for joy and laugh, for I, the Creator, am truly subject to all creatures.
MECHTILD OF MAGDEBURG

One of the first things to do
is learn to accept, and to
expect this Power to flow
through everything we do.
ERNEST HOLMES

intimacy, and they may prefer working with solo creative visualization. This process, described carefully and brilliantly by Shakti Gawain in her book *Creative Visualization,* is actually a working partnership with the Universe itself. We clarify a wish, dream, desire, or goal. We ask the Universe to manifest this for us. We commit to listening for guidance and acting on it in return for this universal funding of our dreams.

We are not meant to be so passive that we deaden the yearnings of our heart. Nor are we meant to be so desperate that we try to yank our dreams from the Universe like apples that are not yet ripe and ready to fall. If we are willing to dream, and to let the Universe dream with and through us, then we can begin to accept the presence of those dreams in our lives. However, this is often more difficult than it sounds. Many of us are too frightened to dream. We have been badly hurt by having our dreams not materialize as we wish and we are frightened to allow them to assume reality for us again.

(It may take a gentle but powerful book like Barbara Sher's *Wishcraft* or Sonia Choquette's *Your Heart's Desire* to coax your heart into articulating its buried dreams.)

Michael Weller wrote a harrowing play called *Ghosts on Fire.* It centers on a blocked director and his tremendous emotional pain. I have always taken the "ghosts on fire" to be the director's buried dreams. It is my teaching experience that all of us have dreams that, like embers stirred to life, can burn us. Sometimes they seem to lie just under the surface of our lives like subcutaneous bruises, and when we brush against them, the pain shoots through our system like fire. This is what is meant by a burning desire.

Ouch! Why should we reawaken our yearnings? Why should we risk again, love again, live again? Answer: because the alternative is a living death. It is my experience that when we ask our hearts to grow again, they do so. We are large enough to encompass our losses. We are brave enough to dream again, risk again, love again. We just need the assurance that we really can do so, and this assurance will come to us in a thousand forms, large and very small, if we ask for it. But ask we must.

I have a song lyric which goes:

The master key is willingness,
The mistress of all things.
Learn to trust the Universe
And see the gifts she brings.

When we believe in a stingy Universe, when we believe in a God bent on denial, it is frightening to articulate our dreams. Drawing them too clearly to mind can seem like furnishing photos of your beloveds into enemy hands. Giving over your dreams to a toxic Universe can make you feel like an informer: if I let God know what I really want, then I will never get it.

There are two ways in which we can work on this dilemma. The first is to examine and alter our God concept. We have done this. The second is to allow ourselves and our new God to deliver a few small parts of our dreams.

Remember, I said "ourselves *and* our new God." This is a partnership. We must ask and be willing to receive. Without our willingness, the Universe cannot deliver.

If we are addicted to the stress and worry of trying to make things happen, we are positively phobic about avoiding the free-fall feeling of letting things happen. Surrender control? Not if we can help it. For people who are addicted to worry, which gives them a sense of safety because it is so familiar and prevents them from letting their imagination roam too freely, the willingness to receive the "part" of partnership can be nearly as hard as the asking.

This is why starting small is such a good idea. The big dream might be going to graduate school. Starting small might be finding out about schools and sending off for brochures. There is usually one small step we can take in the direction of a dream. When we do, the Universe often takes several more. Our willingness is following this lead.

The dream is to write a musical. We start our work on it. A friend offers free theater tickets to two musical shows which would be great to use as Artist Dates. Do we say, "Yes, thank you," or "Oh! I couldn't let you do that . . ."

We could let the "U" do that. We need to remember that the

True intuition is subtle and graceful and will leave you secure if you listen.

SONIA CHOQUETTE

Today I live in the quiet, joyous expectation of good.

ERNEST HOLMES

Universe is the source of our supply, and that other people are its conduits. Too often we mistake people themselves for the Source. "I'll owe them!" we think, panicked. We hate to owe anyone. Again, it feels out of control. Practice allowing people to give to you.

In thinking about what we owe people, most of us need to spend a little more time thinking about what we might owe ourselves. (Support, for one thing. A chance to go to the theater, for another.) If we have spent a great deal of time as batteries for other people, we may owe ourselves a nice, long rest. If our energy has fueled the creative endeavors of others, perhaps we should allow them to return the favor in whatever form they can.

"I wish my husband would support my dreams," a student complained to me. "He did offer to pay for me to take my master's, but I'd like his emotional support."

For some people, money *is* their version of emotional support. We must learn to let people give what they can instead of demanding they give what we wish.

The language of the heart has many tongues. Sometimes it speaks in cash on the barrelhead: "Let me pay for your move out of that house. . . ." Other times, it speaks in barter, "I could watch your kids on Saturday mornings if you want to do that pottery class, and you could pick my kids up Thursdays so I could get into the city for my class. . . ." Still other times, it speaks with silence. Instead of volunteering your time to others when you need it for yourself, you keep quiet. And finally, it can speak in phrases and behavior unfamiliar to you.

To practice acceptance, we must practice *accepting*. In other words, start saying "yes" and "thank you" when you are offered gifts, opportunities, and support. Do not say, "Oh, I couldn't!"

Oh, yes you could!

∼ Task: Accepting Gifts. ∼

Practice accepting gifts in whatever form they come to you. Complete the phrase, "It would be really nice if _____" twenty times. Post this where you will see it.

Be alert for the gifts that arrive in response to this Wish List.

~ Task: Synchronicity Notepad. ~

Purchase and carry a small Synchronicity Notepad. For this task, I like using a tiny pocket-sized notepad, the kind with a spiral along the top. It can easily be carried in a purse or pocket and entries can be recorded and dated (e.g., "January 14, 1995. Started work on *Avalon* rewrite. Instantly, by 'sheer coincidence,' got three sources of information on plants and sound—Wright Smith, Maclean, and Sonia.")

~ Task: The God Jar. ~

Make, find, or designate a "God Jar." What, you may ask, is a God Jar? A God Jar is anything you wish it to be in which you can put your wishes, dreams, problems, prayers, and questions. You may want to think of it as a spiritual mailbox. You may want to think of it as a sort of magic box. Whatever you think of it as, it is important that what you use feel magical and potent to you. My God Jar is a very large, very old, blue-and-white Chinese vase with two dragons curling around it amid clouds and wind. (Dragons are the Chinese symbol of creativity.)

You may want to make not a God Jar but a God Box, using a shoe box or any good-sized box that you can paper with images of strength, magic, and significance to you. When I told Sonia about the Creativity Room I work in, she exclaimed, "You've made a God Room! A Magic Room!" The point is that you want a container where your dreams can be guarded and incubated by a helping universe.

In this way, during the periods when you feel you are waiting too long to receive some longed-for good, you can tell yourself, "It's in the God Jar. Magic is afoot."

Listen to what Marion Weinstein wrote in *Positive Magic:*

> The most difficult part about working magic, and sustaining one's belief in it, is dealing with that apparent time lapse which sometimes occurs when nothing seems to be happening, but that is precisely the time when everything is actually happening—in the Invisible World.

The Creator is Author of all arts that are truly arts.
JOHN THE SCOT

*Matter is transparent and
malleable in relation
to spirit.*
PIERRE TEILHARD DE
CHARDIN

*Authentic initiation is
marked by the compassion,
generativity, and ethical action which issues out of it.*
ROBERT MOORE

～ Task: Accepting Help. ～

Practice accepting help in whatever form it comes to you. Complete the phrase, "I could really use some help with _____" twenty times. Post this where you can see it.

Be alert for help.

～ Task: Watch Your Tongue. ～

For one week monitor your language. Notice how many times you turn aside the abundance of the Universe. A compliment? ("This old thing?") An offer to open the door? ("No, thanks. I can get it.") An offer of payment that you weren't expecting? ("Oh, no, really . . .")

Start saying, "Oh, thank you!" *And accept what is being offered!*

～ Task: Walk Prayerfully Daily. ～

You remember at the beginning of this book, we talked about the power of taking a weekly gratitude walk? For one week, this week, walk in gratitude *daily*. Consciously, vocally, enumerate your blessings or do what I did—write a little song of praise. Mine goes: "*O grazie.* Oh, thank you! Oh, thank you!"

Breaking Camp

Because the Kingdom of Spirituality is an inner kingdom, it will remain with you as you travel onward. Like the Imagic-Nation, it is easily accessed through intention and the simplest of practices. Morning Pages, Artist Dates, Daily Walks—all are continued *physical* keys to this kingdom. Let us look for a moment at the psychological ones we have also acquired.

We have clarified our personal God concept and put that into a physical form, inventing a creativity God and a creativity totem. We have cleared space in our lives for guidance through setting aside special time and silence. We have gone back into our Narrative Time Lines to find and write about our spiritual experience. We have devised a personal card deck invoking our private spiritual sources. We have focused on greater open-mindedness, undertaking tasks that moved us physically into the realm of spirit. Lastly, we have practiced the art of gratitude, opening ourselves to receive and acknowledge a greater flow of universal support.

In short, in our time in the Kingdom of Spirituality, we have increased the capacity of our psyches to receive inspiration and the power to carry that out. (In grail tradition, we have purified the cup.) Thus prepared, we now enter the Kingdom of Possibility.

The Kingdom of Possibility

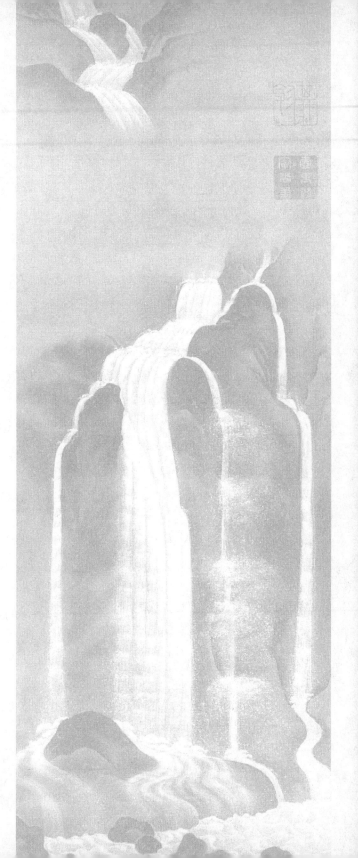

It is one of the paradoxes of a spiritual journey that as we end our pilgrimage we find ourselves not at the end but at the beginning. Jungian Robert A. Johnson tells us: "We have to leave the Garden of Eden before we can start the journey to the Heavenly Jerusalem. It is true that the two are the same place, but the journey must be made."

Having traveled through many kingdoms, we have now arrived at the most awesome of them all. We stand at the doorway to our heart of hearts and, entering, we find the Kingdom of Possibility. While this is the innermost of realms, the *sanctum sanctorum*, it is also the realm where we begin to realize our true size and scope. Dreams and ideas that once appeared grandiose and foolhardy now stand revealed not as follies but as options.

The Kingdom of Possibility is the physical, material fruition of the Imagic-Nation. It is the outward manifestation of our inner creative world. It is as expansive and powerful as our imaginations will allow. Entering this realm with the knowledge of our true spiritual endowment, we reach the furthest horizon of our daring and discover that we have actually come home.

Passion

One of the lies we tell ourselves is that if we do not let ourselves love completely, then we will be less hurt. Loving in a halfhearted manner, pursuing our dreams in a halfhearted manner, we are divided against ourselves. We do ourselves the indignity of not taking ourselves seriously, and we do our creative projects the serious injustice of refusing to visualize them with clarity. Because clarity of vision is a trigger to manifestation, our self-protective desire to hedge our bets can result in our projects not coming to fruition.

Desire is good. Passion is good. A passionate desire focuses the will, which allows energy to move. The will is actually a conducting rod for energy. When it is clear and non-conflicted, it moves energy very quickly and efficiently, like a magic wand. The phrase "seeing is believing" can also be usefully reversed: believing is seeing.

Synchronicity is often triggered by a clear, *passionate* wish. When we have the courage to desire with passion and precision, the Universe responds. Precision is important here.

To believe clearly is to see something clearly in our mind's eye. This clear vision of what we desire is something which fills our heart with yearning. Often, rather than feel a yearning for our dreams, we refuse to know what it is we truly desire. We keep our dreams and longings vague, feeling this is self-protective. We say ignorance is bliss, but that is not my experience. Ignorance is a half-lived life, a tossing away of our capacity to discern and to love with discernment.

It is much closer to my own experience to postulate that clarity is bliss. When we are able to be clear with ourselves, then we are able to be clear with the world. When we are able to be clear with ourselves and the world, then we find ourselves more able to esteem ourselves. This self-esteem allows us to receive more readily the gifts that the Universe offers in return for clarity. In other words, like a clear musical tone, we are able to be more harmonious with other pure tones. We seem to attract them.

An example.

I live in a small New Mexico town in which a world-class chef recently opened a restaurant. Almost every night I go to the restaurant for dinner. The kitchen is exposed to the dining room and has a wooden bar surrounding it, so that you can sit and watch the chef, René Mettler, in his element.

Mettler is a maestro, make no mistake. His food is exquisite and his command of his kitchen is as absolute, focused, and fierce as a matador's command of the ring. He does, in fact, resemble a matador—hair slicked tightly back into a pigtail, a proud posture, and a picador's precision with a knife.

I go to Mettler's restaurant for the food and for the passion. I love watching him do what he loves. One night, I went to the restaurant early and took a ringside seat. I was midway through writing about passion, and maybe my own intensity was particularly keen.

"Let me show you something," Mettler suddenly offered. "I have a book and I seldom show people, but—"

He brought out a very large photo album, which I ate with my eyes between bites of my blueberry country pie. In picture after picture, Mettler's artful cuisine was succulent and astounding. Pâtés, appetizers, roasts, game birds, and seafood phantasmagorias filled page after page. While I had known him to be an artist in the kitchen, I had not realized how literal my phrase really was. In the album I saw butter, ice, and tallow sculptures that rivaled the work of any sculptor. I saw Mettler himself grinning beside a many-sailed ice schooner at the Japanese world championships in ice carving. What I saw most of all was a life led with passion.

If only human beings could . . . be more reverent toward their own fruitfulness . . .

RAINER MARIA RILKE

The passion to make and make again.

ADRIENNE RICH

What sort of God would it be who only pushed from without?

JOHANN WOLFGANG
VON GOETHE

Each piece you complete is an act of faith in the process and value of creativity, a great big Molly Bloom yes to your curious, creative, courageous side. . . .

BONNI GOLDBERG

"Food is my art," Mettler confirmed. "I *love* my work."

Now the man to my left spoke up as Mettler turned back to his work.

"I know what he means," the man said. "I love my work, too."

I turned to look at him. He had fierce, quick eyes, a hawklike nose, wiry body, and gnarled, dry worker's hands.

"You're a builder?" I asked.

"Yes. Adobe. I make things. Ever since I was four years old, I have had a passion for making things, and that is what I am lucky enough to be able to do."

For the next hour we talked about adobe and the journey that had brought this man, Claude Hayward, from New York to an isolated New Mexico valley. I talked a little bit about my writing, and we laughed over how we both loved making things and we both did it with our hands. Meanwhile, a half dozen feet from where we sat, Mettler sautéed his brook trout, drizzled his escargot, and chopped his veal chops with a samurai's focused passion.

It is a myth that we protect ourselves by refusing to be passionate. What we do instead is cripple ourselves. My wise friend Julianna McCarthy once advised me, "If you're going to love, do it with your whole heart. If it doesn't work out, it will hurt just as badly either way."

I do not regret any of the things and people that I have had the courage to love deeply. My passion did not make them exquisite, but it made me available to see how exquisite they were, and as the old song goes, "They can't take that away from me." Some of what they can't take away from me is a set of memories as lucid as Walker Evans photographs.

I have a nineteen-year-old daughter who is old enough now that I am able to tell her some of what is important to me—and passion is important enough to me that it earmarks and explains my life. Over this Christmas break, which marked the nineteenth anniversary of her conception, I told Domenica how passionately I had loved her father. Sitting at the kitchen table, thinking about the many ways in which she resembles him, I told her that his feet—the prototypes for her feet—had delighted me erotically. In all the years those feet have moved away from me now, I have never stopped loving them—and that is good. I wish my daughter a wholehearted love, large enough and small enough to cherish every particular.

Cherishing everything, at least trying to, opens the door to art. While we want to make believe, and we are certainly taught, that the door to art is intellectual, my own experience is that the door to art opens in the heart.

We often talk about women being muses for male artists, and it is my experience that the men in my life have been muses for me as well. Their presence has caused me to blossom and create. Sometimes, when I have been involved with another artist, our love has caused a mutual seeding process and we each have walked into richer, more fecund work. Sometimes my brainchildren are the children I have offered my loves, knowing that they helped seed them.

A closed and protected heart produces a muffled and careful art. As an artist, then, I believe in love.

Rumi, the mystic poet, minces no words: "Never be without love or you will be dead." And again, "Wherever you are and in every circumstance, try always to be a lover and a passionate lover. Once you have possessed love, you will remain a lover in the tomb, on the day of resurrection, in paradise and forever."

When we admit that we love something or somebody, we are also loving ourselves. We are affirming, "It is I who love this." The "I" is also the "eye." Part of having a creative vision is allowing ourselves to see what we love. By celebrating what we love in this manner, we never have an unrequited love. Love becomes its own reward. What I love in you is the me that I find in you and the you that I find in me. I would say, if you want to be an artist, be a lover. Lovers love specifically: the curve of her neck; the red-black glint of the hairs on his forearm . . .

One of the strongest spiritual experiences of my life was a trip "through" the body of the man I loved. I heard and saw him as the most exquisite music. Every hair, every cell, sang to me. The beauty was exquisite and excruciating and divine and particular.

Love is in the details, and so is God. If love and God are in the details, so is art. We are meant to pay passionate attention!

We are the flow; we are the ebb. We are the weavers; we are the web.
SHEKINAH MOUNTAINWATER

Oh, what a catastrophe, what a maiming of love when it was made a personal, merely personal feeling, taken away from the rising and the setting of the sun, and cut off from the magic connection of the solstice and equinox! . . . [W]e are bleeding at the roots, because we are cut off from the earth and sun and stars, and love is a grinning mockery, because, poor blossom, we plucked it from its stem on the tree of Life, and expected it to keep on blooming in our civilized vase on the table.
D. H. LAWRENCE

*We are here to witness the
creation and to abet it.*

ANNIE DILLARD

*The deepest secret in our
heart of hearts is that we are
writing because we love the
world, and why not finally
carry that secret on with our
bodies into the living rooms
and porches, backyards and
grocery stores? Let the whole
thing flower: the poem and
the person writing the poem.
And let us always be kind in
this world.*

NATALIE GOLDBERG

Task: Valentine to Your Past.

Make a valentine to one of your great loves. For this task be sure to include everything you received from this love. Was this the one who gave you your subscription to *National Geographic?* Did you go to concerts? Did this love share or awaken your love of the outdoors with a trip to Yosemite? Use this valentine to celebrate the win, not the loss, of this love.

Task: Valentine to Your Present.

Make a valentine to yourself. For this task, use your imagination in support of your own personality. Using collage or simply beautiful tidbits of lace, ribbon, and frippery, make a collage that honors what is most lovable to you and in you.

Task: List 100 Things That You, Personally, LOVE.

This is one of my favorite tasks and I suggest that you give it the works. First, cue up your Expansion Music. Next light some incense or a good scented candle. Number your pages all the way up to 100 first. (This is a little trick. For an even better trick, number to 150. That leaves you "running" room.)

Now, make that list. Use the animal kingdom. The plant kingdom. All five senses. (And that rapidly developing sixth one, too.) Use your friends. Your family. Any of the arts. Use memories. Hopes. Places. Sounds. Actions. Activities. Attitudes.

Return to your Narrative Time Line or your Vein of Gold Quiz if you run short on items. Allow yourself to be specific: red tulips and parrot tulips and dark violets and light or dark lilacs . . . Walker Evans photos, fresh raspberries, Elizabeth Bishop's poetry, Edward Hirsch's poetry, my sister Libby's paintings, "Louise" my '65 Chevy truck, Grandma Scorsese's lemon-and-garlic chicken, needle-point . . .

This is a deceptively powerful exercise. It places you as the "I" at the "eye" of your own Universe. This is where all of us, actually, always are, but we very often lose sight of this fact. Losing sight of this fact, we often lose the feeling of our own power. Since love is the most powerful energy available to us, focusing on what we love puts us squarely back into our own power.

Risk

You must do the thing you think you cannot do.
ELEANOR ROOSEVELT

I believe in risk. I don't believe in luck. I do believe in synchronicity.

You may call this semantic quibbling, but I don't think so. Luck is something that happens to us. Synchronicity is something that begins in our consciousness. Risk is something we undertake. Luck is passive. We *trigger* synchronicity. We trigger it through risk.

Goethe—statesman, scholar, risk-taker—told us, "Until one is committed, there is hesitancy, the chance to draw back, always ineffectiveness." He was not kidding.

All of us want a net. And we can have it, too. We just can't have it ahead of time. Listen to explorer William Hutchinson Murray on that:

> Concerning all acts of initiative or creation, there is one elementary truth, the ignorance of which kills countless ideas and splendid plans: that the moment one definitely commits oneself, *then* Providence moves too.

Murray, like Goethe, is making us a promise here: "Leap, and [then] the net will appear."

We'd really like it the other way around. Show us the net and then we'll leap. Give us the job, the beau, the deal, and then we'll commit. What do you take me for, a sucker? Only a fool would go off half-cocked chasing some dream. Only a fool—or maybe Goethe, or maybe a mountain climber like Murray.

Here goes Murray again, talking about what happens *after* we foolishly commit:

> All sorts of things occur to help one that would otherwise never have occurred. A whole stream of events issues from the decision, raising in one's favor all manner of incidents and meetings and material assistance which no man would have believed would come his way.

In order to risk, we have to be willing to look bad. We have to be willing to be a sucker. We have to be willing to look like fools.

This is the sticky part: our net is the invisible. It is the unseen. It is there, but we must believe it to see it. In a moment of faith, our dreams shimmer into view. We see them clearly, glistening with hope. For that moment, we know that they can be ours. And then the moment passes; we step back into the shadows of doubt.

In order to risk, many of us need the help of believing mirrors, those people who see our potential and mirror it back to us. Disbelieving mirrors see only our doubts and mirror those back, magnified. Many of us grew up with disbelieving mirrors. I call that "growing up in the Fun House." In the Fun House (which is not fun at all) our creative aspirations are mirrored back to us as monstrous or foolish.

"I'd love to be a writer."

"Who'd want to read anything *you* wrote?"

"I'd like to be a painter."

"Sweetheart, maybe you could teach art."

Not only in our upbringing but also in our current lives, believing mirrors can be hard to find, and once found, can be invaluable—and scary. They help us to call our own bluffs, wear down our resistance a blurt at a time. The dialogue with a believing mirror friend might go something like this:

Everything is so dangerous that nothing is really very frightening.

GERTRUDE STEIN

Now traditionally, magicians are not only the manipulators of reality but evokers of wonder as well.

STEPHEN LARSEN

I have to move, or die.

JAMES WRIGHT

"I am thinking of moving to Seattle but I don't know anybody."

"You've always made friends easily."

"But I'd need a job."

"I'm sure you'd find one."

"I'd be so far from my family."

"Not such a bad idea . . ."

If we cannot locate any believing mirrors among our friends, we may need to find them in a book or in stories. We may need to find them in the words of Goethe or Joseph Campbell, who tells us that when we "follow our bliss" we will find ourself mysteriously aided by "a thousand unseen helping hands."

Make two of those your own.

Trust that the universe is working FOR you and WITH you.
SANAYA ROMAN

Making changes is as natural a human endeavor as speaking.
PETER LONDON

Just as we learn how to start and not finish, we can learn to complete what we begin.
SARK

~ Task: Taking Your Life ~ into Your Own Hands.

For this task, you will need a large piece of poster board, your two hands, and a stack of magazines. You will also need Elmer's Glue or glue sticks, perhaps some Magic Markers, drawing inks, even watercolors or acrylic paints. You may want glitter or tiny stickum stars. You want lots of playthings.

Looking back through your own Narrative Time Line, single out three times when you took a risk that you felt "guided" to take and that it paid off. These risks can be of any sort that feels significant to you. Allow yourself to recall each of these risks in their entirety. Now tear from the magazines images that reflect each of the situations, your feelings and surroundings as you went through them. Additionally, you may wish to include photos of yourself from the time periods involved.

When you have assembled your images, trace your hands, palms up, onto the poster board. Place them in any position you choose—supporting your images from beneath, coming down to help for above, cupping your images between them like a chalice . . .

Now place your images of risk in clusters that please you and glue them into place. What we are after here is a collage that reminds you at mere sight that you have taken your life actively into your own hands with great success and that you can do the same thing again when you choose to. One of the most interesting things about doing this collage is that when you have finished it, you will see that your own hands look equally like the helping hands of a benign and supportive Universe.

Ceilings

We are all far more gifted and far more variously gifted than we imagine. Oh, we may think we have a gift for one thing and a knack for something else, but most of us also have some Impossible Dream, some area we *really* wish we were gifted in that we believe—firmly believe—that we are not. For me, that area was music.

Some years ago I noticed that if I asked for guidance in my Morning Pages and then listened, I very often got clear guidance that seemed to come from a wiser source than myself. Over the years, I have come to rely on this guidance. I ask. I listen. I use it. But trusting it? And trusting the *me* that would trust it? That has been a very gradual process having to do with what I call "creative ceilings." So often the guidance suggests a move that seems too expansive, too daring, too uppity, too scary . . . until I follow the guidance and find myself supported all along the way.

Let me give you an example.

About a year ago, I got the guidance that I was to go to London for the summer. I thought this was a little odd. I have never felt particularly drawn to London. Nonetheless, London it was, and so I dutifully cleared my teaching calendar and told people I would be unavailable—in London—for the summer.

Why London? I wondered. Then my book *The Artist's Way* sold in

England, and I thought, "Ah, that's why! I'm going to London to in-troduce the book." Next, I met a British man I liked and I thought, "Ah, he's why. I'm going to London so we can get to know each other."

Meanwhile, my guided writing volunteered, "You will be writ-ing radiant songs in London." To say the least, I was dubious. For two decades I have served as a lyricist to multiple songwriters, but I did not play an instrument myself, could not read music, and have a voice that I always thought of as "not much of one."

Further, both of my brothers are musicians, one is a composer, several of my sisters are musical, and I have always been our family's musical ugly duckling. ("Who's the one with the funny voice? Julie, is that you?")

Me? Radiant songs? *Not likely,* my thinking ran. I figured that if music had any business with me I would long ago have been in-formed. As a child, I had yielded the piano to my officially more tal-ented siblings. While I loved singing in choir, learning the alto part to *Ave Maria* to carol from the choir loft of St. Joseph's Catholic Church, I had felt far from gifted. I had, however, felt ecstatic—a clue I dismissed.

"Wouldn't it be fun to write a musical about Merlin?" my Morn-ing Pages persisted. I dismissed the thought like a wisp of smoke.

In May, visiting with friends in Boulder, Colorado, I went for a walk on their mountain property. I discovered a crystalline stream running amid boulders. As I sat on the edge of that stream, a song— lyrics *and* melody—ran through my head.

I liked this song. In fact, it made me giddy. Not only the words but the melody were mine. At least, they both came to me. If only I could not lose them! No one was within earshot, so I sang it. It cer-tainly made me *feel* radiant. It *was* a radiant song. There was a sort of Druidic magic smoking through it. But I knew I would lose it just like smoke as well.

It took a friend's suggestion for me to realize I could sing the melody line into a tape recorder and hang on to it that way. Listening to the song played back, I realized it sounded Celtic to me. The yearn-ing of its opening gave way to a merry round midway through. Mer-lin, or Talisman the Bard, might have liked it.

You must do the thing you think you cannot do.
ELEANOR ROOSEVELT

Within our dreams and aspi-rations we find our opportunities.
SUE ATCHLEY EBAUGH

My green heart is filled with apples.
Your dark face is filled with stars.
I'm the one that you've forgotten.
You're the one my heart desires . . .

So dance when you think of me!
Sing to remember me!
Sing 'til your heart can see
Who we are.
Dance when you think of me!
Sing to remember me!
Sing 'til your heart can see
Who we are.

I'm the Lake that has no bottom.
You're the Sword that leaves no scars.
I'm the water sunlight dapples.
You're the light from distant shores.

I saw the music!
DAVID TAME

Not only did the song have a Celtic lilt, it had an Arthurian resonance to it. I remembered the phrase from my guidance writing.
I had asked what I might write about next, and the guidance had
again shot back, "Wouldn't it be fun to write a musical about Merlin?"

Yes, I had thought. It would. If only I were remotely musical . . .

Within a week after the first song, a second song came to me.
It was another song of the greenwood, and again I sang it onto tape.
Meanwhile I was teaching, packing for London, shepherding my
daughter Domenica through her graduation. Almost as an after-
thought, in the last few days before leaving Taos, I made an
appointment to see Pam Hogan, my Taos neighbor and a channeler
of national repute. (One of the distinctive features of living in Taos
is that every second person is an artist or a New Age devotee, a channeler, an astrologer, a naturopath, a psychic, an herbalist, an aro-
matherapist. Dinner parties closely resemble Whole Life Expos.)
Distrusting my own guidance, I wanted to hear her version of why I
was going to England.

I asked about the book, my teaching there, my interest in the British man. At session's end, I asked her about me and music.

The music lit up the game board. In a great *whoosh*, all manner of spiritual encouragement came rushing through. Music would be a focus of my life and my work from here on out. I was to write and sing "heart songs." Music . . .

Despite Pam's encouragement, music still seemed to me like an impossible and improbable dream far above my creative ceiling. Then I went to London.

Within days of my arrival, I noticed that music seemed to float in the air for me there. For the first time it occurred to me that I could buy a tiny rinky-tinky keyboard and pick out what I was hearing. I bought such a keyboard. One night, with much fear and trembling, I took a Magic Marker and labeled the keys with the alphabet letters of their notes. (I remembered middle C from grammar school and my short-lived few months of piano lessons.) Then I tried to match the sounds in my head with the alphabet under my fingers and write out the resulting code.

It was primitive. It was scary. *But it was music.* I could actually read my alphabet minestrone back, pick out the keys again, and hear a song! My song!

"Oh, my God!" Tears trickled down my face. A song! If I made the code into notes on a staff, anybody could play it! I felt like Helen Keller as I wept with gratitude over being given a language. Somehow, *just as I'd been told*, I was given an inner key that opened the door to music. I actually *could* write radiant songs. When friends came to visit, I sang to them. Somehow my voice was unlocking, too. I wasn't a bad alto but a very high soprano.

The next weeks tumbled by in bliss. I was listening and learning, hearing and transcribing. Yes, the songs did feel like a musical, and it was about Merlin. Yes, yes, yes!

When I stopped saying, "Yeah, but . . ." I was moved into a new creative realm, one that I had always longed for and which had always seemed *far* beyond my reach. In other words, when I reached my hand up and out in faith, some other helping hand or hands reached down and touched me back, pulling me

But have the courage to write whatever your dream is for yourself.   MAY SARTON

We have seen too much defeatism, too much pessimism, too much of a negative approach. The answer is simple; if you want something very badly, you can achieve it.

MARGO JONES

through my creative ceiling and into the wide-open realm of divine creativity.

The new meaning of soul is creativity and mysticism. These will become the foundation of the new psychological type and with him or her will come the new civilization.

OTTO RANK

AVALON

Just close your eyes and you'll see it.
Just cross the bridge and it's there.
Open your heart—that's the dangerous part—
The Other World's there if we dare.

It's never been story or legend.
It's part of who we are.
It's never been myth or invention.
We're the ones drifted too far.

Isle of apples,
Sunlight dapples,
Starshine, moonglow—
The starry night
Is very bright
So look and I'll show you.

See the way the emerald green is glowing?
Close your eyes and you'll catch the drift.
See the way the Other World is showing?
We're the ones who let the magic slip.

So, "A" is for Avalon.
The boat that we travel on
Is waiting at the shore.
And "B" is begin again
To be what we can as men,
And "C" is for see something more.

Did you ask your soul what dreams it's had lately?
Did you know all your dreams can come true?
The soul gets its dreams and its schemes
On the beams of the Other World's light sifting through—

Just close your eyes and you'll see it.
Just cross the bridge and it's there.
Open your heart—that's the dangerous part—
The Other World's there if you dare!

Lest you forget,
That's the reason we met!
Take my hand,
Make a stand,
As we planned!

～ Task: Remembering the Possible Dreams. ～

Name an "impossible" dream you would like to reclaim. This is an exercise that is best done gently. Look back over your Narrative Time Line notes to refresh your memory. Exactly what arts did you practice, or want to practice, as a child?

Writer Donna Zerner recalls, "It's hard to believe it now, but once upon a time I was a dancer, musician, sculptor, actress, and painter. It was when I was very young, too caught up in the joy of expressing myself to know I that I wasn't particularly talented. But once I got the message that my creative endeavors weren't quite up to the level of 'professional artist.' All those cherished activities came to an end."

Claim your cherished activities. Write a page or two reclaiming the memory of a beloved creative pastime.

～ Task: Playing at Dreams. ～

Allow yourself to play at a dream you have given up. "Play" is the operative word here. Go to the five-and-dime. Costume yourself. Dress as your little kid's idea of a sculptor. Buy modeling clay. Get a cheap set of watercolors or oils. Find a silly smock. Dress as your little kid's idea of a painter. Remember, "Art" with a capital "A" is somebody your sister dated. This is playtime. Be as childish as possible!

If you find yourself balking at this task, read these words of anthropologist Stephen Larsen and see if they persuade you to try it:

God knows no distance.
CHARLESZETTA WADDLES

The foundation for life in the new world is built on the understanding that there is a higher intelligence, a fundamental creative power, or energy, in the universe which is the source and substance of all existence.

SHAKTI GAWAIN

The concern of the Primary Imagination, its only concern, is with sacred beings and sacred events. The sacred is that to which it is obliged to respond.

W. H. AUDEN

The gentile, the "spoilsport," the positivist who cannot or will not play, must be kept aloof. Hence the guardian figures that stand at either side of the entrances to holy places: lions, bulls or fearsome warriors with uplifted swords. They are there to keep out the "spoilsports," the advocates of Aristotelian logic, for whom A can never be B; for whom the actor is never to be lost in the part; for whom the mask, the image, the consecrated host or tree or animal cannot become God but only a reference. Such heavy thinkers are to remain without.

Doesn't that make you want to be one of the ones who can play?

Once you are in your costume, let your "pretend" artist play with the materials of the Impossible Dream. Remember, this is not intended to be anything other than fun. Remember, too, that "clothes make the man" and that costumes are another form of the bridge that we can use to move ourselves into our Imagic-Nation.

I believe the lasting revolution comes from deep changes in ourselves which influence our collective life.
ANAÏS NIN

God, guard me from those thoughts
Men think in the mind alone
He that sings a lasting song
Thinks in the marrow-bone.
WILLIAM BUTLER YEATS

~ Task: I Trust Myself Dance. ~

Put on drum music or some music with a strong, propulsive energy. Take a blank sheet of unlined paper and draw a large circle. In that circle write twenty things you would do if you trusted yourself. Outside that circle write all of the fears that keep you from trusting yourself. (*You* are the circle's perimeter.)

Put the paper with its dreams and fears on the ground. For at least five minutes, dance out of your fears and into your dreams. You may vocalize as well:

> *I think I can! I know I can!*
> *I think I am! I know I am!*
> *I am! I am!*

Breaking
Camp

Tribal Rules

I want to thank you here for the courage that you have had in working with these tools and also, for many of you, the tools of "The Artist's Way." It is my belief that we are building, collectively, a sort of hospital or hospice where we can nurse the creative spirit back to health.

It is my belief that the creative spirit within each of us is the medicine necessary for our own and planetary healing. I believe that we intuitively know this and that this is why we are gathering together to work tribally, as the artists we know at soul-level we are, to reclaim our divine birthright and our right to guide and co-create our planet's future.

ARTIST'S TRIBAL RULES

Survival Rule Number One is Acceptance: "I seem to want to be an artist." Accept the fact that you're an artist and stop second-guessing yourself. Just do it.

Survival Rule Number Two: Don't Judge It. Focus on process, not product.

Survival Rule Number Three: Defend Your Process. Sooner or later, you're going to run into somebody who won't want you to do it, or will want you to do it only a certain way. Consider the source. Are they making *your* art? Do what *you* need to do.

Survival Rule Number Four: Never Let Anybody Tell You What to Create. Create for you. Create *something* every day.

Survival Rule Number Five: Maintain Your Creative Health. Artists are athletes. Creativity is like distance running. Log ten slow miles for every one fast mile. Consistency—process—builds stamina, what horse people call "bottom," what we might call the bottom line. This brings us to:

Survival Rule Number Six: Grieve Your Losses. In any creative life there are losses. Some of them are grievous. Only one thing makes them go away—more creativity.

Survival Rule Number Seven: Create for Revenge. Be a spiritual midget. Skewer the bastards. Create right at them.

Survival Rule Number Eight: Remember That the Part of Us That Creates Is an Inner Youngster. Allow your creative child to have playmates and playthings.

Survival Rule Number Nine: Find Your Believing Mirrors and Stick Close to Them. You deserve a cheering section.

Survival Rule Number Ten: Ignore the Odds. We are all equally sourced in an abundant Universe. Our dreams come from the God within, and that God has the power to fulfill them. Trust yourself. Accept divine help from whatever human source offers it, remembering always that God is the Great Creator—and artists love other artists.

A Guide for Starting
Creative Clusters

When *The Artist's Way* was first published, I expressed a wish for Artist's Way groups to spring into being. I envisioned them as peer-run circles—"creative clusters"—where people would serve each other as believing mirrors, uniting with the common aim of creative unblocking. It was my vision that such circles would be free of charge, that anyone could assemble one, using the book as a guide and a text. Many such peer-run circles did form and many more are forming still. Such artist-to-artist, heart-to-heart help and support is the heart of *The Artist's Way* and *The Vein of Gold*.

Not surprisingly, many therapists, community colleges, wellness centers, universities, and teachers soon began running facilitated Artist's Way groups, for which they charged a fee. These Artist's Way groups were led rather than simply convened. To the degree to which they adhered to the spiritual principles of creative recovery and introduced people to the use of the tools, they were—and are—valuable. Any group that starts with such a leader should, however, rapidly become autonomous, "graduating" to a peer-run, nonprofit status.

There are *no* "accredited" Artist's Way or Vein of Gold teachers. I chose not to franchise the books but to offer them as a gift, free of charge. It is my belief that creative recovery at its best is a non-hierarchical, peer-run, collective process. In this it differs from the academic and therapeutic models. Any professional using *The Artist's Way* or *The Vein of Gold* should realize that autonomous, peer-run creative clusters must remain the eventual goal. Facilitated groups can serve as a sort of bridge to this end.

In my years of teaching and traveling, I have frequently encountered excellent results from peer group clusters. On occasion, I have encountered facilitated situations where *The Artist's Way* has been unduly modified. Whenever there is a misplaced emphasis on intellectual "analysis" or therapeutic "processing," there is the risk of undermining creative unfolding.

Both *The Artist's Way* and *The Vein of Gold* are experiential books. They are intended to teach people to process and transform life through *acts* of creativity. Both books and *all* creative clusters should be practiced through creative action, not through theory. Very often, what could be interpreted as "neurosis" or a deep-seated problem is simply creative resistance. As an artist, I know this. *The Artist's Way* and *The Vein of Gold* are the distillate of thirty years of artistic practice.

It is my belief and my experience as a teacher that all of us are healthy enough to practice creativity. It is not a dangerous endeavor requiring trained facilitators. It is our human birthright and something we can do gently and collectively. Creativity is like breathing—pointers may help, but *we do the process ourselves*. Creative clusters, where we gather as peers to develop our strength, are best regarded as tribal gatherings, where creative beings raise, celebrate, and actualize the creative power that runs through us all.

GUIDELINES

1. Use a Weekly Gathering of Two to Three Hours. The Morning Pages, Daily Walks, and Artist Dates are required of everyone in the group, including facilitators. The exercises are done in order in the group, with everyone, including the facilitator, answering the questions and then sharing the answers in clusters. Do not share your Morning Pages with the group or anyone else. Do not reread your

Morning Pages until later in the course, if you are required to do so by your facilitator or your own inner guidance.

2. Avoid Self-Appointed Gurus. If there is any emissary, it is the work itself, as a collective composed of all who take the course, at home or otherwise. Each person is equally a part of the collective, no one more than another. While there may be "teachers," facilitators, who are relied on during the entry period to guide others down the path, such facilitators need to be prepared to share their own material and take their own creative risks. This is a dialectic rather than a monologue—an egalitarian group process rather than a hierarchical one.

3. Listen. We each get what we need from the group process by sharing our own material and by *listening* to others. We do not need to comment on another person's sharing in order to help that person. We must refrain from trying to "fix" someone else. Each group devises a cooperative creative "song" of artistic recovery. Each group's song is unique to that group—like that of a pod or family of whales, initiating and echoing to establish their position. When listening, go around the circle without commenting unduly on what is heard. The circle, as a shape, is very important. We are intended to witness, not control, one another. When sharing on exercises, small clusters of four within the larger groups are important: five tends to become unwieldy in terms of time constraints; three doesn't allow for enough contrasting experience. Obviously, not all groups can be divided into equal fours. Just try and do so whenever you can.

4. Respect One Another. Be certain that respect and compassion are afforded equally to every member. Each person is to be able to speak his own wounds and dreams. No one is to be "fixed" by another member of the group. This is a deep and powerful internal process. There is no one right way to do this. Love is important. Be kind to yourself. Be kind to one another.

5. Expect Change in the Group Makeup. Many people will—some will not—fulfill the process. There is often a rebellious or fallow period, with people returning to the disciplines later. When they do, they continue to find the process unfolding within them for a year, a few years, or many years later.

6. *Be Autonomous.* You cannot control your own process, let alone anyone else's. Know that you will feel rebellious occasionally—that you won't want to do all of your Morning Pages and exercises at different times in the twelve weeks. Relapse is okay. You cannot do this process perfectly, so relax, be kind to yourself, and hold on to your hat. Even when you feel nothing is happening, you will be changing at great velocity. This change is a deepening into your own intuition, your own creative self. The structure of the course is about safely getting across the bridge into new realms of creative spiritual awareness.

7. *Be Self-Loving.* If the facilitator feels somehow "wrong" to you, change clusters or start your own. Continually seek your own inner guidance rather than outer guidance. You are seeking to form an artist-to-artist relationship with the Great Creator. Keep gurus at bay. You have your own answers within you.

A Word To Therapists, Teachers, Art and Writing Instructors, and Other Artist's Way Group Leaders. Thank you for the wonderful work you do. While I know that many of you are using *The Artist's Way* and *The Vein of Gold* to run groups, I hope and expect that you will go on to explore your own interests using both books for your process, also. I encourage you to follow your own creative vision, to strive for your own True Note. You will find that the facilitation process continues your own growth experience. I cannot state emphatically enough that neither *The Artist's Way* nor *The Vein of Gold* name and path should be used in ways that differ substantially from the techniques as spelled out in the books. I have tested the tools for a decade and a half in order to find them roadworthy. I ask that you refrain from presenting yourselves publicly as Artist's Way or Vein of Gold "experts," though you may use the book within your practice. I ask that you remember that the wisdom of *The Artist's Way* and *The Vein of Gold* is collective, non-hierarchical experience. I have heard of abuses of this principle, such as a group leader's requiring the Morning Pages to be read in the group. This is not in the spirit of the book. Facilitated groups should "graduate" into free, peer-run clusters.

A Word to Therapeutic Clients. Please remember that the book itself remains the primary source of the Artist's Way and Vein of Gold teachings, and that it is your interpretation, and *your* work with the books and their tools, that are central to you in your recovery. I remind you that the work is your own, not just something done under the influence of a magic teacher. Please "own" your recovery as *your* recovery.

Thank You. I am delighted *The Artist's Way* and *The Vein of Gold* are used in the many contexts in which they are. I again offer the reminder that the Artist's Way and The Vein of Gold are intended to be used in keeping with the spirit of the books, as written. In both cases, there is always the book itself to refer to. This is an individual's journey that may be facilitated by the group process. If you cannot find or start a group, consider yourself and the book to be one!

Pass It On. To those forming a peer-run cluster, you do not need to make the Artist's Way or The Vein of Gold a money-making venture, for me or for you. If you follow the spiritual practice of tithing, both myself and my longtime partner Mark Bryan recommend buying the book and passing it on.

Artist's Way and Vein of Gold Glossary of Tools

ARTIST MYTHOLOGY: Artists are an elite tribe of special people (they wear black and live in New York, south of Fourteenth Street) who were born knowing they were real artists, never experience any real self-doubt, are well connected, well recognized, "focused, disciplined, visionary, published, galleried, full time, recognized, famous and rich. . . ." Not like us.

ARTIST DATE: A once-weekly, solitary expedition with your "creative self" into new, interesting, and expansive territory. Expeditions do not need to involve "high art." They might be a trip to an aquarium store, a concert, a used-record store, a drive in the country—anything that "fills the well"—for you. Artist dates are undertaken alone.

ARTIST REALITY: We are all creative, far more creative than we know or acknowledge. It is the *process* of making art, not the product we produce or its recognition and remuneration, that makes us artists.

ARTIST TRUTH: We are *all* intended to create. Creativity is our spiritual DNA.

CINEMA SELF: A larger-than-life, movie version of you. This is the silver-screen version where your life has been enlarged, spiffed up, glamorized—in directions you would actually enjoy and approve of. ("What kind of car does your Cinema Self drive? What skills does he/she have that you don't yet? What is Cinema Self's signature item of clothing? What three adjectives were most used at Cinema Self's funeral? Who would play Cinema Self in the movie?")

CONSIDER THE ODDS: The phrase most often used by self or others to keep an artist from committing art. (QUESTION: "Yeah, but what are the odds of your selling an original screenplay?" ANSWER: "A lot higher if I do write it!")

CREATIVE CEILING: The often arbitrary and frequently low ceiling that we set for ourselves and our abilities. ("I could never learn to play the piano at my age." "I'm probably not really funny enough to try improv." "I could never learn to sight-read." "I think a novel is just too much for me. . . .")

CREATIVE CHAMPION: Someone who has contributed positive support to you and your creative dreams. ("Of course you can write a novel. You write all the time and I love to read what you write." "Why couldn't you go back to graduate school? Lots of people have." "I don't see why you couldn't go to Italy.")

CREATIVE CLUSTER: A deliberately gathered band of people interested in expanding your and their creativity. Once-weekly meetings, lasting two to three hours, are suggested. (Clusters can also be done by phone or even by letter, but person to person is the most powerful.)

CREATIVE MONSTER: A toxic figure from the past or present who has damaged your self-worth around your creativity. ("This paper is awfully good, John, did someone else write it for you?" "Mary, I don't really know if you have the talent to pursue fine art . . . perhaps a career in teaching?"

EXPANSION MUSIC: The piece of music that most lifts your heart and imagination, allowing you to dream a larger self. This can be anything from Vangelis's "Chariots of Fire," to Mozart, Beethoven, or Rodgers and Hammerstein. Again, this is your piece of "I can do it" music—no one else's.

IMPOSSIBLE DREAM: The act of art we would most like to commit, but tell ourselves we could not possibly accomplish.

MORNING PAGES: Three pages of longhand morning writing. These are strictly stream of consciousness, not "art." They are a Western form of meditation that prioritizes the day, clears and focuses the mind, and offers alternative routing to the solution of many problems.

NARRATIVE TIME LINE: A handwritten stream-of-consciousness autobiography—your life as told to you by you. Fifteen or more pages—often many more. This tool allows you to discover your own version of you, not the official family one we so often—mistakenly—own and parrot. ("Then we moved to that wonderful house in the country. . . ." "Wait a minute! I hated that house. I was lonely. It took me three years to find any friends.")

POISONOUS PLAYMATES: Those people around us, frequently creatively blocked themselves, who undercut our plans for expansion and growth by their own poisonous, well-placed doubts. ("I don't know, hon, you really think you'd be any good at that?")

POSSIBLE DREAM: Same as Impossible Dream. We just need to learn the tools and raise our creative ceiling.

READING DEPRIVATION: A week of media deprivation that allows you to contact—and listen to—your own inner guidance instead of the thoughts, opinions, and guidance of others. Often a threatening concept, reading deprivation is an extremely powerful tool, a kick-start for stalled projects and decisions. For many of us, media is a negative addiction. We glut our own appetite for life with the vicarious experience of others.

SAFETY MUSIC: The piece of music that makes you feel the most safe and protected. This can be anything from Michael Hoppé's "The Yearning" to "Brahms's Lullaby" or "Rock-a-bye Baby" or "Amazing Grace." Do not feel it must be music that anyone else would be impressed by. This is a very idiosyncratic, personal choice.

SECRET SELVES: Inner personas that have a guiding hand in your life decisions, frequently killjoys, but also undervalued positive parts of ourselves. "Do I need to add this cast?" can be in opposition. (Martyred Mary: "I don't think you should let yourself get that coat, it's so expensive." Bon-Bon: "You'll love that coat! Get it and eat tuna fish if you have to!")

SHADOW ARTIST: A person who has used his/her creativity in the service of someone else's art or has chosen a career field parallel to or in service of the real dream. (An artist's manager who really wanted to be an actor, an editor who has always longed to write, etc.).

THE VEIN OF GOLD: That area in which you are most truly yourself and from which your gifts and interests mesh and interact most smoothly and powerfully (e.g., Robert DeNiro in movies about male bonding; Kevin Kline in comedies).

WALKING: An invaluable creative tool, used for developing creative ideas, plans, and projects. Next to Morning Pages and Artist Dates, the most potent tool for contracting inner guidance and creativity.

Discography

The following discography is intended as a mere introduction to the world of healing music. Please use it as a gate to the world you may wish to explore far more fully.

Heart Music: The selections in this category work to open the heart.

Journey Music: These selections alter and expand spiritual consciousness.

Toning and Vocal Music: These selections focus on the voice as a spiritual instrument of healing.

Movie Sound Tracks: Perhaps because these are written to visuals, movie sound tracks are often superb for opening the imagination.

HEART MUSIC

Bunting, Edward. The Chieftains. *The Celtic Harp—A Tribute to Edward Bunting.* BMG Classics. Vigorous and evocative.

Enya. *The Celts, Watermark, Shepherd Moons.*

Hoppé, Michael. *The Yearning.* Teldec Classics International GMBH, Schubert Strasse 5-9, D-22083, Hamburg, Germany 011-49440229320. Atlantic Classics. A profoundly healing album of piercingly romantic melodies which open the heart. Compositions and keyboards by Hoppé. Inspired alto flute by Tim Wheater.

Hoppé, Michael. *The Dreamer. Romances for the Alto Flute*, Vol. 2. Deeply resonant and evocative. Hoppé on keyboards. Tim Wheater plays virtuoso alto flute. Teldec Classics International GMBH, Schubert Strasse 5-9, D-22083, Hamburg, Germany 011-49440229320. Atlantic Classics. Available on CD and cassette at record stores nationwide or by calling 1-800-490-5465.

Hoppé, Michael. *The Poet.* Profoundly nostalgic and grounding. Deepens the heart. Keyboards and cello. Teldec Classics International GMBH, Schubert Strasse 5-9, D-22083, Hamburg, Germany 011-49440229320. Atlantic Classics.

Wheater, Tim. *Green Dream.* Audio Alternatives, P. O. Box 405, Chappaqua, NY 10514. Spirited and expansive quest music, healing and heart-centered. Also excellent for journeying. 1-800-283-4655.

Wheater, Tim. *Timeless.* Audio Alternatives, P.O. Box 405, Chappaqua, NY 10514. 1-800-283-4655. Opening and releasing music, aerating for claustrophobic, clock-driven lives. Also, excellent journey music.

Wheater, Tim. *Whalesong.* Mysterious and evocative music for planetary healing, profoundly moving. Audio Alternatives, P.O. Box 405, Chappaqua, NY 10514.

JOURNEY MUSIC

Beasts of Paradise. *Gathered on the Edge.* City of Tribes, 3025 17th Street, San Francisco, CA 94110. Powerful, grounding, and mysterious.

Big Bang, The. Masterworks of world drumming music. Three hours of percussion recordings. The Sounds True Catalogue, Dept. FC8, 735 Walnut Street, Boulder, CO 80302.

Darling, David. The Native Flute Ensemble. *Ritual Mesa Talking.* Taco Records.

Darling, David. *8 String Religion, Hearts of Space Music.* The cello as healing instrument.

Drummer's Path, The. *African and Diaspora Percussive Music.* Destiny Recordings, 1 Park Street, Rochester, VT 05767. Music to enter ecstasy.

Global Meditation. *Authentic Music From Meditative Traditions of the World.* Excellent spiritual anthology.

Gross, Ed. *Shamanic Journey Drumming.* Journey Records, P.O. Box 13375, Dinkytown Station, Minneapolis, MN 55414.

Halpern, Steven. *Inner Peace.* Audio Alternatives, P.O. Box 2644, San Anselmo CA 94979. A consciousness-shifting journey album.

Hart, Mickey. *At the Edge.* Rykodisc. Pickering Wharf, Bldg. C-3G, Salem, MA 01970. Rich musical gumbo of world sounds.

Hart, Mickey, and Taro. *Music to Be Born By.* Rykodisc. Pickering Wharf, Bldg. C-3G, Salem, MA 01970. Propulsive, energizing, and grounding.

Kater, Peter, and Carlos Nakai. *Migration.* Masterful Native American music. Silver Wave Records.

Moses, Harold. *Edges of the Soul.* Exquisite and expansive. Crucible Sound, P.O. Box 19191, Boulder, CO 80308. 303-784-5941.

Nakai, Carlos. *Journeys.* Native American flute. Canyon Records. 4143 N. 16th St., Phoenix, AZ 85016.

Olatunji, Babatunde. *Drums of Passion: The Invocation.* Rykodisc. Pickering Wharf, Bldg. C-3G, Salem, MA 01970. Name tells it all.

Roth, Gabrielle. *Bones.* Consciousness-altering "body/mind" music. Raven Recording.

TONING AND VOCAL MUSIC

Benedictine Monks of Santo Domingo de Silos. Chant. Angel Records. 1750 N. Vine St., Hollywood, CA 90028. Grounding and mesmerizing.

Bollman, Christian, and the Dusseldorf Overtone Choir. Pure overtone singing, instrumentation including flute and tambura. Network.

Campbell, Don. *Healing Yourself with Your Own Voice.* The Sounds True Catalogue,

Dept. FC8, 735 Walnut Street, Boulder, CO 80302. About the natural power of the human voice and its role in establishing a balanced, healthful life.

Gardner, Joy. *The Healing Voice—Toning Meditations*. Available from Help Yourself, P.O. Box 3414, Santa Cruz, CA 95063.

Gardner, Kay. *Sounding the Inner Landscape*. The Sounds True Catalogue, Dept. FC8, 735 Walnut Street, Boulder, CO 80302.

George, Michele. *River of Song, River of Life*. Overcome your fear of singing. Easy-to-learn techniques. The Sounds True Catalogue, Dept. FC8, 735 Walnut Street, Boulder, CO 80302.

Goldman, Jonathan. *Healing Sounds—Instructional Tape. Harmonic Journeys,* Vol. 1, *Vowels as Mantras*. Spirit Music, Inc. P.O. Box 2240, Boulder, CO 80306. Clear and grounded instructional tape.

Gyuto Monks, The. *Freedom Chants from the Roof of the World*. Rykodisc. Pickering Wharf, Bldg. C-3G, Salem, MA 01970. Sacred chants of the Gyuto Monks. Kitaro, Philip Glass, and Mickey Hart also appear.

Gyuto Monks, The. *Tibetan Tantric Choir*. Windham Hill Records, Windham Hill Productions, Inc. P.O. Box 9388, Stanford, CA 94305.

Gyuto Monks, The. Tantras of Gyuto. (Folkways).

Hykes, David, and the Harmonic Choir. *Hearing Solar Winds*. Ocara, 3364 S. Robertson Blvd., Los Angeles, CA 90034. Hypnotic and enchanting.

Vetter, Michael. *Overtones*. Harmonia Mundi, 3364 S. Robertson Blvd., Los Angeles, CA 90034. Groundbreaking work.

von Bingen, Hildegard. *The Music of Hildegard von Bingen*. Female vocals. The Sounds True Catalogue, Dept. FC8, 735 Walnut Street, Boulder, CO 80302.

Wheater, Tim. *Heart Land*. Almo Sounds, Inc., 360 N. La Cienega Blvd., Los Angeles, CA 90048. An anthem for spiritual transformation and planetary healing. A portal to the deep heart and a stairway to heaven. A tour de force of world music. Sublime toning vocals and choral arrangements.

Wilde, Stuart. *Cecelia*. Voice of the Feminine spirit. White Dove International, P.O. Box 100, Taos, NM 87571. Featuring Cecelia Knudsen's sublime soprano vocals and Wheater's incomparable virtuoso flute, green-hearted melodies, and muscular compositions. Wilde's lyrics.

MOVIE SOUND TRACKS

August. Anthony Hopkins. Debonaire Records. Haunting, evocative, and masterful music.

Baraka. An eclectic world tour. Mila Records.

Black Orpheus. Antonio Carlos Jobim. Mercury Records, 825 Eighth Avenue, New York, NY 10019.

Chariots of Fire. Vangelis. Polygram, 825 Eighth Avenue, New York, NY 10019. Vigorous, uplifting, and triumphant.

The Good, the Bad, and the Ugly. Ennio Morricone. Liberty, 1750 N. Vine St., Hollywood, CA 90028.

The Last of the Mohicans. Robert Summers (1977 version). Inspirational and uplifting themes.

The Last Temptation of Christ. Peter Gabriel. WEA, 75 Rockefeller Plaza, New York, NY 10019. Passionate and powerful.

The Last Waltz. The Band. Warner Brothers, 75 Rockefeller Plaza, New York, NY 10019. Rich and eclectic showcase of heart-centered rock and roll. Title theme profoundly healing.

The Mission. Ennio Morricone. Piercingly beautiful themes. Virgin Records America, Inc., 338 N. Foothill Road, Beverly Hills, CA 90210.

Music for the Native American. Robbie Robertson. Capitol Records, 810 Seventh Avenue, New York, NY 10019. Deeply evocative and spiritually grounded.

Once Upon a Time in the West. Ennio Morricone. RCA, 1540 Broadway, New York, NY 10036.

Out of Africa. John Barry. MCA Records, 1755 Broadway, New York, NY 10019. Deeply romantic, majestic, and expansive.

The Piano. Michael Nyman. Virgin Records America, Inc., 338 N. Foothill Road, Beverly Hills, CA 90210. Haunting and passionate.

La Strada. Nino Rota. Sony Music Entertainment, 550 Madison Avenue, New York, NY 10022.

Themes. Vangelis. Polygram, 825 Eighth Avenue, New York, NY 10019. Transcendent.

SELECTIONS

Take seriously the idea that music can rep-
resent emotional states, liberate your body in
this world, and save your soul in the next.
—Jon Barlow

These are useful in experiencing the healing powers of music.

I wish to acknowledge the guidance received from Carol Bush and Hal. A. Lingerman, and the musical assistance of Alexander Cassini and Joseph McClellan.

Bach, Johann Sebastian. Mass in B Minor, "Qui Tollis." Karl Richter, Munich Bach Choir and Orchestra. Musikfest 413 688-2. Reverential.

Bach, Johann Sebastian. Orchestral Suite No. 3 in D Major, movement II (Air). Matthias Bamert, BBC Philharmonic. CHAN 9259. Soaring.

Bach, Johann Sebastian. Two Flute Concertos. James Galway. RCA 65172. Exhilarating.

Bartók, Béla. Music for Strings, Percussion and Celesta, movement I. Benny Goodman, Bernstein. CBS MK-44707. Evocative.

Beethoven, Ludwig van. String Quartet in C Major, Opus 131. Safety.

Beethoven, Ludwig van. Symphony No. 7, movement II. Pablo Casals, Marlboro Festival Orchestra. Sony Classical SMK 45893. Grounding.

Beethoven, Ludwig van. Symphony No. 9, movement I. Eugene Ormandy, Philadelphia Orchestra. CBS MYK 37241. Energetic.

Beethoven, Ludwig van. Symphony No. 9. *Choral, Fidelio* overture. Sony Music Entertainment, Inc. Exultant.

Berlioz, Hector. *Symphony fantastique*, movement II. Martinon, ORTF National Orchestra. EMI CZS762739-2. Evocative.

Brahms, Johannes. Piano Concerto No. 2, Allegro non troppo. George Szell, Cleveland Orchestra. CBS MYK 37258. Opening.

Brahms, Johannes. Symphony No. 1, movement III. Seiji Ozawa, Saito Kinen Orchestra. Resolution.

Brahms, Johannes. Symphony No. 2, movement III, Andante. George Szell, Cleveland Orchestra. CBS MYK 337258. Expressive.

Brahms, Johannes. Symphony No. 3 in F Major, Opus 90, movement I. George Szell, Cleveland Orchestra. CBS MYK 3777. Structuring.

Brahms, Johannes. Symphony No. 3, movements II and III. Clarifying.

Coltrane, John. *A Love Supreme*. MCA-5660. Exultant.

Debussy, Claude. *Prélude à l'après-midi d'un faune*. Pierre Boulez. Cleveland Orchestra. MB2K 45620. Nostalgic.

Delius, Frederick. Two selections: "On Hearing the First Cuckoo in Spring," "Song Before Sunrise." Norman Del Mar, Bournemouth Sinfonietta. CHAN 6502. Discovery.

Gounod, Charles. *Messe solennelle en l'honneur de Sainte Cecile*. Radio France Orchestra. Angel CDC-47094. Sublime.

Handel, Georg Friedrich. *Water Music*. Pierre Boulez, Hague Philharmonic. Elektra/ Nonesuch H-71127. Refreshing.

Hazen, Gusdo. *Missa Luba*, "Sanctus." Philips. Reverent, moving.

Haydn, Joseph. Cello Concerto in C, Adagio. Yo Yo Ma, English Chamber Orchestra. Sony Classical SK 36 674. Comfort.

Holst, Gustav. "Mars Music" from *The Planets*. Leonard Bernstein, New York Philharmonic. CBS MYK-37226. Propulsive. "Venus Music" from *The Planets*. Love.

Hoppé, Michael. *The Yearning*. Teldec Classics International; Atlantic Classics. Healing, heart-centered.

Liszt, Franz. *Liebesträume*. Daniel Barenboim. DG-415118-2. Spiritually transformational.

Mahler, Gustav. Symphony No. 5, Adagietto. Leonard Bernstein, New York Philharmonic. CBS MYK-38484. Poignant.

Mahler, Gustav. Symphony No. 5, movement III. Barbirolli, New Philharmonic Orchestra. EMICDM7 69186-2. Spiritual.

Mendelssohn, Felix. Violin Concerto in E Minor. Heifetz, Munch, Boston Symphony Orchestra. RCA 5933-2-RC. Healing, heart-centered.

Mozart, Wolfgang Amadeus. *Laudate Dominum*. Frederica van Stade, The Mormon Tabernacle Choir. London 436 284-2. Exultant.

Mozart, Wolfgang Amadeus. Requiem. Sir Neville Marriner, Academy of St. Martin-in-the-Fields. Philips 432087.

Nelson, Willie. *Stardust Melodies*. Columbia JC-35305. Heart-centering.

Orff, Carl. *Carmina Burana*. James Levine, Chicago Symphony. Deutsche Grammophon 415136.

Pachelbel, Johann. Canon in D. RCA 65468. Reassuring.

Rachmaninoff, Sergei. Symphony No. 2, Adagio. Eugene Ormandy, Philadelphia Orchestra, MILK 64 056. Romance.

Ravel, Maurice. *Daphnis et Chloé*, Suite No. 2, part 1. Leonard Bernstein, New York Philharmonic. CBS 36714. Yearning.

Ravel, Maurice. *Introduction and Allegro*. Martinon, Chicago Symphony. RCA AGK1-5061. Vibrant.

Rubinstein, Anton. *Melody in F.* Heart-centered.

Schubert, Franz. *Ave Maria*. RCA 7964-2-RG. Spiritually opening.

Schubert, Franz. *Marches militaires*. DG 419217-1 GH. Energizing.

Stravinsky, Igor. *Rites of Spring*. Leonard Bernstein, New York Philharmonic. CBS MK44709. Buoyant.

Stravinsky, Igor. *Firebird Suite*, "Finale." Leonard Bernstein, New York Philharmonic. CBS MYK-37221. Expansive.

Tchaikovsky, Pyotr Ilich. Piano Concerto in B Minor. Van Cliburn. RCA LSC-2252. Assertive.

Vivaldi, Antonio. *Gloria* in D Major, *Et in terra pax* II. Simon Preston, The Academy of Ancient Music. L'Oiseau-Lyre 414-678-2. Transcendent.

Wagner, Richard. *Tristan und Isolde*, Prelude and *Liebestod*. George Szell, Cleveland Orchestra. CBS MYK-38486. This tone poem explores the erotic and spiritual polarities, male and female.

Wagner, Richard. Wagner Overtures. George Szell, Cleveland Orchestra. CBS MYK-38486. Imaginative.

Wagner, Richard. *Lohengrin*, Prelude to Acts 1, 3. Schwarz, Seattle Symphony Orchestra. Delos, DCD-3053. Transcendent.

Wheater, Tim. *Eclipse*. Side B. Haunted and haunting, great depth of feeling. Audio Alternatives, P.O. Box 405, Chappaqua, NY 10514.

Wheater, Tim. *Green Dream*. Spirited and expansive quest music. Audio Alternatives, P.O. Box 405, Chappaqua, NY 10514.

Wheater, Tim. *Whalesong*. Mysterious and evocative. Audio Alternatives, P.O. Box 405, Chappaqua, NY 10514.

Vaughan Williams, Ralph. *Fantasia on "Greensleeves."* Sir Neville Marriner, Academy of St. Martin-in-the-Fields. Argo 421227-1#ZH. Reflective.

Vaughan Williams, Ralph. *The Lark Ascending*. Iona Brown, violin; Sir Neville Marriner, Academy of St. Martin-in-the-Fields. Argo 414596. Heaven-storming.

Vaughan Williams, Ralph. *Pastoral Symphony*. Bryden Thomson, The London Symphony, CHAN 8594. Emotionally resonant.

Wilson, Ransom. *Koto, Flute*. Ransom Wilson flute and koto orchestra. Angel 4XS-37325. Elemental.

Yogananda. *Divine Gypsy* (Instrumental Arrangement of Cosmic Chants). Spiritually opening.

Note: Additionally, these composers bear exploration for their common ground of music that soothes and liberates the spirit.

Adams, John

Copland, Aaron

Crumb, George

Gershwin, George

Gorecki, Mikolaj

Hovhaness, Alan

Päat, Arvo

Piazzola, Astor

"Pop"ography

... The greatest priests on Fifty-second Street and on the streets of New York City were the musicians. They were doing the greatest healing work and they knew how to punch through music that would cure and make people feel good.

—Garth Hudson

The following list is sound-healing. Thank you, Mark Bryan, Alexander Cassini, Richard Cole, Bill La Vallee, Al Ojas, and Domenica Cameron-Scorsese for lending me your ears. Apologies to greats omitted.

The Allman Brothers Band: *"Blue Skies," "Little Martha."* Blondie: *"Denis."* Badfinger: *"Day After Day."* The Band: *"Unfaithful Servant," "Daniel and the Sacred Harp," "The Weight."* Kathleen Battle: *"Honey and Rue."* The Beach Boys: *"I Get Around," "Help Me Rhonda," "Sloop John B."* The Beatles: *"You've Got to Hide Your Love Away," "Good Day Sunshine," "And Your Bird Can Sing," "Here Comes the Sun," "Sgt. Pepper's Lonely Hearts Club Band."* The Bee Gees: *"To Love Somebody," "Lonely Days Odessa."* Blind Faith: *"Can't Find My Way Home," "Presence of the Lord."* Blood, Sweat and Tears: *"I Can't Quit Her."* The Bo-Deans: *"In the Still of the Night."* David Bowie: *"Suffragette City," "Five Years," "Absolute Beginners."* Jackson Browne: *"Late for the Sky," "For America."* Buffalo Springfield: *"For What It's Worth," "Mr. Soul."* The Byrds: *"Mr. Tambourine Man," "Turn! Turn! Turn!," "Eight Miles High," "My Back Pages."* Maria Callas: as Medea. The Cars: *"My Best Friend's Girl."* Johnny Cash: *"I Walk the Line," "Folsom Prison Blues."* Ray Charles: *"You Are My Sunshine."* Chicago: *"If You Leave Me Now," "Baby, What a Big Surprise."* Eric Clapton: *"Bell Bottom Blues," "Layla."* Merry Clayton: *Dylan's Gospel* (album). Jimmy Cliff: *"The Harder They Come."* Patsy Cline: *"I Fall to Pieces," "Walking After Midnight."* Joe Cocker: *"Feeling Alright," "With a Little Help from My Friends."* Leonard Cohen: *"Suzanne," "Sisters of Mercy."* Judy Collins: *"Both Sides Now."* John Coltrane: *"Lush Life."* Ry Cooder: *"On a Monday."* Elvis Costello: *"Watching the Detectives."* Cream: *"Sunshine of Your Love," "Crossroads," "Badge," "Sittin' on Top of the World," "Politician," "White Room."* Creedence Clearwater Revival: *"Midnight Special," "Bad Moon on the Rise," "Have You Ever Seen the*

Rain?" Crosby, Stills and Nash: *"Suite: Judy Blue Eyes," "Helplessly Hoping," "Southern Cross."* Sonia Dada: *Sonia Dada* (album). Miles Davis: *"Kind of Blue."* Bo Diddley: *"Who Do You Love?"* Celine Dion: *"Because You Loved Me," "River Deep, Mountain High."* Dire Straits: *"Sultans of Swing," "So Far Away."* Donovan: *"Season of the Witch," "Sunshine Superman."* Bob Dylan: *"Highway 61 Revisited," "It Ain't Me, Babe," "Like a Rolling Stone," "A Hard Rain's Gonna Fall."* The Eagles: *"Take It to the Limit," "Desperado," "Hotel California."* Duke Ellington: *"Black, Brown and Beige."* The Eurythmics: *"Sweet Dreams Are Made of These."* Bill Evans: *"Quintessence."* Marianne Faithful: *"As Tears Go By."* Fleetwood Mac: *"Station Hand News," "Dreams," "Go Your Own Way."* The Flying Burrito Brothers: *"White Line Fever," "Colorado," "Wild Horses," "Sin City."* The Four Seasons: *"Sherry," "Baby," "Big Girls Don't Cry."* Aretha Franklin: *"Think," "Respect."* Peter Gabriel: *"Mercy Street," "Sledgehammer."* Judy Garland: *"Over the Rainbow," "Born in a Trunk."* The Grateful Dead: *"Uncle John's Band," "Casey Jones," "St. Stephen."* Joel Grey: *"Money," "Cabaret."* Emmy Lou Harris: *"Sin City," "Sweet Dreams," "Stan's Jewel Crown."* George Harrison: *"If Not for You," "Dark Horse."* Jimi Hendrix: *"Purple Haze," "Foxey Lady," "Voodoo Chile."* Billie Holiday: *"Strange Fruit," "God Bless the Child," "Ain't Nobody's Business."* Janis Ian: *"Society's Child," "At Seventeen."* Jane's Addiction: *"Up the Beach."* Jefferson Airplane: *"White Rabbit," "3/5 of a Mile in 10 Seconds."* Jethro Tull: *"Aqualung."* Joan Jett: *"Crimson and Clover."* Elton John: *"Tiny Dancer," "Levon," "Rocket Man."* Robert Johnson: *"Crossroads Blues," "Come On in My Kitchen," "Walking Blues."* Al Jolson: *"Swanee," "Mammy."* Janis Joplin: *"Piece of My Heart," "Me and Bobby McGee," "Ball and Chain," "Mercedes-Benz."* The Kinks: *"You Really Got Me," "A Well-Respected Man," "Lola," "Apeman," "20th Century Man."* Patti LaBelle: *"Lady Marmalade," "You Are My Friend."* Cyndi Lauper: *"House Full of Stars."* Led Zeppelin: *"Ramble On," "Good Times, Bad Times," "Babe I'm Gonna Leave You," "Dazed and Confused," "Kashmir."* Leadbelly: *"Good Night, Irene."* John Lennon: *"Imagine," "Just Because," "Remember."* Annie Lennox: *"Diva."* Gordon Lightfoot: *"If You Could Read My Mind," "Early Morning Rain."* Little Feat: *"Dixie Chicken," "Let It Roll."* Little Richard: *"Slippin' and Slidin'."* Madonna: *"Like a Virgin."* Mahavishnu Orchestra: *"Meeting of the Spirits."* Paul McCartney: *"Band on the Run," "Maybe I'm Amazed."* Bette Midler: *"Friends," "Wind Beneath My Wings."* Glenn Miller: *"Take the A-Train," "Pagan Love Song."* Liza Minnelli: *"The World Goes Round."* Joni Mitchell: *Blue* (album). Thelonius Monk: *"Crisscross."* Van Morrison: *"Caravan," "Tupelo Honey," "Brown Eyed Girl," "T.B. Sheets," "Astral Weeks," "Ballerina," "Wavelength."* Tracey Nelson: *"Down So Low."* Willie Nelson: *Stardust Memories* (album). Bob Neuwirth: *Bob Neuwirth* (album). Laura Nyro: *"Eli's Coming," "The Poverty Train," "And When I Die," "Super Summer Sugar Coppin' in the Morning..."* Sinead O'Connor: *I Do Not Want What I Haven't Got* (album). Anita O'Day: *"The A Train."* Charlie Parker: *Complete Dial Session* (album). Dolly Parton: *"Coat of Many Colors," "Jolene."* Edith Piaf: *"Je n'regrette rien."* Pink Floyd: *"Brain Damage," "Shine On, You Crazy Diamond."* Elvis Presley: *"Blue Suede Shoes," "Hound Dog," "Amazing Grace," "Oh, Listen to All of It."* Procol Harum: *"A Whiter Shade of Pale," "Conquistador (live)," "A Salty Dog," "The Devil Came from Kansas."* Bonnie Raitt: *"Matters of the Heart," "Let's Give Them Something to Talk About."* Lou Reed: *"Walk on the Wild Side," "Sweet Jane."* R.E.M.: *Green* (album). Righteous Brothers: *"You've Lost That Lovin' Feeling."* Minnie Ripperton: *"Inside My Love," "You Feel What I'm Saying."* The Rolling Stones: *"Under My Thumb," "Think," "Play With Fire," "Let's Spend the Night Together," "Ruby Tuesday," "Gimme Shelter,"*

"*Let It Bleed,*" "*Midnight Rambler,*" "*You Can't Always Get What You Want,*" "*Brown Sugar,*" "*Wild Horses.*" Linda Ronstadt: "*Hard Like a Wheel,*" "*Desperado.*" Diana Ross/Supremes: "*Where Did Our Love Go?*" "*Love Is Like an Itching in My Heart.*" Run DMC: "*King of Rock.*" Tom Rush: "*Jamaica, Say You Will.*" Sex Pistols: "*My Way.*" Ravi Shankar: "*Improvisation on the Theme Music from* Pather Panchali." Paul Simon: *Rhythm of the Saints, Graceland* (both albums), "*Loves Me Like a Rock,*" "*Mother and Child Reunion.*" With Art Garfunkel: "*Homeward Bound.*" Frank Sinatra: Anything, especially "*My Way.*" Jimmy Smith: "*Walk on the Wild Side.*" Bruce Springsteen: *Asbury Park, Thunder Road, Nebraska* (albums). Barbra Streisand: "*People,*" "*The Way We Were,*" "*Don't Rain on My Parade.*" Elaine Stritch: "*Here's to the Ladies Who Lunch.*" Talking Heads: *Stop Making Sense* (album). The Temptations: "*(I Know) I'm Losing You,*" "*Get Ready.*" Traffic: "*Empty Pages,*" "*Stranger to Himself,*" "*John Barleycorn Must Die,*" "*Dear Mr. Fantasy.*" Tina Turner: "*We Don't Need Another Hero (Mad Max),*" "*Private Dancer,*" "*What's Love Got to Do With It?*" U2: *Rattle and Hum* (album). The Velvet Underground: "*Waiting for the Man,*" "*White Light/White Heat,*" "*All Tomorrow's Parties,*" "*I Heard Her Call My Name.*" Muddy Waters: "*Mannish Boy,*" "*Two Trains Running.*" Weather Report: "*I Sing the Body Electric.*" The Who: *Tommy,* "*Summertime Blues,*" "*Shakin' All Over,*" "*My Generation,*" "*Magic Bus.*" Stevie Wonder: "*Maybe Your Baby,*" "*Superstition.*" Tammy Wynette: "*Stand By Your Man.*" Lester Young: *Lester Leaps In* (album). Neil Young: "*Tonight's the Night,*" "*Cinnamon Girl,*" "*After the Gold Rush.*" Warren Zevon: "*Excitable Boy,*" "*Werewolves of London.*" Show Tunes: Leonard Bernstein–Stephen Sondheim: "*Something's Coming.*" George Gershwin: "*Summertime,*" "*I Love You, Porgy.*" Alan Jay Lerner–Frederick Loew: "*I Could Have Danced All Night.*" Cole Porter: "*Night and Day.*" Galt McDermott–Gerome Ragni–James Rado: "*Aquarius.*" Richard Rodgers–Oscar Hammerstein III: "*Hello, Young Lovers.*" Andrew Lloyd Webber: "*Memories.*" New and Notable: *Afghan Whigs, Alice in Chains, Tori Amos, Bush, Ani di Franco, P. J. Harvey, Jewel, Natalie Merchant, Alanis Morrisette, Rage Against the Machine, the Smashing Pumpkins, Soundgarden, Stone Temple Pilots.*

Filmography

Note: While directors are often referred to as auteurs, or authors, they are more accurately thought of as composers/conductors whose films, like musical compositions, clarify and carry certain energies. What follows is a "musical" sampler of movies. While they could be spoken of in strictly musical terms (e.g., Robert Altman: Sardonic jazz), instead they are identified in terms of their dominant themes, a.k.a. "Vein of Gold." Thank you to Alexander Cassini and Jay Cocks for "spotting" me on this list.

Allen, Woody: Despoiled innocence, bruised sophistication. *Manhattan, Annie Hall, The Purple Rose of Cairo.* Altman, Robert: Betrayal. *The Player, Nashville.* Anderson, Lindsey: Inequality. *If, This Sporting Life.* Antonioni, Michelangelo: Being and nothingness. *Blowup, La Ventura.* Armstrong, Gillian: Individuality. *My Brilliant Career.* Attenborough, Richard: Social agendas, heroics. *A Bridge Too Far.* Beatty, Warren: Against all odds. *Reds.* Bergman, Ingmar: Shape-shifting. *Persona, The Seventh Seal.* Beresford, Bruce: Personal honor. *Breaker Morant, Tender Mercies.* Bertolucci, Bernardo: Corruption and transcendence. *The Conformist, 1900.* Bogdanovich, Peter: Innocence. *The Last Picture Show.* Buñuel, Luis: Societal infirmities, spiritual malaise. *Discreet Charm of the Bourgeoisie, Belle de Jour.* Burton, Tim: Outsider. *Beetlejuice, Edward Scissorhands.* Cameron, James: Doom. *The Terminator, Aliens, Titanic.* Campion, Jane: Love in the ruins. *The Piano, Sweetie.* Capra, Frank: Value of the individual. *It's a Wonderful Life, Mr. Smith Goes to Washington.* Cassavetes, John: Communication and commitment. *Woman Under the Influence, Husbands.* Cimino, Michael: Loyalty. *The Deer Hunter.* Clarke, Shirley: Connection. *The Connection.* Cocteau, Jean: Eros as spirit, truth as beauty. *Beauty and the Beast, Orpheus.* Coen, Joel and Ethan: Community. *Raising Arizona, Miller's Crossing, Fargo.* Coppola, Francis Ford: Power as blindness. *Godfather, Godfather II, Appocalypse Now.* Costa-Gavras: Injustice. *Z, Missing.* Cronenberg, David: Mutation. *Dead Ringers.* Cukor, George: Male-female, class polarities. *Holiday, The Philadelphia Story, A Star Is Born.* De Sica, Viottorio: Purity within decay. *Bicycle Thief, Garden of the Finzi-Continis.* Demme, Jonathan: Odd alliances, societal inequity. *Melvin and Howard, Silence of the Lambs.* Donaldson: Passion. *Smash Palace, No Way Out.* Donen, Stanley: Heart ties. *Two for the Road, On the Town* (with Gene Kelly). Edwards,

Blake: Comedy of eros. *Pink Panther* series. Eisenstein, Sergei: Injustice. *Potemkin.* Fellini, Federico: Jungian tribal rites. *8 1/2, La Strada.* Ford, John: Destiny. *The Searchers, Stagecoach.* Fosse, Bob: Love and death. *All That Jazz, Cabaret.* Frears, Stephen: Connection. *My Beautiful Laundrette.* Friedkin, William: Juggernaut of will. *The French Connection, The Exorcist.* Godard, Jean-Luc: Outsiders. *Breathless, Alphaville.* Griffith, D. W.: Epic energies. *The Birth of a Nation.* Hawks, Howard: Male-female polarities. *His Girl Friday, 20th Century.* Herzog, Werner: Power. *Aguirre, the Wrath of God; Fitzcarraldo.* Hitchcock, Alfred: Identity. *Notorious, North by Northwest.* Huston, John: Odds. *Treasure of the Sierra Madre, The African Queen.* Jones, Chuck: Mischief. *Bugs Bunny* et al. Kazan, Elia: Social injustice. *On the Waterfront, Panic in the Streets.* Kelly, Gene: Joie de vivre. *Invitation to the Dance.* Korda, Alexander: Pomp as circumstance. *Thief of Baghdad.* Kubrick, Stanley: Societal forces. *Dr. Strangelove, A Clockwork Orange.* Kurosawa, Akira: Identity. *Rashomon, The Hidden Fortress.* Keaton, Buster: Ego as id. *The Navigator, The General.* Lang, Fritz: Progress as poison. *Metropolis, Big Heat, M.* Lean, David: Transcendence, destiny. *Passage to India, Lawrence of Arabia.* Lee, Spike: Rigged game. *Do the Right Thing, She's Gotta Have It.* Leigh, Mike: The naked truth. *Naked.* Leone, Sergio: Honor among thieves. *The Good, the Bad and the Ugly, Once Upon a Time in the West.* Losey, Joseph: Class. *The Servant.* Lubitsch, Ernst: Divine comedy. *Trouble in Paradise, The Shop Around the Corner.* Lumet, Sidney: Injustice. *Serpico, Dog Day Afternoon, Q&A.* Lupino, Ida: Underdog. *Not Wanted.* Lucas, George: Communal transcendence. *American Graffiti, Star Wars* trilogy. Lynch, David: Outcasts. *Eraserhead, Blue Velvet.* Malick, Terrence: Fate. *Badlands, Days of Heaven.* Malle, Louis: Passion and compassion. *Murmur of the Heart, My Dinner With André, Atlantic City, Pretty Baby.* Mann, Michael: Fire in the belly. *Thief, The Last of the Mohicans, Heat.* Marshall, Penny: Male-female polarities. *Big.* Miller, George: Heroism. *Lorenzo's Oil, Road Warrior.* Minnelli, Vincente: Passion. *An American in Paris, The Clock, Lust for Life.* Monty Python: The human condition. Any! Murnau, F. W.: Discernment. *Nosferatu.* Newell, Mike: Obsession. *Dance with a Stranger.* Nichols, Mike: Decadence. *Carnal Knowledge, Virginia Woolf.* Ophuls, Max: Passion and society. *Earrings of Madame Deux, Lola Montes.* Pabst, G. W.: Mystic feminism. *Pandora's Box.* Pakula, Alan: Dignity. *Klute.* Pasolini, Pier Paolo: Underdogs. *Accatone!, Teorema.* Peckinpah, Sam: Desperate honor. *The Wild Bunch, Straw Dogs.* Penn, Sean: Love. *The Indian Runner, The Crossing Guard.* Polanski, Roman: Corruption. *Chinatown, Repulsion.* Pollack, Sydney: Fated love. *Out of Africa, The Way We Were.* Powell, Michael/ Emeric Pressburger: Spiritual law as destiny. *Black Narcissus, I Know Where I'm Going, Red Shoes.* Preminger, Otto: Obsession. *Laura, The Man with the Golden Arm, Exodus.* Rafelson, Bob: Individuality. *Five Easy Pieces.* Ray, Nicholas: Existential loneliness. *In a Lonely Place, They Live by Night, Rebel Without a Cause.* Ray, Satyajit: The human condition. *The River.* Reid, Sir Carol: Honor as fate. *The Third Man.* Riefenstahl, Leni: Power. *Triumph of the Will.* Reiner, Rob: Tender comrades. *Spinal Tap, Princess Bride.* Renoir, Jean: Human transcendence. *Grand Illusion.* Resnais, Allan: Destiny. *Hiroshima, Mon Amour.* Ritt, Martin: Human value. *Hud, Sounder.* Roeg, Nicolas: Devastation. *Performance, Don't Look Now.* Rosselini, Roberto: Soulfulness. *Paisan, Open City.* Russell, Ken: Extreme polarities. *Women in Love.* Sirk, Douglas: Honor. *Magnificent Obsession.* Sayles, John: Love. *Baby, It's You, Brother from Another Planet.* Schlesinger, John: Decadence. *Darling, Midnight Cowboy.* Schrader, Paul. Spiritual/Sexual Identity. *Mishima, Hard Core.* Scorsese, Martin: Betrayal of self and others, spiritual courage and cowardice. *Mean Streets, Taxi Driver, Raging Bull, GoodFellas.* Sheridan, Jim: Dignity. *My Left Foot.* Silver, Joan Micklin:

Connection. *Hester Street, Chilly Scenes of Winter*. Spielberg, Steven: Heroic transcendence, community and communication. *Close Encounters of the Third Kind, Jaws, Sugarland Express, The Indiana Jones* movies. Sternberg, Josef Von: Seduction and will. *The Blue Angel, Shanghai Express*. Stevens, George: Heartlands. *Giant, Penny Serenade*. Stone, Oliver: Deception. *Salvador, JFK*. Streisand, Barbra: Individual destiny. *Yentl, Prince of Tides*. Szabo, Istvan: Comedy of eros. *Coca-Cola Kid*. Tati, Jacques: Irony as truth. *Mon Oncle, Monsieur Hulot's Holiday*. Tarantino, Quentin: Apotheosis (Pop). *Reservoir Dogs, Pulp Fiction*. Towne, Robert: Personal integrity. *Tequila Sunset*. Truffaut, Francois: Heart and soul. *400 Blows, Jules and Jim*. Van Zandt, Gus: Alienation. *Mala Noche, Drugstore Cowboy*. Verhoeven, Paul: Personal integrity. *Soldier of Orange*. Vidor, King: Destiny. *Duel in the Sun*. Visconti, Lucino: Grandeur of fate. *Death in Venice*. Wajda, Andrzej: Human resilience. *Ashes and Diamonds, Kanal*. Warhol, Andy/Morrissey, Paul: The bottom line. *Trash*. Weir, Peter: Spiritual law, mysticism as destiny. *The Last Wave, Green Card, The Year of Living Dangerously, Gallipoli, Witness*. Welles, Orson: Hubris. *Citizen Kane, Touch of Evil*. Wenders, Wim: Transcendence. *Wings of Desire, American Friend*. Wilder, Billy: Self-deception. *Double Indemnity, Sunset Boulevard, The Lost Weekend*. Wyler, William: Power. *Jezebel, The Collector*. (Apologies to the many brilliant filmmakers omitted.)

Bibliography

Please consider this list as a "sampler" of titles that may entice you.

WRITING

Aftel, Mandy. *The Story Of Your Life—Becoming the Author of Your Experience.* New York: Simon & Schuster, 1996. Persuasive and useful.

Bennett, Hal Zina. *Write from the Heart: Unleashing the Power of Your Creativity.* Novato, Calif.: Nataraj Publishing, 1995. Kind and comforting.

Brande, Dorothea. *Becoming a Writer.* 1934. Reprint. Los Angeles: Jeremy P. Tarcher, 1981. The best book on writing I've ever found.

Burnham, Sophy. *For Writers Only.* New York: Ballantine Books, 1994. Prickly and provocative "field report" on writers and writing.

Capacchione, Lucia M. A. *The Power of Your Other Hand.* North Hollywood, Calif.: Newcastle Publishing Co., Inc., 1988.

Goldberg, Bonni. *Room to Write: Daily Invitations to a Writer's Life.* New York: A Jeremy P. Tarcher/Putnam Book, 1996. A masterfully provocative and wise writer's tool.

Goldberg, Natalie. *Wild Mind—Living the Writer's Life.* New York: Bantam Books, 1990.

Goldberg, Natalie. *Writing Down the Bones—Freeing the Writer Within.* Boston: Shambhala Publications, Inc., 1986. Simply the best into-the-water book ever written.

Metzger, Deena. *Writing for Your Life: A Guide and Companion to the Inner Worlds.* San Francisco: HarperSanFrancisco. A Division of HarperCollins Publishers, 1992.

Rico, Gabriele Lusser. *Writing the Natural Way.* Los Angeles: Jeremy P. Tarcher, Inc., 1983.

Selling, Bernard. *Writing from Within: A Unique Guidee to Writing Your Life Stories.* Alameda, Calif.: Hunter House, 1988.

Shaughnessy, Susan. *Walking on Alligators.* San Francisco: HarperSanFrancisco. A Division of HarperCollins Publishers, 1993. Excellent daily companion in a writer's life.

Ueland, Brenda. *If You Want to Write.* 2nd ed. 1938. Reprint. St. Paul, Minn.: Schubert, 1983.

VISUAL ARTS

Cassou, Michell, and Stewart Cubley. *Life, Paint, and Passion: Reclaiming the Magic of Spontaneous Expression.* New York: A Jeremy P. Tarcher/Putnam Book, 1996. Passionate and experienced into-the-water book for visual artists.

Diaz, Adriana. *Feeling the Creative Spirit.* San Francisco: HarperSanFrancisco, 1992.

Franck, Frederick. *Zen Seeing, Zen Drawing.* New York: Bantam Books, 1993.

Klotsche, Charles. *Color Medicine.* Sedona, Ariz.: Light Technology Publishing, n.d.

London, Peter. *No More Second Hand Art: Awakening the Artist Within.* Boston: Shambhala Publications, Inc., 1989. A manifesto for personal art as process, not product.

Noble, Vicki. *Motherpeace—A Way to the Goddess Through Myth, Art, and Tarot.* San Francisco: Harper & Row Publishers, 1983.

von Rohr, Ingrid S., and Wulfing von Rohr. *Harmony Is the Healer.* Rockport, Mass.: Element, Inc., 1992.

Walker, Barbara G. *The Woman's Dictionary of Symbols and Sacred Objects.* San Francisco: Harper & Row Publishers, 1988.

MUSIC AND SOUND HEALING

Andrews, Ted. *Sacred Sounds.* St. Paul, Minn.: Llewellyn Publications, 1993.

Bassano, Mary. *Healing with Music and Color—A Beginner's Guide.* York Beach, Mass.: Samuel Weiser, Inc., 1992.

Berendt, Joachim-Ernst. *The World Is Sound: Nada Brahma.* Rochester, Vt.: Destiny Books, 1991. Eloquent and persuasive book on sound theory.

Bonny, Helen. *Music and Your Mind.* Barrytown, N.Y.: Helen A. Bonny and Louis M. Savary, 1973, 1970.

Bush, Carol A. *Healing Imagery and Music.* Portland, Oreg.: Rudra Press, 1995. A profoundly useful guide to listening for healing.

Campbell, Don. *Music Physician, For Times to Come.* Wheaton, Ill.: The Theosophical Publishing House, 1991.

Campbell, Don. *Music and Miracles.* Wheaton, Ill.: The Theosophical Publishing House, 1992.

Campbell, Don G. *The Roar of Silence.* Wheaton, Ill.: The Theosophical Publishing House, 1994. Seminal book on sound healing—clear, passionate, and useful. All of Campbell's many books are important and persuasive, but this one remains a primer. Be alert for his broad scope book, *The Mozart Effect,* to be released in spring 1997.

Chatwin, Bruce. *Songlines.* New York: Penguin Books, 1987. An exquisite, mysterious, and powerful book.

Cole, Richard, and Richard Trubo. *Stairway to Heaven: Led Zeppelin Uncensored.* New York: HarperCollins, 1992. Riveting account of the high cost of sex, drugs, and rock and roll.

Crowley, Brian, and Esther Crowley. *Words of Power.* St. Paul, Minn.: Llewellyn Publications, 1992.

Drake, Michael. *The Shamanic Drum: A Guide to Sacred Drumming.* Bend, Oreg.: Talking Drum Publications, 1991. A clear and practical work.

Gardner, Kay. *Sounding the Inner Landscape.* Stonington, Mass.: Caduceus Publications, 1990.

Goldman, Jonathan. *Healing Sounds: The Power of Harmonics.* Rockport, Mass.: Element Books, Inc., 1992. Powerful and gentle teaching book on sound healing techniques.

Gardner-Gordon, Joy. *The Healing Voice.* Freedom, Calif.: The Crossing Press, 1993. An openhearted and friendly book on vocal practices.

Hart, Mickey. *Drumming at the Edge of Magic.* San Francisco: HarperCollins, 1990.

Kelley, William Melvin. *A Drop of Patience.* Hopewell, N.J.: The Ecco Press, 1965, 1996. Music as spiritual path. Arguably the finest novel ever written about jazz.

Keyes, Laurel Elizabeth. *Toning: The Creative Power of the Voice.* Marina Del Rey, Calif.: DeVorss & Co., 1973. The groundbreaking primer on toning that launched sound healing in America.

Khan, Hazrat Inayat. *The Music of Life.* New Lebanon, N.Y.: Omega Press, 1988.

Khan, Hazrat Inayat. *The Mysticism of Sound.* Netherlands: Servire BV, 1979. Name tells all.

Lingerman, Hal A. *The Healing Energies of Music.* Wheaton, Ill.: The Theosophical Publishing House, 1983. Excellent book on music as medicine, learned yet friendly.

Mathieu, W. A. *The Listening Book: Discovering Your Own Music.* Boston: Shambhala Publications, Inc., 1991. A companionable book that demystifies music as a life path.

Mathieu, W. A. *The Musical Life: Reflections on What It Is.* Boston: Shambhala Publications, Inc., 1994.

McClellan, Randall, Ph.D. *The Healing Sources of Music.* Rockport, Mass.: Element, Inc., 1994. A kindly yet wide-ranging source.

Rael, Joseph, with Mary Elizabeth Marlow. *Being and Vibrating.* Tulsa, Okla.: Council Oak Books, 1993.

Tame, David. *The Secret Power of Music.* New York: Destiny Books, 1984. A lucid, introductory overview.

SPIRITUALITY/INTUITION AND ECO-SPIRITUALITY

Arrien, Angeles, Ph.D. *The Four-Fold Way.* New York: HarperCollins Publishers, 1993.

Berry, Thomas. *Dream of the Earth.* San Francisco: Sierra Club Books, 1988.

Bradley, Marion Zimmer. *The Mists of Avalon.* New York: Ballantine Books, 1982. A powerfully evocative novel of female spirituality in pre-Christian England. Mesmerizing novel of goddess worship in Arthurian times.

Burnham, Sophy. *A Book of Angels.* New York: Ballantine Books, 1990. Eloquent and moving book of spiritual experience and exploration.

Carr-Gomm, Philip. *The Druid Way.* Rockport, Mass.: Element Books, Inc., 1993.

Choquette, Sonia. *The Psychic Pathway.* New York: Random House. Crown Trade Paperbacks, 1994, 1995. Safe, grounded, practical guide to opening to spiritual gifts.

Choquette, Sonia. *The Heart's Desire.* New York: Random House, Crown Trade Paperbacks. 1997. An extremely clear, step-by-step guide for manifesting dreams as working reality.

Coelho, Paulo. *The Pilgrimage.* New York: HarperCollins Publishers, 1995. Allegorical novel of mindful living.

Duerk, Judith. *Circle of Stones—Woman's Journey To Herself.* San Diego: LuraMedia, 1989.

Eisler, Riane. *The Chalice and The Blade.* San Francisco: Harper & Row Publishers, 1987.

Fox, Matthew. *Original Blessing.* Santa Fe, N.M.: Bear & Company, 1983; seventh printing, 1986. An important, corrective book on Christian tradition; brilliant, impassioned, compassionate.

Gawain, Shakti. *Creative Visualization.* New York: Bantam Books, 1985. Seminal and lucid book on creative manifestation.

Gawain, Shakti. *Living in the Light.* Mill Valley, Calif.: Whatever Publishing, Inc., 1986.

Grof, Christina. *The Thirst for Wholeness—Attachment, Addiction, and the Spiritual Path.* New York: HarperCollins Publishers, 1993.

Hall, Nor. *The Moon and the Virgin*. New York: Harper & Row Publishers, 1980.

Harvey, Andrew. *The Way of Passion—A Celebration of Rumi*. Berkeley, Calif.: Frog, Ltd., 1994.

Heywood, Rosalind. *ESP: A Personal Memoir*. New York: E. P. Dutton & Co., Inc., 1964.

Holmes, Ernest. *Creative Ideas*. Los Angeles: Science of Communications, 1973. A tiny, powerful, and important book of spiritual law as applied to creative manifestation.

James, William. *The Varieties Of Religious Experience*. New York: Penguin Books, 1982.

Kornfield, Jack. *A Path with Heart*. New York: Bantam Books, 1993. A compassionate book that humanizes Eastern traditions for Westerners.

Mariechild, Diane. *Open Your Mind—Women's Daily Inspiration for Becoming Mindful*. San Francisco: HarperSanFrancisco, 1996.

Maclean, Dorothy. *To Hear the Angels Sing*. Hudson, N.Y.: Lindisfarne Press, 1990. A lovely book, a fascinating spiritual autobiography by one of the founders of Findhorn.

Maclean, Dorothy. *To Honor the Earth*. New York: HarperCollins Publishers, 1991.

Miller, Ronald S., and the editors of *New Age Journal. As Above So Below*. Los Angeles: Jeremy P. Tarcher, Inc., 1992.

Nahmad, Claire. *Earth Magic*. Rochester, Vt.: Destiny Books, 1994.

Peck, M. Scott, M.D. *The Road Less Traveled*. New York: Touchstone/Simon & Schuster, 1978.

Roman, Sanaya. *Spiritual Growth: Being Your Higher Self*. Tiburon, Calif.: H.J. Kramer, Inc., 1989.

Roman, Sanaya, and Duane Packer. *Opening to Channel: How to Connect with Your Guide*. Tiburon, Calif.: H.J. Kramer, Inc., 1987.

Rosanoff, Nancy. *Intuition Workout: A Practical Guide to Discovering and Developing Your Inner Knowing*. Lower Lake, Calif.: Aslan Publishing, 1991.

Sark. *Living Juicy—Daily Memories for Your Creative Soul*. Berkeley, Calif.: Celestial Arts, 1994. Playful yet practical heart-opener for creativity.

Sher, Barbara, and Annie Gottlieb. *Wishcraft: How to Get What You Really Want*. New York: Ballantine Books, 1979. A potent, catalytic book for creative living. Seminal to my own work and thinking.

Starhawk. *Truth or Dare—Encounters with Power, Authority, and Mystery*. San Francisco: Harper & Row Publishers, Inc., 1987.

Starhawk. *The Fifth Sacred Thing*. New York: Bantam Books, 1994. Mesmerizing novel of spiritual ecology.

Stein, Diane. *Stroking the Python—Women's Psychic Lives*. St. Paul, Minn.: Llewellyn Publications, 1988.

Szekely, Edmond Bordeaux. *The Gospel of the Essenes*. 10th impression. Saffron Walden, U.K.: C.W. Daniel Co., Ltd., 1993.

Swan, James A. *The Power of Place*. Wheaton, Ill.: The Theosophical Publishing House, 1993.

Vaughan, Frances E. *Awakening Intuition*. New York: Doubleday, 1979.

Weinstein, Mario. *Positive Magic: Occult Self-Help*. Custer, Wash.: Phoenix Publishing, Inc., 1981.

Wright, Machaelle Small. *Behaving as if the God in All Life Mattered*. Jeffersonton, Va.: Perelandra, Ltd., 1987. A spiritual autobiography about work with "earth" and other energy forms.

Andrews, Ted. *Magickal Dance: Your Body as an Instrument of Power.* St. Paul, Minn.: Llewellyn Publications, 1993.

Cowan, James G. *The Elements of the Aborigine Tradition.* Rockport, Mass.: Element, Inc., 1994.

Drury, Nevill. *Vision Quest: A Personal Journey Through Magic and Shamanism.* New York: Avery Publishing Group, Inc., 1989.

Gersi, Douchan. *Faces in the Smoke.* Los Angeles: Jeremy P. Tarcher, Inc., 1991.

Halifax, Joan, Ph.D. *The Fruitful Darkness: Reconnecting with the Body of the Earth.* New York: HarperCollins Publishers, 1993. A provocative book by a wonderful writer and thinker.

Halifax, Joan, Ph.D. *Shamanic Voices: A Survey of Visionary Narratives.* New York: Arkana/Penguin Books, 1979. Last printing, 1991.

Harner, Michael. *The Way of the Shaman.* New York: HarperCollins Publishers, 1990. The seminal text on shamanism for interested beginners.

Heinze, Ruth-Inge, Ph.D. *Shamans of the 20th Century.* New York: Irvington Publishers, Inc., 1991.

Kalweit, Holger, *Dreamtime and Inner Space. The World of the Shaman.* Translated by Werner Weunsche. Boston: Shambhala Publications, Inc., 1988.

Kalweit, Holger. *Shamans, Healers, and Medicine Men.* Translated by Michael Kohn. Boston: Shambhala Publications, Inc., 1992. Excellent and eloquent.

King, Serge Kahili. *Kahuna Healing.* Wheaton, Ill.: The Theosophical Publishing House, 1983; sixth printing, 1994.

King, Serge Kahili, Ph.D. *Urban Shaman.* New York: Fireside/Simon & Schuster, Inc., 1990.

Keeney, Bradford. *Shaking out the Spirits.* Barrytown, N.Y.: Station Hill Press, Inc., 1994.

Larsen, Stephen. *The Shaman's Doorway—Opening Imagination to Power and Myth.* Barrytown, N.Y.: Station Hill Press, 1976, 1988. A lovely book due to its clear, grounded writing.

Mann, John, and Lar Short. *The Body of Light.* Rutland, Vt.: Charles E. Tuttle Co., Inc., 1990.

Matthews, Caitlin. *Singing the Soul Back Home: Shamanism in Daily Life.* Rockport, Mass.: Element, Inc., 1995. A wonderfully rich book for grounded spiritual practice.

Matthews, John. *The Celtic Shaman—A Handbook.* Rockport, Mass.: Element, Inc., 1991.

Noble, Vicki. *Shakti Woman—Feeling Our Fire, Healing Our World.* New York: HarperCollins Publishers, 1991.

Rael, Joseph E., and Lindsay Sutton. *Tracks of Dancing Light.* Rockport, Mass.: Element, Inc., 1993.

Roth, Gabrielle, and John Loudon. *Maps to Ecstasy—Teachings of an Urban Shaman.* Novato, Calif.: Nataraj Publishing, 1989.

Starhawk. *The Spiral Dance: A Rebirth of the Ancient Religion of the Great Goddess.* New York: HarperCollins Publishers, 1979, 1989. A brilliant book on theology and creativity.

Stevens, Jose, Ph.D., and Lena S. Stevens. *Secrets of Shamanism—Tapping the Spirit Power Within You.* New York: Avon Books, 1988.

Walsh, Roger N., M.D., Ph.D. *The Spirit of Shamanism.* New York: Tarcher/Perigee Books, 1990.

SPECIAL INTEREST
THESE BOOKS ARE INTENDED AS SPECIAL HELP ON ISSUES THAT FREQUENTLY BLOCK CREATIVITY.

Alcoholics Anonymous. *Came to Believe*. New York: Alcoholics Anonymous World Services, 1973. Useful and touching book about embryonic faith.

The Augustine Fellowship. *Sex and Love Addicts Anonymous*. Boston: The Augustine Fellowship, Sex and Love Addicts Anonymous Fellowship-Wide Services, 1986. One of the best books on addiction. The chapters on withdrawal and building partnership should be required reading.

Beattie, Melody. *Codependent No More*. San Francisco: Harper & Row, 1987. Excellent for breaking the virtue trap.

Bryan, Mark, and Julia Cameron. *The Money Drunk—90 Days to Financial Freedom*. New York: Ballantine Books, 1992. Money through lens of addiction theory.

Hallowell, Edward M., M.D., and John J. Ratey, M.D. *Driven to Distraction*. New York: Touchstone Books/Simon & Schuster, 1994; first Touchstone edition, 1995. Invaluable book on attention deficit disorder.

Louden, Jennifer. *The Women's Comfort Book (A Self-Nurturing Guide for Restoring Balance in Your Life)*. San Francisco: HarperSanFrancisco, 1992. Applicable to either sex as a practical guide to self-nurturing.

Orsborn, Carol. *Enough is Enough: Exploding the Myth of Having It All*. New York: G. P. Putnam's Sons, 1986. Excellent for helping dismantle the heroic workaholic personality.

RESOURCES

Sounds True
413 South Arthur Avenue
Louisville, CO 80027
1-800-333-9135
A wellspring of spiritual sound and wisdom from all world traditions.

The Transformative Power of Sound School, with Don Campbell
3010 Hennepin Avenue South, #269
Minneapolis, MN 55408
1-800-490-4968
612-377-5700
Don Campbell is the dean emeritus of American sound healings. His work is thoroughly grounded, researched, and road-tested through many years of teaching experience.

Transitions Bookplace
1000 West North Avenue
Chicago, Il 60622
1-312-951-7323
Largest American clearinghouse for titles like these.

W., Bill. *Alcoholics Anonymous: The Story of How More Than One Hundred Men Have Recovered from Alcoholism*. Akron, Ohio: Carry the Message, 1985.

AVALON

Lyrics and music by
Julia Cameron
Music arrangement © 1996
by Tommy Eyre

Just close your eyes and you'll see it. Just cross the bridge and it's

there. Op - en your heart—that's the dan - ge - rous part— The

Oth - er World's there if we dare. It's ne - ver been sto - ry or

le - gend. It's part of who we are. It's

ne - ver been myth or in - ven - tion. We're the ones drif - ted too

far. Isle of ap - ples, Sun light dap - ples, star - shine moon -glow—The

star -ry night Is ve - ry bright So look and I'll show you.

See the way the emerald green is glow - ing? Close your eyes and you'll catch the

Index

About the Author

Julia Cameron has been an active artist for more than thirty years. Additionally, she has served on numerous film faculties, Northwestern University and Columbia College among them, and has taught and refined the methods of the Artist's Way and the Vein of Gold for nearly two decades. She has extensive credits in film, television, and theater. Her essays have been anthologized and she is a published poet. Also an award-winning journalist, she has written for such diverse publications as the *New York Times*, the *Washington Post*, the *Los Angeles Times*, the *Chicago Tribune*, the *Village Voice*, *Rolling Stone*, *American Film*, *Vogue*, and many more. The focus of her current work is music and sound healing.